REVIEWS FOR OVERSEER

I have finished reading your remarkable manuscript, *Overseer* and enjoyed the whole, wild, exciting and thoroughly captivating journey. I quickly came to the conclusion you could be a cross between a modern-day Muhammad Ibn Battuta and the more contemporary Louis Theroux, such is the extent of your knowledge of the fascinating places to which you ventured. The road less travelled certainly comes to mind. The day-to-day detail is remarkable. Your story is something that a lot of people will find fascinating and as such I thoroughly recommend it to anyone. I enjoyed reading every page.

— Doug Pinnington, Sunshine Coast, Queensland.

Bill Stanford's *Overseer* will be a nostalgic ride for Australian backpackers of the 1960s and 1970s, the exploding generation of world wanderers. As in his major work, *Skirmish Hill*, Stanford writes in a personal style that is impressive in its recall of days lived over fifty years ago. He captures perfectly the wonders of a first-time visitor to places both renowned and remote. We are treated to many delightful, touching and occasionally frightening encounters with strangers that challenge his innocence while also building wisdom. *Overseer* reads as an invitation to all those who have an itch to travel lightly and create their own adventures.

—Janet Loneragan, Ph. D, Washington, United States of America.

In *Overseer*, Bill Stanford shows himself to be a real traveller rather than a mere tourist. He takes risks and looks beneath the surface. His curiosity often leads him into danger but also a real engagement with other peoples and their complex histories. He begins with a snapshot of a very different Australia and its almost forgotten social mores, some of them harsh by today's standards and others admirable. He finds work in the outback, hard physical work that runs from dawn to dusk. He vividly evokes the harsh outback conditions and often encounters people from beyond the Black Stump. Later adventures include mining in remote Western Australia. Leaving Australia he begins to work his way across Europe with no set itinerary and eventually crossing into the Soviet Union. There, he and a friend are caught in a vast repressive system, dogged by cruelty and corruption and in an extraordinary episode just make it back from the confines of the KGB via a cargo ship sailing from Odessa in the Ukraine to Bulgaria. In Istanbul he wangles his way into the Turkish Army's largest fort and explores the rooms occupied by Florence Nightingale in the Crimean War. In Iran and Pakistan he and his wife were stoned by Muslims while in Kashmir his wife and a friend were stoned by Muslim children. He describes the violence, danger and squalor of travelling through Afghanistan and the historical context, the many conquerors and civilisations that passed that way. *Overseer* is a celebration of curiosity, of travel for travel's sake, trying something new, witnessing tragedy and hardship, having adventures and unexpected situations. Well worth reading and managing to be both educational and entertaining. Perhaps it might inspire some intrepid person to head out into the unknown and see what happens.

— Luke Harris, author of *Goldenscale*, Melbourne, Victoria.

Reviews for Overseer

I have been amazed at the adventurous life you described including your marriage to the lovely and charming Janice. Your memory of the events and description of the things you observed is truly astonishing. The way you travelled through strange countries was masterful and illuminating. Congratulations on producing a well written, exciting and informative document.

— Jim Silkman, Leura, Blue Mountains, NSW.

In his new book, Overseer, Bill Stanford quotes one of my favourite sayings by Mark Twain,

Twenty years from now you will be more disappointed by the things that you didn't do than by the ones you did do. The author clearly proves that he took those words to heart because Bill's life is full of the things he *did* do and in Overseer, he introduces the reader to the best recipe for adventure and insight into other cultures you can imagine. From his early life in Australia and his first real job as a jackaroo (by someone who had no experience of horses) you realise this is a unique character whose roaming of the world in his subsequent years embraced the chance to follow any interest that flashed into his mind. Often accompanied by his equally intrepid English wife, Janice, he visited 120 countries over the years, such as Bhutan, North Korea, Ethiopia, Ukraine and others by land and sea. His desire to sail in a 1911 built barquentine as voyage crew to Antarctica and on to South Africa (almost) dispelled my horror at the thought let alone when he and Janice later sailed around Cape Horn east to west for 47 testing days and nights. I started looking for a country or region to which his curiosity hadn't taken him.

His interest in seemingly minor events or national characteristics of a culture brings a deep understanding of why we are here.

I defy anyone who reads this book not to be planning an adventure of their own by the time they put it down. Do read it and admire a man who has followed his own path around this world purely to satisfy his own understanding of mankind.

—Myra Fonceca, Dragon Cottage, Devon, England.

OVERSEER

BILL STANFORD

First published in Australia 2025
This edition published 2025
Copyright © Bill Stanford 2025
Cover design, typesetting: WorkingType (www.workingtype.com.au)

The right of Bill Stanford to be identified as the Author of the Work has been asserted in accordance with the Copyright, Designs and Patents Act 1988.

All rights reserved. No part of this publication may be reproduced, stored in a retrieval system, or transmitted, in any form or by any means without the prior written permission of the author, nor be otherwise circulated in any form of binding or cover other than that in which it is published and without a similar condition being imposed on the subsequent purchaser.

Stanford, Bill, *Overseer,*
ISBN: 978-1-7644282-2-4

Attribution: Owing in part to Russia's KGB not returning the author's camera after he was arrested and charged with spying the book does contain photos connected to the text that have been obtained online. The original source of said images has not been found and the author apologises for that shortcoming. If any of my readers are able to identify the original source/s, please notify me and attribution will be made in the following edition.

INTRODUCTION

Overseer is written by Bill Stanford not as an autobiography but as the work of a memoirist, in that here he writes of the first ten years of his life after leaving school.

He has since made numerous journeys around or across the world and in 2019 he was invited to conduct the Armchair Travel class at Dubbo's University of the Third Age. Due to his acquired knowledge of some remote and different lands and people of interest those classes continue to this day.

Upon leaving school he was a jackaroo at Wingadee Station, north of Coonamble, NSW, where the 150,000 acres ensured a working knowledge of the station's 5,500 cattle and 60,000 sheep along with the self-replacing herd of station-bred horses. He followed that with more rural life at Ebor, via Armidale and also Mudgee. He then gained a position in a mining camp on Koolan Island, off the Western Australian Kimberley coast. Bill started at the bottom as a tradesman's apprentice and rose through the ranks to being in charge of the major drilling rig on the island.

Whatever he may have achieved on Wingadee Station and Koolan Island he attributes to the discipline he inherited by way of the overseers of the day. It was understood that there was work to be done no matter the hours required, the working conditions or the weather, for in both endeavours one should acknowledge Mother Nature, let alone all manner of mankind.

Many of his fellows amongst the workforce of 200 Koolan island men came from overseas and he was interested in the backgrounds of those who risked their lives to escape from Eastern Europe where they had been ruled by the harsh and narrow Soviet Union ideology.

Before he left Australia he avoided his own early death when he walked away from a plane in Alice Springs that moments later crashed on take-off, killing all on board. He bought a one-way ticket on a Russian ship to England, teamed up with an Australian bull-dozer operator who had been working in New Guinea and set off to see the lie of the land. He worked on a vineyard in Chianti, Italy, as a civilian employee at the headquarters of the American Army for Europe at Heidelberg, Germany where for a while he was the civilian overseer and as a tour guide operating in and out of England and then a club manager.

In Istanbul he made his way into the headquarters of the Turkish First Army after spending two days gaining military permission to visit the Fort. A Turkish Army Lieutenant-Colonel and another officer escorted him to the immaculately preserved rooms that were granted to Florence Nightingale during the Crimean War. He also found the home of Mary of the Mongols who had married Abaqa Khan, great-grandson of Genghis Khan.

Bill was stoned by Muslims in Iran while visiting a mosque and also stoned in Pakistan. His wife and a friend were stoned in Kashmir by Muslim children for no obvious reason. He was involved in various incidents in Afghanistan, Moldova, Ukraine, the Soviet Union, Germany and Bulgaria that necessitated unexpected departures.

After ten years of freedom he married an English girl in London and along with others they travelled for their honeymoon on a retired single-decker bus from London to Kathmandu where he encountered the Living Goddess before island-hopping to Australia. Bill readily acknowledges his fortunate life is in the main due to the company of his wonderful wife, Janice. To this day he relishes the early love and attention granted him by his grandfathers and their equally devoted wives and abides by the discipline instilled in and accepted by him courtesy of the overseers.

A DEDICATION

I dedicate Overseer to my grandchildren and hope they gain as much from life as I have.

To Oliver, Zara and William Reynolds and to Reuben and Hugh Stanford.

CONTENTS

Chapter One	Wingadee station	1
Chapter Two	Panda	38
Chapter Three	Koolan Island	64
Chapter Four	Shota Rustaveli	88
Chapter Five	The KGB	126
Chapter Six	Opposite the Blind	164
Chapter Seven	Men of Iron	192
Chapter Eight	Morocco on twenty cents a day	224
Chapter Nine	El Cid	245
Chapter Ten	Jack the Ripper	268
Chapter Eleven	Mary of the Mongols	304
Chapter Twelve	Afghanistan	335
Chapter Thirteen	Varanasi	359

Bill at age 18   *Bill, aged eighty*

CHAPTER ONE

Wingadee station

Overseer; Person whose job it is to make certain employees are working or that the activity is being done correctly.

There is no greater agony than bearing an untold story inside you. Maya Angelou, memoirist.

No one can bear undeclared grief.
Major David Starling SAS.

It is often said that in the first moments, mere minutes at most, of an interview, addressing an audience or hoping to attract someone's personal attention that you present yourself with an air of intrigue, an implication that you are able to offer a worthwhile difference or an attribute lacking in others. I am going to take the chance that for the first few pages I can get something off my chest, warts and all, as in the above quotations and you will still be here riding alongside me for the rest of the journey.

I saw it on my father's desk as I walked by. It was the last of my thirty school term reports over the past ten years, in my day the school year consisted of but three terms, and I stopped to read my teachers' comments. I knew I wasn't the prominent plank in the woodshed but I did pass the Leaving Certificate in English, history, geography and French. I didn't realise it at that time but those four subjects would be of immense value to me when and why I was later travelling many parts of the world. The sciences of physics and chemistry were not my strong suit and whilst I coped well with straight mathematics I confess I was at a loss, and still am, as to the merits of algebra and trigonometry.

The remarks were overall satisfactory but it was the last line, at the bottom of the page that caught my eye. Truth to tell I don't remember a single word my teachers had to say about me but in the past sixty and more years since then I have never forgotten the six words the Headmaster felt worthy of his time to compose. He said, *Bill will mature later in life*.

He being so prescient and accurate I didn't take it in at the time but as the years and I progressed his judgement began to sink in. Where for a long time I was a part of the crowd with my fellows I now see myself positioned on the edge, watching from afar as the world evolves and observing while reflecting on past days. I am fully aware that my life also can change for the worse in the blink of an eye. Therefore I take nothing for granted and am grateful for the road I have travelled. I see life from a different perspective that surrounded me when I was growing, working, and tackling the usual challenges and continuation of everyday life. Planning ahead, moving out of my comfort zone at times and self-discipline have been rewarding but the best blessing of all has been the God-given opportunity to meet and immediately marry one of the most wonderful women ever created.

Chapter One *Wingadee station*

Neither my teachers nor my parents suggested I might go to University, not that I expected such encouragement. My father rarely spoke to me, in a lifetime. In my ten years at boarding school he never came to see me, never wrote to me and never phoned me. I did not know why he was that way. I wasn't happy about it but not being enlightened by anyone else I accepted it, with two exceptions.

The first came about when I was quite young. One morning I found my mother in the kitchen and after talking with her I heard

Bill with his mother, Judy and his sister Wendy

chatter and laughter coming from my parent's bedroom. I was drawn to the apparent merriment and enticed by it I entered the room to find my younger sisters in bed with my father. As I moved forward he looked at me and rather abruptly said, *There is no room in here for you*. Without saying a word I turned and left, shaken but not stirred. His was a momentous statement that would not leave me. As it was readily on my mind the day soon came when I realised what he actually meant was, *There is no room in my life for you*.

His stand-off action had cautioned me but the day came when I weakened and at the age of fourteen and having witnessed the loving parents of my friends' families I burst into tears in my parents' presence. My mother never stood up to my father but when she

S. J. Stanford, Bill's grandfather

asked why was I crying I told her because my father did not love me. She turned to him and said, *Tell Bill you love him Jimmy, tell him.*

She repeated her plea but she might have conversed with one of the Maui, the stone-faced statues that stand tall, silent and aloof on Easter Island. He didn't blink and he refused to utter a single word. That was the first time in my life that I cried.

His parents, my paternal grandparents, Stanley and Ethel Stanford, were attentive and helpful to me. At the most unexpected of times I would find my grandfather nearby and keeping watch over me, such as when I was batting during a cricket match and as I looked around the field placings there he was on the square leg boundary keeping an eye on me. He was a man who did not speak often, usually leaving that social attribute to his wife although I always felt he was there if I needed him and that gave me feelings of comfort and confidence. The horrible day my grandfather died was the second and the last time I cried. The grandparents paid for my school fees and perhaps my father resented that, although he did pay for my three sisters to attend good schools. It became obvious my moody father had a chip on his shoulder all his life about something but the only time he mentioned it was rather late in the day, when he was on his deathbed, dying, at age eighty-four. He revealed that he was illegitimate, saying to my mother and I, *My father was not my father.*

I think it fair to say that in today's society that is not a big deal, certainly not a fraction of what it was in 1915 when my father was born, in an era when only 2 to 3 per cent of births were listed in that category. In 2013 the Australian Bureau of Statistics reported that 33 per cent of Australian babies were born out of wedlock while the more recent report from America in May, 2024, stated that 39.8 per cent of American children are illegitimate, a figure that is mostly likely now matched by Australia.

I have a cousin who is deeply into researching genealogy. She told me of a Scottish family member who was walking along a Glasgow street during World War One when he came across a seemingly fit and healthy young man openly crying. Looking to offer assistance he asked what is the matter? While gasping for breath and words the young man said he had just applied to join the Army but had been rejected out of hand. How can that be? asked the other.

With good intentions he had produced his identity card, not realizing the significance of the diagonal red line drawn across the face of the card. Such an ID card was required to be shown to prospective employers and various government departments. The red line informed one and all that the card holder was illegitimate and consequently he was not wanted by the military. I imagine my father also felt the associated stigma and could never get it off his chest. If that was the case and he had made the effort I have little doubt we would have had a better relationship, any relationship for that matter.

My maternal grandparents were also of a loving nature. As they lived in Melbourne we did not see them often enough and although I was young I sensed that my father was averse to visiting my mother's parents, sadly for her and myself. My Melbourne grandfather would make the most of every opportunity to take me into his study, sit me on his lap and read to me the intriguing stories of The Classics, such as Horatious, aka Horatio, at the Bridge. The Classics introduced me to the ways of the ancient Romans and Greeks, their civilisations, philosophy, archaeology, languages and history. I feel that introduction was the reason I later studied Latin for two years, even though it was difficult for me. I still enjoy coming across English words in which I recognise their derivation from the Latin. Most of all I have no doubt that my grandfather's description of Roman and Greek history instilled in me a latent desire for travel to historically interesting parts of the world.

Bill's Melbourne grandparents, Dr. Hedley and Mrs. May Ham

My grandfather's name was Hedley Harefoot Ham, one of the six sons of the politician and Ballarat investor in no less than 175 gold mining enterprises, David Ham. It is on the record that when David Ham died everyone in Ballarat attended his funeral, even the children. All his sons were remarkably successful in their careers: Fred Ham, barrister of Ballarat; Dr. Nathaniel Burnett Ham, first Commissioner of Queensland Health; W. S. Ham, sharebroker of the Melbourne

Stock Exchange; William Ham, stock and station agent of Brisbane; David Jonathon Ham, farmer and Boer War soldier and Hedley Ham, dentist. Hedley studied dentistry in Paris and Rome before working in Bucharest for three years where he was private dentist to Queen Elisabeth of Romania. In America he obtained the degree of Dental Surgery at the University of Pennsylvania. In England he gained his Licentiate of Dental Surgery at the Royal College of Surgeons before establishing his decades-long dental practice in Collins Street, Melbourne, next to the Independent Church.

When Hedley was ten years of age he was one of the few members of the public to witness the hanging of Ned Kelly at 10 a.m. on 11th November, 1880, in Melbourne Gaol. He accompanied his well-connected politician father, David Ham. In later years, while Hedley was attending the Royal College of Surgeons in London he would walk from his nearby lodgings to the Royal College

Bill's paternal grandfather at rear centre holding a baby, Bill's father, at a gathering at Cooma when the baby was born in 1915

via the pathways of Hyde Park. On many of those mornings he fell into the habit of every day greeting a regal lady who came his way in a phaeton, an open carriage popular in the late 19th century. He would tip his top hat to her and wish her good morning. She came to acknowledge him and responded by always smiling upon recognising him. The lady in question was Queen Victoria of England. I imagine few people could have said they had seen the visages of two such disparate people as bushranger Ned Kelly and Queen Victoria.

I earlier mentioned University and I find that topic relevant today as some 55 per cent of Australian students who now complete Year 12 go on to University or a similar under-graduate course. I left school at the end of 1962 and in those days 4 per cent of Year 12 students went to university and when I think about the comparative figures something seems wrong regarding today's education system. The 96 per cent who did not proceed to university went to work and work they did. There was no welfare state such as exists today. The 1960s produced a record 5.3 per cent of GDP, Gross Domestic Product growth by the nation for the whole decade while the individual per capita growth for those ten years was 3.2 per cent, a record for that amount of time which still holds today. President Trump has declared the United States of America will now proceed to have a decade of three per cent growth in GDP Gross Domestic Product. Apparently America has never been able to do that but Australia has, in the past but certainly not these days.

Halfway through 2024 the GDP for Australia was 0.1 per cent for the previous twelve months and that was inflated by unprecedented immigration numbers, multiple amounts of State and Federal

Chapter One *Wingadee station*

Government hand-outs of money and subsidies while the more worthwhile per capita growth figures for the past seven quarters have all been negative. The 1960s was the strongest performing decade of the 20th century in Australia, with a measured post-war increase in population of actual working people and a definite transition to something we sadly lack nowadays, that being manufacturing.

I think we know that Australian Universities have for some time now been lowering their entry levels for many students such as the fifteen universities around the country that have enrolled school leavers with ATAR scores below 60---the lowest twenty per cent of students. The University of Tasmania has offered a place in a primary school teaching degree to an applicant with a raw ATAR of 39.35----a rank reflecting the bottom 4 per cent of high school results. The elite Monash University enrolled an applicant with an ATAR of 60. I thought the teacher was meant to be smarter than the student.

I shall put the lecture aside now and proceed with the first part of my life story, as a memoirist.

My first job was in the administrative section at the Sydney Head Office of QBE at 80-82 Pitt Street, a short walk up from Circular Quay. Two nights a week I attended a nearby business college and studied accountancy. My accommodation was a single room in a boarding house at Cremorne Point. Even if I had a car I would not have used it to go to work as what could be better than a brisk walk down the road to the ferry, where I sat on an outside bench and to then travel across Sydney Harbour and past the Opera House, buoyed by salt water and refreshed by the tang of the sea spray on one's face. On the opposite side of 82 Pitt Street stood the narrow-fronted but three-story high rabbit warren of a pub, the Angel Hotel. It is long gone now, in fact the Angel was knocked down while I was there but it is remembered because it had character in spades.

Mick was a fellow about my age who also resided in the boarding house and he had a motor bike, which I thought was really cool. I don't ride motor bikes but I admire those who can handle them at the extraordinary speeds they produce. I remember watching Casey Stoner, one of several Australians who won the world championship title. He was asked how he handled fear when riding at maximum pace and he said he didn't know what fear is. The speed and the inherent risk did not affect him one iota. I imagine you have to be born to it.

My grandparents had moved to a unit at Manly and on week-ends Mick and I would ride over there. Mick had a good friend at Manly, Terry, who had a car. It was a Ford Prefect Saloon and it ran well. The Prefect had roof-racks made for surfboards and with Terry's mate, Dean, the four of us would fill the car, inside and on top and check out every beach from Manly to Newport looking for the best waves. That car carried us to so many happy places, from The Steyne Hotel at Manly to the beer garden at the Newport Arms and of course to all those fabulous northern beaches in between but mostly to Manly and Freshwater.

I had a surfboard made by Gordon Woods of Brookvale but my grandparents' unit was too small to keep it there. I was lucky because they knew a real estate agent by the name of Rex Phillips. Rex was a well- built man with an excellent physique and a member of the Manly Surf Club, which was the first surf club to hold a beach competition in Australia.

Rex had a shed behind his Manly office and he told me I could leave my board in there. As he was closed on Sundays he kindly gave me a key and allowed me to come and go as I pleased. In his day Rex was the Australian Beach Sprint Champion, run over 100 yards, for four successive years and when I met him in 1961 he was made a life member of the Manly Surf Lifesaving Club. For 1967-68 and 1968-69 he was the President of the Manly Surf Lifesaving Club. I don't know why he took to me but I was ever so grateful. I still have that surfboard with its 1961 and 1962 Manly Council rego stickers. A good twenty five years ago a Sydney businessman offered me $1,000 so he could have it on show in his surf museum but I could never let it go. Some parts of your life are not for sale.

Another Manly icon who was still a regular at Manly was 'Snow' Mcalister. Snow would have been about 58 and still rippling with muscle when I met him at the beach and he generously gave me

Snow McAlister surfing at Manly

Fifty-eight year old Snow McAlister of Manly

tips about board riding and surfing. He was well qualified for the subject of board riding as he won the Australian surfboard riding title three times and was the first man to be inducted into the Australian Surfing Hall of Fame. When I knew him he was still riding surfboards standing on his head. I believe he passed away in 1988 and for the past twenty seven years an annual winter surfing competition in his name has been held at Manly.

I also saw Bernard 'Midget' Farrelly now and again at Manly. In 1963 he won a major event in Hawaii and the following year he captured the first World Surfboard riding championship title, which just happened to be held at Manly. They were all good in their own way but for me Rex Phillips was special.

I wasn't around to see Midget win for I was long gone. As much as I loved body surfing and board riding I was of the opinion that for me big cities would be somewhere to visit and enjoy but not to live, with all due respect to insurance and accountancy. The sea had much to offer as I would later come to appreciate but I could not make a living off it and I intuitively felt the need for more space elsewhere.

I soon landed a position at Wingadee Station, Coonamble, as a jackaroo, a type of apprentice farm manager where one learns the business of agriculture but at the owner's expense, which is why the pay is on the low side. I might come to that in due course. Coonamble is 560 km north-west of Sydney and Wingadee would be forty km further north, starting off on the road to Walgett and then turning off on to the track to Come-by-Chance.

Wingadee, then owned by the New Zealand and Australian Land Company was so prominent that there was a time when the Council was named Wingadee Council, before it became Coonamble Council. The Coonamble district was honoured when it was reported as having the highest enlistment per head of population, in NSW, for military service in World War One. As a result it was later recognized by a visit from His Royal Highness, Edward, Prince of Wales, who duly stayed at Wingadee, where he was accorded a guard of honour consisting of the station stockmen, jackaroos, Aboriginals and neighbours. The Prince was accompanied by his Aide-de-Camp, Lord Louis Mountbatten who was a second cousin once removed of Queen Elizabeth 11 and also an uncle of Prince Philip the Duke of Edinburgh. Mountbatten would later be an

Admiral of the Fleet and the last Viceroy of India before he was assassinated by the IRA.

Wingadee has since been cut up but when I arrived it consisted of 150,000 acres or 60,000 hectares as measured today. The level country had never been farmed and consequently it was a quality livestock grazing property, consisting mostly of highly prized Mitchell grass along with some areas of Old Man saltbush which was handy for keeping Merino sheep in good condition in times of drought. One paddock of 13,000 acres or 5,260 hectares stood apart from all else. This was the much talked about Bullock paddock which consisted of lignum scrub, a stock feed peculiar to Australia and comprising a tangled mass of perennial shrubs that together form dense thickets that keep most other vegetation at bay. It thrives in often dry areas which now and again flood and in this case the Castlereagh river cut through that section of Wingadee. The Castlereagh is somewhat unusual as most of its water flows below ground rather than above. Lignum normally grows to 2.5 metres in height and it creates an outstanding hiding place for animals, even cattle when they are sitting or lying down. If the cattle stay quiet one has to all but ride on them to realise where they are and it is a perfect haven for snakes, wild pigs and foxes.

Wingadee ran 5,500 head of cattle, 60,000 sheep and enough horses to breed, replenish and break-in all that were needed. I had not ridden a horse prior to going there but we rode nearly every day and after two years and a few mishaps I was quite content with my progress. Every man had three horses to last him three months, after which he received three fresh horses and so on. We had two Landrovers for the manager and the overseer. There were several Bedford trucks.

Wingadee employed six station hands, five jackaroos and because of its size and long distances to be covered, five boundary riders. The latter lived out on the boundary at various points of the compass and when sheep and cattle had to be brought in to the main stockyards, those men would muster the stock they were responsible for and start moving them in to the station yards. At the same time we would be riding out to meet them and then bring them in to complete the day's droving. The jackaroos were told what do by their overseer and you should not underestimate the authority of those men. They are descended from the hortators or encouragers you see in Roman galleys cracking the whip to ensure adherence to duty and eternal discipline. I don't think anyone complained because we soon realised it was the way to have things done properly and quickly with the end result being high productivity and therefore satisfaction all around. I gained much by learning discipline from the overseer regime and I believe that type of education stood me in good stead in future years no matter what line of work I was involved in.

Fellow jackaroo Malcolm 'Springheel' Robertson has a hold on Bill at Wingadee Station

There were other men who did singular jobs, such as the blacksmith, the groom who when not mustering ensured that the horses were well-treated and healthy, the cook who did the obvious and his off-sider who killed sheep for our rations and especially when the shearing team arrived, the bore-drainer who used to hitch his draught horses up to a large and heavy iron implement known as a delver, somewhat in the shape of a cow-catcher on 19th century American trains. He would manoeuvre the beast of a thing into a bore-drain that was clogging up with silt and other matter and then command his powerful draught horses to pull the delver through the drain, cleaning it out as they progressed, day after day. This ensured the next flow of above ground water from the bore would provide comparatively clean and heathy stock-water. Poly pipe was not in use for water transfer back then.

As we were nearly always engaged in stock work we were not required to do any fencing and on 60,000 hectares there are always sections of fence that require repair, especially from the non-domestic animals such as the wild pigs, kangaroos and emus. We had them in abundance and spent many a night spot-light shooting. I could say we did it because we had to feed our dogs, which at times

Delving a bore drain as done on Wingadee Station, where Bill Smith, the life-long blacksmith, did his delving single-handed.

were invaluable to our work but I know we all enjoyed the action of shooting. Making head shots at night without using a scope but having a spotlight teaches one to be accurate and to put a quick end to the target. Those nights were the rare times we were allowed to use a Landrover.

I ended up with a few rifles over the years but the pick of them by far was a Brno 22, a repeater rifle made in Czechoslovakia. It was an amazing rifle, so damned accurate and a well-regarded brand throughout Europe. I recall I bought mine in the Johnny Burns Menswear clothing shop in Coonamble and I know I paid $22. I kept it for decades, only surrendering it when I sold the farm and moved into town, into Dubbo. The police knew I had moved because almost straight away they came around to ask what had I done with my rifles and also my treasured double-barrelled shotgun. I sold them to a gun-shop owner who was late informing the police he now had them, as required by law. I could have joined a gun club and kept the rifles but just living in town curtailed a lot of my freedom and I put the guns in the past part of life category.

Imagine my surprise when I recently looked the Brno up on the internet. Second-hand Brno rifles from the same era, either side of 1960, same type without a telescopic sight, are listed for sale from $750 to $1,250.

The Brno took me away from the fencing story on Wingadee, sorry about that. I mostly just write as it comes to me. We did not do the fencing but the station employed a contract fencer. He was a white man, Geoff, and first thing every Monday morning he would arrive in his work truck with six full-blood Aborigines in the back along with his fencing and camping gear. The overseer would tell Geoff what he wanted done for the week and then off they would go in the truck. Late Friday afternoon they returned to the station office to report on the week's work and then they were off to Coonamble for the week-end at home.

Truth to tell, home included the pub. Those six men would drink so much alcohol over the week-end they were incapable of lining up for work on the Monday. It was like that every week, never the same six men two weeks in a row but Geoff handled it and he always ensured the allocated job was done courtesy of another six.

We rarely saw the manager but there was a full-time accountant who also ran a small store where he handled the mail, sold tobacco, roll-your-own papers, boot polish etc and handed out the pay slips. We had one Saturday afternoon off work every month and for that we were paid £5 and ten shillings a week, which put simply without inflation and natural increase today equals $11 per week. If I conservatively say we worked fifty-five hours per week then we were being paid twenty cents an hour. Obviously that is not realistic in today's terms but it is interesting to know that people in various trades or professions are now being paid $100 per hour, or more. You might care to give a thought as to what future wages will be although ever since Prime Minister Keating's recession struck in 1990 things changed. Westpac had lent far too much money to building developers who, labouring under interest rates of 18 per cent or more, could not repay their loans. To avoid going broke Westpac had to have a massive capital raising and was forced to pay the American banker Bob Joss an absolute fortune, millions, to come in and save the bank. I believe since then we have been paying ourselves too much along with a dramatic drop in productivity.

Chapter One *Wingadee station*

There were occasions when the boss let us go down to the nearby billabong at the far end of the horse paddock on Sunday afternoons after work and lunch and do some water ski-ing. As with horse-riding I had never water skied but I can immodestly say I took to it instantly and after a couple of runs I was up on one ski. The billabong was probably 600 metres in length and fortunately it widened at the far end. With a good boat driver and if you positioned yourself well and made a tight turn, at speed, you could ski around that end of the billabong and then have an exciting run home. If you misjudged it and went wide on the bend you found yourself ski-ing and disappearing, in amongst the two to three metre tall cumbungi that lined that entire far end of the billabong.

Cumbungi is native to Tasmania and often known as bullrushes. Its new white/green shoots can be eaten raw and if left to become young green cobs they can be consumed like sweet corn. The yellow rich protein from the male flower spike can be mixed with flour or starch from the rhizomes to form cakes that you can cook in hot ashes while it is possible to use the brown female flower spike as a mild anaesthetic for toothache.

When the 1965 drought was raging the Gungalman water ski club at Carinda, which is at the northern end of the wetlands known as the Macquarie Marshes and about 100 km west of Wingadee, ran out of water and Con Mooy of Gungalman, asked if he and his men could come and ski at Wingadee. Our boss agreed, probably in part because drought can be devastating and one needs a good social outlet to keep up one's spirits. Our billabong had the advantage of not having water flow into it like a river or creek and therefore to lose it in the same way. It held its water, be it groundwater, rainfall, soak or heavenly. Con and his men were well pleased to ski with us and in turn they did us a favour. They brought with them their water-ski jump. It was a monstrous affair, a home-made heavy timber sloping ramp on empty but sealed 200 litre drums. They positioned it some 100 metres before the end of our home run so that we finished our run by doing the jump in front of an audience.

As with everyone else I had to get back on two skis for the jump and I was apprehensive for if I made a mistake in approaching the ramp let alone while moving at speed on to it, the end result was not going to be pretty. The boat driver helped with the speed side of things and I concentrated on lining my approach up. I can still feel the sensation of approaching the ramp at an angle then pulling hard on the rope and straightening up my run to gain sufficient speed, bending zee knees, zooming up the ramp and taking off. All of a sudden I was flying though the air and making the landing. Like most of life it is a matter of facing it and doing it.

Of course we did receive board and lodging, along with two weeks annual leave. Once again I had a small room to myself, one with the most basic of furniture but I had little in the way of clothing to be concerned about and only rarely having somewhere worthwhile to go and the roof did not leak. The only air-conditioning in those days occurred when you hung your canvas water-bag on the front bumper of the vehicle and drove rather fast and/or wound the windows down. However it was dry heat and at that age, eighteen/nineteen, I don't believe the weather was a problem. Young people take it in their stride.

For most of us a day in the week started at 7.30 a.m. at the stables, with your packed lunch, your horse and yourself ready to receive the orders of the day from the overseer and to then ride out. However you had to have your horse available in the first place and for the jackaroos that required extra effort.

The horses we rode for three months at a time were kept in the horse paddock and they therefore had the billabong for their water supply but they did not trot up to the stables on demand every morning. Each jackaroo in turn for one week at a time was required to be up at 5.30 a.m. or perhaps 6.00 depending on the season and be the horse-tailer. You went to the stables where the night-horse was wide awake and eagerly waiting to be saddled up. His name was Hammerhead. If you look at racehorses finishing off their race, some will let down and extend their body, driving forward in long, low strides with a lovely rhythm. Others will go fast and furious with as many strides as possible and urging themselves on by pushing their head forward and as their legs carry them on the head seems to roll back before being pushed forward again at a great rate. The latter was Hammerhead's style but at a ferocious pace, hence his name. It was a wonder his head didn't snap off for it went to and fro with the speed of a chain saw. If he had been in a Melbourne Cup he would have led all the way to victory, such as Lord Fury did in 1961, the aptly named Might and Power in 1997 and Twilight Power in 2023.

Hammerhead was as strong as an ox but he did not buck or veer to the side. He had no interest in trying to dislodge the rider as long as he could be allowed to run free and as fast as he could, so that he could harass the stock horses by way of his sheer determination and speed. The slight problem for the rider was that there were times when searching for the horses Hammerhead would use his strength to take a look in amongst the trees and the horseman would need to ride like a jockey, stretched out along his back with head on the horse's neck. Otherwise you could be knocked clean out of the saddle. Once we found the horses and were behind them you could relax. The pace was still flat out but now all Hammerhead wanted to do was to boss the horses and drive the mob to the yards at maximum speed and that I have to say was exciting. If you hadn't been awake you certainly were then. In a cloud of dust and the absolute thunder of hooves of some thirty-three horses we galloped past the jackaroos quarters and into the open yards by the stables.

Lest you might think we always rode like that I can assure you that at the end of a day's work we obeyed the golden rule. If you had delivered cattle to a paddock ten or twenty km away no matter what distance or how late in the day your horse was not permitted to trot, canter or gallop home. Once we turned for home the horses knew their job was done and they wanted to return as quickly as possible. Everyone, man and beast, had to adhere to the discipline and walk home and we often came back by the light of the moon.

As the drought set in the manager decided we would sell off the cattle, which were still in good condition and keep the sheep. That meant feeding them wheat which we did not have, every second day.

That was a big decision as it came on top of the regular work. We bought wheat from the Coonamble silos and after emptying those cleaned out the Gulargambone silos, manufactured our own troughing to place on the ground and then dropped the wheat into the troughs so as to have as little as possible of it ending up on the ground. We did not have an auger to convey the wheat up and into the large bin on the back of the truck so we had to dig a hole in the ground below the bottom chute of the silo, stand in the hole and manually fill bags with wheat, fifty kilo bags, then lift them up to ground level, then lift the bags up on to the trucks and finally lift them further up and into the hoppers from where we let the wheat out to fill the troughing as the truck drove alongside. Very physical work. As for the cattle we would muster a selected mob, draft off the best of them to fill a truckload or two, send them off to be sold and return the rest to their paddock. A few days later we would do the same to another mob and when we weren't feeding sheep do yet another mob of cattle, all the time reducing the pressure on the remaining feed and cattle. The process was relentless but eventually the cattle were gone and because of their good condition they sold well.

I would say the exercise of feeding the sheep was not that good. On their rather limited food supply they were steadily losing ground and feeding them every second day in relentless heat was not sufficient to give them the balanced diet they required. In January, 1965, I had been invited to a wedding in Coonamble, before we had been barred from leaving the station for six months. When I entered the church that Saturday morning at 9.45 a. m. a thermometer in the shade of the verandah was already nudging 43 degrees Celsius.

A few weeks later in February we conducted the annual sheep classing. The classer assessed each sheep on its merits and decided to keep or sell them. That assessment was conducted out in the open in a race that had an overhead bough covering to keep the immediate rays of the hot sun at bay for the benefit of the sheep and the classer. It rarely covered us whilst keeping up the supply of sheep. It took two weeks to do all the sheep and believe it or not that year every one of those fourteen days the temperature reached at least 47 degrees. However it was as dry a heat as you could wish for and bearable.

Back to the sheep. They started to die for want of good green grass and the minerals that go with that. We began to send a truck out and we picked up the dead sheep and stacked them in a distant heap for burning. However we could not hide that activity from the merciless crows who were not beyond attacking those animals who were weakened but still alive. Many a crow would descend upon the poor creatures still drawing breath and peck their eyes out. We took some revenge and put a stop to much of their barbaric behaviour by putting Luci-jet, a chemical that contained poisonous Fenthion-ethyl that was regularly used to control blowflies on sheep and the eradication of lice and ticks, on the already dead sheep. Many a crow met their fate there before being consumed on the same funeral pyre.

One day a stranger by the name of Tex rode in. He was in his mid-thirties, as tall as they come, well over two metres and as lean and as hardy as an ironbark post. His hair had not been cut for a few years which was less time since his teeth had been exposed to a dentist. When we saw them I think most of us recoiled. They were misshapen, in various shades of brown and mostly of different sizes. He rode a good style of a horse and led a packhorse that was hitched to a trailer of sorts, well, I should probably say of his worldly possessions.

Tex had ridden in from the Macquarie Marshes I mentioned earlier where he had been camped and literally living off the land, beholden to no man. Now the drought had dried out the wetlands and the wildlife, which included kangaroo meat and emu eggs,

Chapter One   *Wingadee station*

birds and the fish had departed. They were the tucker supply for Tex and his dogs and he was now in need. He asked about a job and Murray, the latest overseer, obliged. Murray was as hard a man as Vince the previous overseer but he could smile once in a while and he had some understanding of individuals. A few years later I heard he married well and was managing a good property at Jerilderie in the Riverina where something went wrong and he died young. On the positive side it was said his wife took over the reins and became an excellent rural manager, so good on her after her tragic loss.

When it was time for the annual lamb marking, that was a big job. It was too far and slow to bring the ewes and their lambs into the station sheepyards so each of the five boundary riders would muster the sheep in their territory to their own set of sheepyards and pen them up. We would normally ride out there but as we needed to start work at 4 a.m. to beat the heat and to have the lambs healing from their cuts and marking before the heat of the day and the flies getting at them, we went out in the Landrovers and trucks. Some of the station hands came with us as not only all due care and accuracy was required but also speed. Tex was in our mob.

We set up and were soon under way, working in well-prepared teams to mark the thousands of lambs each morning. Someone was always required to keep the tally and part of that routine was that every time a hundredth lamb was marked that person would call out in a loud voice, HUNDRED. That score would be written down. When it came time for Tex to do the counting he was different. We used an implement that you hold across the palm of your hand and hold it firmly. One end of it has a knife blade with which you cut off the tail of the lamb and then slice off the top of the purse or ball-bag.

The other end of the item has a hook that you then use to reach around the lamb's balls and pull them out.

Tex would use the knife blade to cut off the tail and slice open the bag but instead of using the hook to remove the balls Tex would lean down, put his face to the purse and pull the balls out with what remained off his teeth. As he stood upright he swallowed the pair and then called, HUNDRED. That was how he counted and it didn't end there. When we finished the morning's work at 11 a.m., had ensured the ewes and their lambs were now all outside the yards on fresh, clean grass and we had tidied up, washed and put everything away we put the billy on and had morning tea. There were supplies of fruit, bread and extras. Most of us had a mug of fresh tea and made a sandwich or two. Tex once again did it his way. He made his own sandwiches as did we all but the difference was that Tex did not have vegemite or cheese and tomatoes. He loaded his sandwiches up with more lambs balls and he eagerly devoured them. Lord only knows what he ate out in the Macquarie Marshes.

The annual shearing was such a big event we would often have tourist buses pull up during the day and disgorge the sightseers and I don't blame them for it is not often you could see at first hand such a large and well-organized rural operation. In earlier days Wingadee had fifty-two shearing stands, with twenty-six on each side of the board. In our time we used just one side of the board but at least it was twenty-six shearers all in one straight line and not many sheds could match that. There were four strong men who pressed the wool and to do that all day was a major task. There were two men to a wool press and they had to fill and press

Chapter One *Wingadee station*

the wool down and into each of the two presses. There were no electric wool presses in the 1960s.

The gun shearers could shear 200 adult Merino sheep per eight-hour day and each day concluded with ninety bales pressed. A large truckload per day. Shearing went on for three weeks provided the weather held good, which it invariably did. Sometimes it doesn't rain when you want it to and then again it does rain when you don't want it to. The jackaroos did the mustering and then returned the shorn sheep to their paddocks. The shearers and the overall shearing team stayed in basic shearers quarters and there were no complaints when the shearing contractor was a knowledgeable and well-organized character, which Bob Dixon of Coonamble was. The most important man of course was the cook. With just one off-sider that amazing character produced three full meals and two smokos for dozens of men every day and faultlessly so. A side product of that was the large number of sheep we killed, hung up and then cut up or dressed every day. If the jackaroos were around the shed for smoko they shared in that although not the main meals but I know they were excellent because the shearing team was definite about that.

I have to tell you briefly about the Bullock paddock. Its 5,260 overgrown hectares demanded that when we had to muster that challenging terrain every man on the station, even the cook, a German by the name of Ingo whom we called Ringo, had to saddle up. You could ride into that paddock easily enough but finding your way out could be a problem, let alone finding sufficient numbers of cattle.

On the week-ends most of the shearing team went into Coonamble or Walgett but an interesting fellow was Dougal, one of the wool pressers. He stayed in the shearers' quarters for those weekend nights so that he could have a good start the next morning. He would take his dogs and go with them into the Bullock paddock. He also took his knives for he went pig-hunting. No rifle for Dougal, that would be too easy. He walked in there until his dogs flushed out some pigs and he was not interested in the young or small ones. When his dogs bailed up a good-sized pig Dougal would get in behind the pig when it was distracted by the dogs. He would jump on the pig's back and hold it from behind. When he had a good grip and felt he could avoid the grunter's deadly tusks he would kill the pig with his knife. I never heard of anyone else being so fearless let alone successful and I say that because Dougal always went into the Bullock paddock bare-foot.

There were others worthy of mention such as the old blacksmith, Bill Smith. He knew his trade as a banker knows your money. Bill had a son Aubrey, born and raised on Wingadee as a station hand in general and a horseman from the moment his mother released him. Apart from my horse-riding experiences in Mongolia I never saw another man who rode near as well as he did. If ever a man was born to his trade that was Aub Smith. He was peerless.

Talking of horsemen, every twelve months Ron Richards, the former Australian buckjump champion, would arrive with his gear and break in our current crop of two-year old station-bred horses. Ron had a good manner with men and horses but I sometimes thought he might have put the rope away too soon. I say that because once Ron had the young'uns to the point where he had ridden them once or twice he then handed them over to us, saying they were all ours now. I just thought he could have given them a bit more work because although we could all ride fairly well he was the one with a lifetime of such experience and had a track record par excellence. More to the point he was the one who better understood the nuances of young horses. I might have expected too much and I suppose we did learn quicker than we otherwise would have but we did take the odd fall because of that which left me with that nagging feeling. I suppose he was testing us.

Each year the young 'uns were named with the next letter of the alphabet. For instance the previous year it was K and the next year L. One of the best horses I was lucky enough to have was a two-year old from that crop by the name of Lightning and so it went each year.

Murray had jackaroos, Malcolm, aka Springheel, Nick and myself riding three of the newly broken-in horses to take a mob of cattle to a distant paddock and he said we could take our time with them, the horses and the cattle. It happened to be a gorgeous day, the scent of the Australian bush hung in the air with trees and vegetation contributing to the drifting aroma. Man and beast alike were savouring the environment and I imagine some of that goes missing when today's stockmen utilize machines such as motor-bikes and helicopters as they more forcefully tend to their livestock.

Unexpectedly the cattle in the lead were disturbed but by what? Half a dozen of them were lifting their forelegs off the ground and appeared to be stamping down on something, causing small clouds of dust to add to the extra movement. Nick was on our left flank so he cantered up to see what was causing the agitation. I followed but walked my horse after him and Malcolm kept control at the rear.

Nick reached the ruckus and I saw him lean down to his right, so that he was all but out of the saddle. His right arm momentarily disappeared from my sight but just as quickly it re-appeared as he extended his arm off to the side, whilst holding a live snake by the tail. No doubt the unfortunate snake had been basking in the early morning sunshine and the cattle had taken it by surprise.

The reptile was a fair size, close to one and a half metres in length. It looked bruised and dusted up, thanks to the hooves of the cattle. I couldn't be sure but it may well have been one of the area's numerous Inland Taipans or possibly a Western or Eastern Brown. It didn't claim the striking copper colour of the Mulga or King Brown and it did not have the strong tones of the red bellied Black snake but then again, it had been touched-up somewhat.

I was coming close to Nick now and he began to swing the snake around and over his head, at a definite arm's length. Faster and faster he swung and I had an insight into what he planned to do. I halted my horse six to seven metres from him and as I did so in that instant he brought his arm down by his side with all the strength he could muster. That sudden change of direction at speed was similar to the method of cracking a whip. The resultant force separated the snake's head from its body and it flew instantly in my direction. I was looking at it as though it was a bullet leaving a rifle barrel. In that split second the head seemed to grow larger and larger as it filled my vision and even though I had half anticipated Nick's move I could not adjust when the moment came. I was fascinated. The head of the snake passed so close to my left ear I heard it hiss.

One day Ringo the cook left Wingadee and that was a serious matter when it was discovered that a replacement could not be found. Murray solved the problem by the simple expedient of delegating the role to the jackaroos. Each one of us was to do the cooking for a week

Chapter One   *Wingadee station*

A Mulga or King Brown snake as on Wingadee Station

at a time. No one had expected anything like that and it was no good protesting. Orders are to be obeyed. Murray did find some cooking and recipe books and left us to it. Imagine. Without worthwhile experience we each and individually had to cook three meals for six station hands and five jackaroos plus provide two smokos for whoever might be about, seven days a week, every fifth week. On top of that we had to do the preparation, washing up and putting everything away after each meal. They were long days. There were several fifth weeks for each of us as it took forever to find another cook. Remarkably we all managed and there was barely a complaint made about our culinary skills.

I do feel obliged however to tell you this. It was during the six months when due to the increased workload of continually feeding sheep and mustering and drafting off sale cattle on top of regular work that the other jackaroos and myself were not allowed to have a single day off work. We began to suffer from sore and discoloured limbs. I was affected above the ankles, around the shins which began to ache, rising up to the knees and the skin thereabouts turned purple. We had contracted what was known locally as Barcoo Rot but was known to sailors in the 18th century as scurvy. There are many aspects of where and how scurvy can affect one's body and they are not pretty if treatment does not come soon. You would know that fresh fruit and vegetables are regarded as an antidote and with time it did work for us.

Another station-hand was Dooley Wallace, an Aboriginal some five years older than I but we hit it off as soon as we shook hands. We clicked. Don't know why but we liked each other. So it wasn't a disaster when we made a slight error. Dooley and I were on the back of a truck feeding out small bales of hay to the sheep. He used his machete to cut the twine and as soon as he had done that I picked up the bale before it could fall apart and threw it over the side of the truck to the sheep, where it then broke up.

I had to be quick as Dooley's job took less time than mine. Consequently I was reaching for the cut twine as normal but as I did so I might have been too quick as Dooley's machete cut my hand as it reached the twine. I was lucky it only sliced into a few fingers but I needed to have them stitched up. I mention it because there are days when the sunlight is on them and after all this time I can still faintly see a couple of stitch marks where the needle went in and out. That made us blood brothers.

I might make light of that last comment but there was a time when I was seriously close to Dooley, like a brother. It was a Saturday afternoon when we should have had our half day off but the work went on and it was near dark when we finished for the day and

Chapter One   *Wingadee station*

arrived in Coonamble. We went straight to Tatts, the Tattersalls Hotel, and had to force our way through the bumper crowd. I ordered five beers and in reply the barman looked over my left shoulder and said, *Is he with you?* Momentarily I halted but I knew what he meant. I half turned, just enough to be sure he was looking at Dooley and I replied, *He is.*

He was equally to the point when he said, *I can't serve him.* There was no gain in arguing the toss, with both of us trying to score points. He had his job to do. I turned my back on the man and said to the others, *Come on, we're going across the road.* To their credit and to Dooley's worth, without hesitation they joined me in pushing our way back on to the street and across the road to the more receptive Coonamble Hotel. That hotel was not bursting at the seams but it did have a reasonable number of Aboriginal patrons and everyone there was on the same level or accepted as such. We stayed till late. Decades later I heard it said that a group of Aborigines bought the Coonamble Hotel but I can't prove that. It is long gone as a pub. Today it is a hardware store.

Over the years since I heard the accepted story that the later owner of the hotel, a white man, barred all Aborigines from his establishment and then he put the pub up for sale.

Prospective purchasers looked the place over and one man, a non-local who had never previously owned a hotel but liked the idea as he rather fancied himself as a hotel proprietor, bought the main street pub. To say he was surprised as the previously barred Aborigines drifted back into his new premises would be an understatement. I endeavour to make sure everything I write is correct. Janice and I have been in Queensland during the past few winters and whilst there I always meet up with an old friend, Doug Pinnington. He confirmed the story is true, telling me the buyer was his uncle.

We made one of our rare Saturday trips into Walgett and again we were held back by working late so it was already sunset when we arrived in that hard town. I normally prefer to drink beer, either VB or if I can find it Resch's. The D.A., Resch's Dinner Ale, has long gone but sometimes I can still lay my hands on Resch's Pilsener. Malcolm had a liking for black rum and insisted I join him in a few rounds. I had previously stayed away from the rum but after I had a few heart-starters of VB I agreed. Suffice it to say we had more than a few. I don't recall how we returned to Wingadee but I do know that when I went to get Malcolm up for breakfast he worried me. He had blood oozing out of his right ear. We put it down to his excessive consumption of rum but otherwise apart from being doughy and temporarily partially deaf, he seemed alright. Which was just as well.

Murray appeared, sober, bright-eyed and bushy-tailed. He even smiled, a rare sight indeed. On seeing our condition, especially Malcolm, he all but laughed as he said after breakfast we are going scrub-cutting and that being Sunday and all. We were to take our chainsaws, climb trees and cut branches all day long so as to provide a change of diet for the sheep.

We all had splitting headaches and the sound of the Landrover's engine was harsh. Murray took us to a copse of trees we had not encountered elsewhere. Wingadee had black box, wilga, coolabah and white cypress pine but he said these are Rosewood trees and the sheep do well on the leaves. I thought Rosewood trees have exceptionally hard, red timber and are excellent for building fence posts and making furniture but what would I know. Not much, so

I didn't say anything. I didn't feel like hearing anyone's voice let alone those chainsaws hammering away in my head all day. I shall let it rest at that except to say it was a living miracle not one of us fell out of a tree. it was the jackaroos who were to be sacrificed not the station-hands for this work and on a Sunday.

On another Saturday afternoon Malcolm, John Savage and I went up to Lightning Ridge to try our hand at finding opals. A lot of digging failed to produce any colour so we inspected the Lightning Ridge house made entirely of large but empty beer bottles. Both attractions induced us to retire to the regular hotel to meet the locals. Another Saturday saw us drive up the road to Come-By-Chance which was only a few km over the Wingadee boundary for the annual Come-By-Chance Picnic Races. Somewhat like the famous Birdsville Races people come from everywhere not only to see the races and the people but to participate as much as possible. It is a great Australian day out.

There was a lesser crowd the Saturday afternoon we went south to the horse racing at Gulargambone but those who were there witnessed a rare event. It was a summer's day, dry, hot and a little windy. So when the fire broke out it raced, what else would it do, around the track. The race track was on fire, it went up in flames but the stand and the saddling stalls were spared with no harm done other than to the precious grass.

The day came when Dennis Muller, a man I had known during my time on Wingadee, asked if I would work with him on his property in the New England district of Ebor, eighty km east of Armidale, in the high country. That sounded different enough to be challenging so I accepted the offer and went over there.

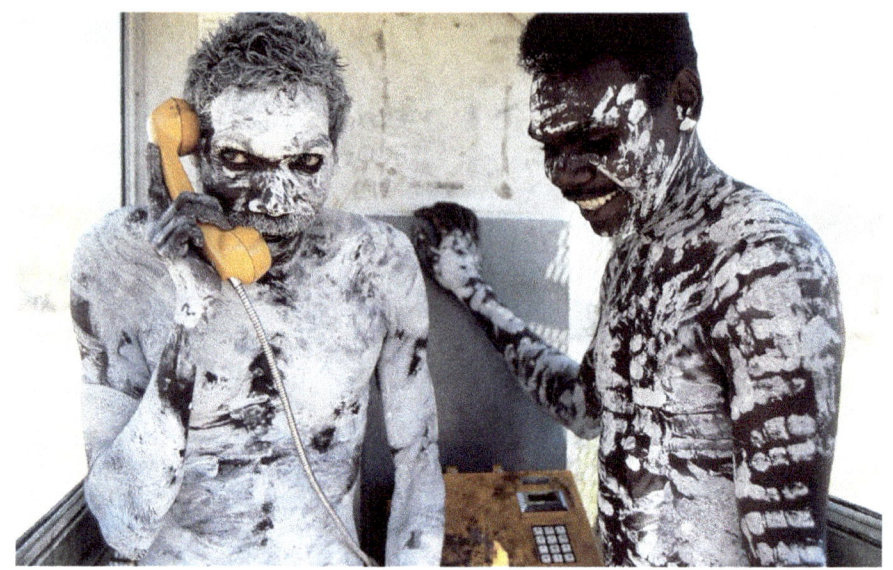

Aboriginal man, Tom, and his son using a phone for the first time, but not on Wingadee.

I thoroughly enjoyed my time at Wingadee Station. I never heard a bad word about or between anyone else, the sheep and cattle work, like the horses was never dull and I learned about animal husbandry. Recently a man said to me we must have earned a lot of overtime money for the hours we put in. He was startled when I told him we did not receive one cent extra for it never occurred to any of us. We were there to do the overseer's bidding and that was it. For myself I also learned horse riding, rifle shooting, water ski-ing, self-discipline, reward for effort, how to dress sheep meat, enjoy hot showers, cook satisfactory meals, engage in friendly wrestling, crack a stock whip, make omelettes from emu eggs, as the barbers were closed whenever we made it to town we cut each other's hair and to shear sheep. The overseer waited until it was shearing time and when we mustered those sheep that had missed last year's shearing and now had two year's heavier and dirtier fleece, those were the sheep we were required to practice on. That was hard for a novice but you learn, you always learn and you sleep like a log.

    You could well say that on the other side of the ledger we did not have motor-bikes, television, any sort of phone let alone mobile phones, other tech devices, alcohol on the station, newspapers, rarely girlfriends and were not allowed to play sport but I would not have swapped those life and work experiences for quids. Money for the benefit of the younger brigade. The experiences that we missed would come around in due course but those that we had encountered and conquered might not.

CHAPTER TWO

Panda

The clock of life is wound but once and no man has the power to tell just where the hands will stop, at late or early hour. To lose one's wealth is sad indeed, to lose one's health is more. To lose one's soul is such a loss as no man can restore. The present only is our own. Live, love, toil with a will. Place no faith in 'tomorrow' for the clock may then be still.

I was now the proud owner of a car, not exactly a rural vehicle but a Mini-Minor and it was transport. As young people in China have discovered a car takes them on their first road to comparative freedom. My venture took me into the high country of the New England tablelands. Coonamble sits at 180 metres of elevation, not that you would notice it, while Armidale resides at 980 metres of elevation and Ebor rules the roost at 1,300 metres. Lucky me. Dennis' property *Glen Alvie* was within rifle range of the village of Ebor.

Everything was different. The first time I rode out we went down a hill and as I reached the creek at the bottom my saddle slid so far forward I was about to go over the horse's head and into the water. I had never ridden a hill, either way and all but came to an embarrassing end in the water. I was never again so lax with the saddle girth. The air temperature was rather low but it felt healthy and the grass was green, everywhere. Dams were full to overflowing, stands of timber stood tall as they surrounded pristine paddocks in which cattle glowed and sheep luxuriated, protected from the weather while putting on weight.

This time I not only had a single room but an entire house to share with Dennis, the highlight of which for me was the enormous stone fireplace. I had never imagined, let alone seen anything like the sheer size of it. It was as though the house had been built around the fireplace and in the mountain climate I soon saw and experienced the sense of it. We hardly lacked for firewood.

A few days later we drove down the far side of the Great Dividing Range to the Dorrigo Plateau, near the New England Escarpment and came to the town of Dorrigo. At a gentle height of 730 metres one might think it a more relaxed environment but it holds the record for the highest rainfall ever recorded in 24 hours in NSW. This was 809 mm which occurred in February, 1954.

The first white man to lay his eyes on the district's magnificent timber was an escaped convict. When the word was out timber cutters moved in and established sawmills to satisfy the high demand for timber, which included blackbutt, tallowwood, ironbark and the highly sought after Australian red cedar. The latter is of deep, rich red colouring and before it was over-used red cedar was popular for furniture, wood panels and items as diverse as coffins and ship-building. The early settlers referred to red cedar as red gold.

I gather Dorrigo's population is holding at around 1,200 people. In 2005 a most unfortunate incident took place, affecting local livestock on a nearby farm. A herd of some eighty cows was sheltering under a tree that was struck by lightning. Apparently electricity spread from the tree onto the surrounding soil and killed sixty-five dairy cows. A tragedy.

Dennis and I drove down to Dorrigo to buy a few horses for stockwork. At length we came upon a farm with good stock and as we were spending Dennis's money he rode them and selected three horses. At that time, similar to Wingadee, Glen Alvie's main enterprise was tied up in sheep and cattle. There was no farming then but with such good soil and adequate rainfall there was barely a need for supplementary feed unless one wanted to increase production.

I won't dwell on the everyday working life as good as it was although I will say the farmers were different from the those in the far west. Many of the eastern men wore patches on the elbows of their coats when they went out, they tended to have more gentrified homes and for relaxation went shooting with a difference. They liked to indulge in trap or clay pigeon shooting and that involves not rifles but the more expensive shotguns.

Those men were polite to me, probably on account of Dennis, made me welcome and invariably someone would lend me a shotgun for the day. I always felt accepted in their company despite being a virtual stranger and from a different background.

Dennis made the rules and unlike Wingadee we would take some time off to indulge in sport, as in Rugby Union. Armidale City was always a strong club while the New England University in Armidale had three highly competitive teams drawn from their best colleges. Dennis played in the centres and was exceedingly robust. I thought if need be he would not be out of place in the forwards' engine room. I might say I was getting better with age but on the other hand I was still young. No disrespect to those teams but the more we thought about it we decided to go with a team from elsewhere but one that played in the same competition. We would compete against all four of the Armidale and other teams. Armidale is eighty km south-west of Ebor and Guyra is eighty km north-west of Ebor, with forty km separating Armidale and Guyra. A no brainer, we signed on with the Guyra Ghosts.

As suggested Dennis played a strong game, although at times he might have been playing his own way. With the ball in hand he was inclined to run straight and as a result many an opposing centre was left on the ground in his wake.

Shortly after I arrived the Armidale University Ball was to be held and Dennis had a partner but I did not know anyone. I said I would sit it out but he and Nancy, his girlfriend, insisted I go and they arranged a blind date for me.

I drove to Julie's house, introduced myself and vice versa and on to the Ball. We met Dennis and Nancy on the lawn in front of the Hall and climbed the stone steps to the main entrance where two young women greeted and made us welcome. They were both extraordinarily attractive and although I caught their names, Mandy and Helen, I was bestowing my attention upon Julie, endeavouring to do the right thing by my blind date. Somehow I felt the need to be of exemplary behaviour to a stranger more than I might to a girl I already knew. It wasn't her fault if she felt she was stuck with someone, such as myself, that she normally might not go out with and be a disappointment to her.

Julie and I made good conversation, we danced and sometimes conjured up a laugh or two but neither of us was going to look deep into the other's eyes. We stayed at the Ball until people began to drift away and then I took her home. When I saw her to the door I lightly put my arm around her waist, drew her to me and gave her a matching kiss on the cheek. She was ok with that but there was no more. Not that I was aware of. It marked the conclusion of a civilized outing and I never saw her again.

I mention that evening for two reasons. The first being that the next day Dennis told me he was pleased that I had paid so much attention to Julie and done the right thing by her. The second and more compelling reason was about to come.

We were right into the football season and the time came for Guyra to play Robb College, the gun team of the University for that year. Robb had a star player by the name of Armidale-born Rick How. Rick played on the right wing but to look at he could have been on the centre stage of a Broadway production. He would have been a good 185 cm in height and whilst I don't know his weight it would have been the perfect match. Girls loved him and men admired him, not just for his startling Greek god good looks but for his demeanour on and off the field. It seemed to me he was incredibly popular right across the board. He was a good Errol Flynn reincarnated.

I nearly forgot. My position was left wing and therefore I was marking Rick How. As I had to confront that situation I simply wanted to have it over and done as quickly and painlessly as possible. I discovered why footballers admired him on the field. I was not fast enough to be worthy of a wing spot so to balance things up I had some time ago made defence the main part of my game. I was put to the test before long. When Rick came my way I moved in and tackled him around the hips before sliding my arms down and around his legs. That was my intention and it had worked on other players. Not this time. When I drove in to Rick I as good as bounced off him for his hips were a concealed weapon. It was as though I was tackling Ned Kelly's iron armour. How could a mere mortal be as flexible as a politician and as fast as a hedge fund manager yet have the hidden strength of a blacksmith's anvil.

I was becoming painfully aware of what made the man a danger. Yet life at times is deceptive. We were still in the first half of the match with our attacking backline spread out on the right-hand side of the ground when from a scrum win our half back kicked the ball downfield on the blind side, i.e. my rather narrow left-hand side of the ground.

I had moved up in an attempt to hopefully collar Rick if the ball went his way and before he had time to set sail. Even so I did not expect our half-back to make the bold move of kicking away possession, least of all in my direction and certainly not towards Rick How. That is exactly what he did.

I was on the move, thankfully for me, and I imagine Rick was more surprised at this turn of events than I was for the ball landed on its point nicely downfield between us but closer to myself. It bounced up and back into my arms. I did not have to deviate or side step and best of all I now had the momentum which carried me past Rick's diving grasp. The line ahead was wide open and the remaining twenty metres vanished like a Menindee mirage.

Several of my teammates gave me a pat on the back and I expected no more but what stunned me was that Rick How walked over to me and said, *Well done, you scored a good try*. I was all but speechless. In five years of grade football no other opposition player said anything positive to me. I managed to say it was due to the bounce of the ball, the Luck of the Draw. I once scored two tries for Mudgee against Parkes, in first grade, one from halfway and the sole acknowledgement for that came as we walked off the field after the match from a spectator I knew who called out to me, *You miserable streak of misery, you got a couple*. I took that as a compliment.

Rick had a few more quick words to me and I was still floating on air when in the second half he went around me with blistering speed and evened the score. With him on the field I felt as though I was on hallowed ground.

Rick was soon selected to play for the Australian Rugby Union team, the Wallabies. The Test match was against Ireland at the Sydney Cricket Ground and as it happened Ireland had its first Test victory in Australia, winning 11-5. Rick might not have had his best of days and he would surely have been nervous but even so it seemed grossly unfair to select a player for one game and then not allow him the opportunity to redeem himself in a second. Perhaps the selectors used him as the scapegoat for their presiding over that initial home loss to the Irish. On the other hand once they make it into an Australian sporting team certain players cannot be levered out with the blade of a bulldozer.

An interesting thing happened after that Guyra/Robb College game. I had showered, changed and was standing outside the sheds taking in the surrounds, especially where Rick had been so thoughtful and generous when a girl, well a young woman, walked up and stopped right in front of me. She said hello. That was all and it made me a little cautious so I replied in the same manner, simply saying hello to her and no more. The surprise strengthened when she then said, *You ignored me.*

There was no doubt she was exceedingly pretty, most attractive and I knew I had briefly seen her at the University Ball but I said nothing of that. I was on the right track as she then told me that she and her friend Helen had been welcoming guests to the Ball and when our group arrived I did not pay any attention to her, as she implied people usually do. I could have told her I was accompanying Julie but I let that slide for the time being and only said, *Is that right?*

She told me her name is Mandy, she is the current Miss University and then as bold as brass she said to me, *Are you going to ask me out?* I gave it a moment's thought and addressing her on my terms, I said, *Amanda, would you like to go out with me*? She accepted immediately and it went from there. Every time I contacted her about going out, wherever and whenever she always said yes.

Funny creatures aren't we. If I had fawned over her she would most likely have ignored me but sensing the shoe was on the other foot and that she was being slighted she must have been determined to right that perceived wrong. I guess it went back to what Dennis said to me, that I had been patient and done the right thing by Julie and consequently I ended up with Mandy for quite some time and she never again displayed that air of expectation when I was with her.

As much as I enjoyed my time at Ebor and Armidale I was becoming restless. Dennis and I were compatible, he was good to work with and I seemed to get along with everyone I met. The New England area is stunning in many respects but there was something like an itch within me.

In due course I took my leave of Dennis and moved to Mudgee where I worked with Andy Pirie at his well-regarded Stock and Station agency business. In World War Two Andy had been a member of the 2/5th Cavalry Australian Commando Squadron, fighting the Japanese in New Guinea and Borneo 1942-1945. He was not known for talking about his exploits but men of his time said he saw a lot of action.

It was not until I had known Andy for thirty years that he finally put pen to paper and wrote his book, entitled *Commando Double Black*. The name signifies the identifying colour patch of those commandos, a double black patch worn on the upper arm. I recently saw Andy's book on sale via the internet at $330 and separately a double black patch was for sale at $250.

Eventually I bought a small block of land at Cooyal, north-east of Mudgee to run a few sheep. In the Aboriginal Guyal tongue Cooyal is the word for dry but otherwise that language has faded away unless somehow it is related to the Guyal language to be found in Saharan Chad. There were sheepyards but no buildings on the Australian version. Ernie Babbage said I could rent a deserted house on his neighbouring land. It can only be described as an old and cold concrete block. I paid four dollars a week for the privilege of not having electricity but enjoying cold water. Fortunately neighbouring wives took pity me on me from time to time and fed and watered me, with hot water.

Ernie had two sons, David and Errol. The former was known to one and all as Blue and he was tall, quiet and with an air of efficiency about him. He became a solid citizen, a good man of the land and the community. Somehow, by nature's whim, Errol was exceedingly short of stature but always with a word to say and it seemed, fearless. He was the smallest player I ever saw on a football field and it was remarkable for he displayed as much courage as I have seen from any player, of any code, amateur or professional. He played half-back for the Mudgee Dragons Rugby League club, first grade of course. He was like an emu or a kangaroo for he never took a backward step on the field of battle. To the world he was *Badger* Babbage. He thrived on confronting the opposing team's forwards and giving them cheek which only incited them all the more to run at him. Because of his lack of height he was compelled to tackle low. That meant he regularly dropped men twice his weight and all but twice his height. If he played today he would be known as a honey badger, of that I have no doubt. The Mudgee Dragons had an outstanding fullback by the name of Friday Reagan. I knew him but not so well as I did Badger. Friday was regarded by one and all as a naturally gifted sensational player, he should have and surely would have risen to great heights but unfortunately he died, a young man.

Whilst I maintained an interest in race-horses Badger did likewise with greyhounds, of which he owned several. He would talk to me so enthusiastically about them that the day came when with his usual relentless chatter he inveigled me into taking a half share in a young and untried but well-bred greyhound. He would own the other fifty per cent and keep it at his place and when it came good on the race-track we would share the profits, along with the costs. Before I came to have second thoughts about the latter the pup escaped from Badger's yard and was sadly run over and died. Thus ended my greyhound association.

Along with partaking of Rugby Union with the Mudgee Wombats

for two winters in reserve grade and then two years in first grade I was able to resume water-skiing during the summer months at Burrendong Dam, between Mudgee and Wellington. I particularly thank Harvey Parsonage who had country at Running Stream, a good sixty-four km south of Mudgee. He then had to travel another forty or so km to Burrendong so it was it was a significant trek, plus the return run, that Harvey and Panda made for our enjoyment. Harvey was, and still is, the proud owner and mechanic to his magnificent speedboat, Panda. In all those summers and for years afterwards Panda never failed to perform at the highest level, all credit to Harvey. I spoke to him recently and he told me Panda is still running, sixty years later. He doesn't go regularly to Burrendong nowadays but more so to the closer Chifley Dam at Bathurst.

As Panda is remarkable in its own right I should like to tell you something of her. Harvey is a farmer, now living at Sofala, but also a more than capable mechanic. He bought Panda in 1965 and she came with the six cylinder Q Dodge engine from a 1957 Chrysler Royal. The term KEW or Dodge Q motor refers to the DP/DQ engine developed by Dodge in 1933-34. It was a straight-6 flathead engine, which means the valves were located in the engine block and not the cylinder head. That format was used by Chrysler in the DeSoto and Chrysler Royal cars as they shared the same design. My father had a DeSoto in the 1950s and I do recall the front seat, a bench seat, being big enough for three adults. As an example of how strong that type of engine is it has been used in fork-lifts and headers, the latter for harvesting grain crops. Panda's engine has enabled her to still be performing today as she has for nigh on the past six decades and the principal reason for that is the thorough rebuild of the motor that Harvey carried out in 1969.

Chapter Two   *Panda*

Panda at scenic Burrendong.

*Panda and her redoubtable, multi-skilled owner-driver,
the farmer/mechanic Harvey Parsonage.*

Harvey modified the engine mounts, put in new pistons, rings and oversized bearings, ground the crankshaft and added twin carburettors from a Holden. All this inherent power made the engine rather tight and difficult to start, requiring much cranking so he added another twelve-volt battery. That made the world of difference and Panda then started up instantly and unleashed even more power. It is no trouble for her to tow two skiers and just to test her and to find out, she has, but carefully, towed three skiers at the one time, but Harvey restricts her to two.

Over the succeeding years Harvey has done this and that to maintain Panda's stamina and reliability but since then she has not required another engine rebuild. That will tell you not only of Panda but also the measure of the man and his ability.

Day after day, summer after summer, year after year, Panda never failed. As he pointed out, on a three-day long week-end Panda would operate from daylight to dark and consume, in today's measurement, a 200-litre drum of fuel through the carburettor, not to emphasise a heavy fuel consumption but an efficient one to reveal how much work Panda performed.

Panda is a clinker boat, meaning the body of the boat and certainly the hull are built of timber planks which when attached ensures the lower edge of each plank overlaps the upper edge of the plank below it. Those overlapping planks are then fastened together with screws, nails or rivets and they create a strong and watertight hull. The Vikings built their longships in the same clinker style, hammering iron nails through roves or washers to join the overlapping planks together from the outside to create a watertight joint. Some Viking builders went further and placed tarred rope or

Chapter Two   *Panda*

Panda in shed with blue engine nearby

Panda behind a red station wagon. In 1991 Harvey bought the vehicle from a Sydney dentist after a conversion specialist had turned a luxury Holden Statesman sedan into a V8 automatic AWD station wagon and Harvey, his wife Annie and their family rumbled around in that for the next ten years.

animal hair between the planks to aid the waterproofing process. I don't believe Harvey does that today.

In other parts of the world the clinker method was applied to traditional fishing boats. In today's era the clinker process enhances a variety of pleasure boats, sailing dinghies, small motor launches and rowing skiffs. This results in strength, durability and elegance.

Our ski group consisted of a hard core of ten blokes and not that it mattered but eight were from the Rugby Union club. At various times of a summer weekend we would meet Harvey and Panda at Burrendong and Harvey, generous to a fault, would take us, and many others as well, out behind Panda. It might seem selfish but with one exception there seemed to be an unwritten agreement that no one was accompanied by a girlfriend. It was never discussed, it just went that way, except that sometimes you might hear the Burrendong get together expressed as a time for the boys. The exception was the Rugby team's half-back, Neil Brodie, who was married to Maureen. Brodie was the only one among us who was married and Maureen never seemed to feel out of place while heavily outnumbered. We all enjoyed her company and that was the natural way of it. She was a good scout. I wouldn't know but it was quite possible the girls were glad we were out of town on those days.

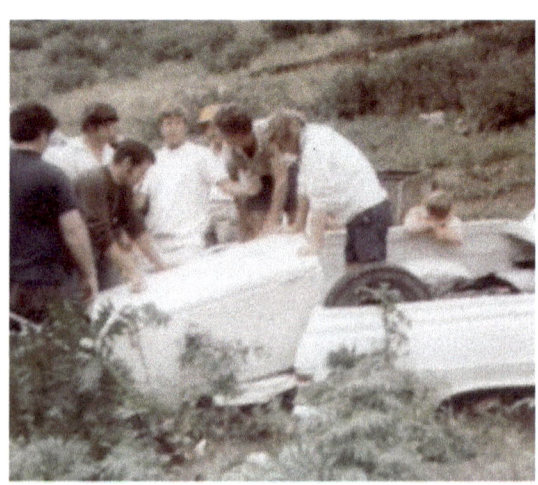
Bill Suttor (facing camera), author unloading fridge from utility.

Burrendong holds three

times the water of Sydney Harbour so it was never crowded and the rolling to level terrain had natural camp sites and local government installed facilities. It was and is a superb site for fishermen, campers, fossickers and nature and water lovers. I won't rave on much more but I would like to mention two incidents.

Late one afternoon most of us were there; Maureen, the Newman boys, Mike and Bill, Drew Pirie, Graham Hawkins, Bill and David Suttor, Tony Sheridan, Ian Thomas. Harvey had taken Neil out for a good, long run and now the boat was returning to shore at a fair pace but we thought Neil was cutting it fine. He was on two skis which he handled exceptionally well but this time his judgement seemed a little out of whack. Instead of letting go of the tow-rope as Harvey turned Panda away from the approaching shore, Neil kept coming, at speed. Finally he let go of the rope but now he could not slow up quickly enough unless he deliberately fell over or turned hard away. He did neither and even though he hit the shore line far too fast the silt and mud did stop his skis in the blink of an eye. Consequently Neil's excessive speed lifted him out of his skis and up and through the air. Open-mouthed we watched in awe as Neil did a magnificent somersault through the air, going above and past most of us and miraculously landed on his bare feet and remained there, rooted to the spot, like a statue in a museum, in front of the keg of beer. He could all so easily have landed on his head and broken his neck or simply landed with a might belly-flop and damaged himself no end but he didn't do that. We couldn't keep the beer in the keg cold enough for long enough so we kept a fridge at the dam and a few of us always brought bagged ice out with us to keep the beer cold in the fridge. That worked well.

Sixty years later the Mudgee boys tell me that flight of fancy by Neil is still talked about. How could that have happened? I have given it some thought and I have a theory how it was possible. Neil was perhaps the best footballer in the Mudgee team. He was that good he had been a triallist for the New Zealand All Blacks. They don't know what they missed. Neil played halfback for perhaps fifteen or twenty years, I can't be sure. He was of average height but of solid build for a halfback and fast on his feet. In his position he was always on the move, either for the next attacking play or defending against and tackling the opposition. As halfback if he was not running the ball himself he was passing it to someone and halfbacks traditionally are regularly required to make long and accurate passes. So Neil had developed a lovely sense of balance aligned with his strength.

My theory is that once the gods had determined he would be landing upright Neil was instinctively able to naturally employ that balance to land on his feet such as the contenders in the final of the Olympic Games gymnastics are capable of. Not that he practiced such but on that amazing afternoon his football techniques and balance, honed over countless years and matches, brought out the true athlete in the man, for when he landed on his feet, he stood as still as a tree stump.

Sunday mornings were often special. Sleeping out as we did the early morning sun invariably woke us to look upon a nautical miracle. If it was truly a blessed day the Burrendong water was perfectly flat with not a ripple of movement on its glistening surface, shining mirror-like and devoid of the slightest early morning breeze.

Usually at that hour we had the water to ourselves and whilst we could not all be the first of the day to take advantage of the pristine conditions the bounty was duly shared around between us, with Harvey and Panda once again making all things possible. In any event there were mornings when the heavens were distracted by the good people going to church and allowed us their morning grace for a thrilling two hours, sometimes a little more before the conditions were brought back to normal and the water once again had an edge to it.

On those mornings the water was perfect, to the point that we could lean over so far on the ski we were all but parallel to the surface of the water. Sometimes we pushed it too far but although the speed and the feeling of being right on top of one's game were sensational we did not have far to fall as we would be all but touching the water with our shoulder anyway. Those Burrendong gatherings with Panda and the boys numbered amongst the best of days.

I also joined the Cooyal Rifle Club. Half the members were former soldiers from World War Two and all the men had strong rural roots. They made for good company, enjoying a long night's campfire after the day's shoot along with the occasional beer and wonderful stories, even some singing but I wouldn't repeat the words.

Having joined the club I purchased a 1942 ex-Army .303 rifle. It was the genuine article with scars and a deep cut on the butt and with open sights, just as used in wartime. I think I could say I took to that type of rifle shooting as I enjoyed it and was sometimes successful as far as competition results went. I won a National Rifle Association Medal over 300 metres but on handicap and at the rarely used distance of 800 metres, actually 900 yards in those days, I did not hit the bullseye but I could regularly hit the target, again with open sights. My left eye is fortunately still good but recently the optometrist said that my eighty-year old right eye, my shooting eye, is strong.

The Cooyal Rifle Range was on a neighbouring property managed by Jack Reeves and his good wife Yvonne. Jack was one of the many Cooyal men who had served in the Army and he, like Andy Pirie, had been at Balikpapan, Borneo but in the infantry. One night he told me that their forward scouts had spotted a detachment of Japanese soldiers in the next valley. The decision was made that the Australians would move out at 4 a.m. the following morning and attack the Japanese just as the rising sun would be in their eyes. The pity of it was that the Japanese already knew where the Australians were camped and they attacked well before 4 a.m. The losses were substantial as they caught the Australians in their tents.

Forty per cent of Jakarta, the capital city of Indonesia, is below sea level and the city is sinking about 15 cm a year, due to the large and increasing population drawing heavily on the underground water supply. In July, 2022, the Indonesian Government began construction of a new capital city, to be known as Nusantara. The closest town to the new capital will be Balikpapan which nowadays is a major oil processing centre. How things change.

Many a night after the rifle shooting Jack would invite me home for dinner and afterwards by the light and warmth of his wood-fire we would talk well into the early hours. If I was expected or not Yvonne always said she had made enough dinner to include the likes of me and not to worry about putting her out. Jack married a good woman indeed. They suited each other to a T and had a strong work ethic. In that rather humble home they had three great children, all brought up right and kids to be proud of.

There were many interesting citizens in Mudgee and they could fill a book between them but I have to move on so I have selected just the one. Tex Priddle was the airline representative in Mudgee, with an office in Market Street. He was similar in age to the decade of the day, the sixties. Tex was gay or at least he appeared to be, in more ways than one for he always, without fail, had an infectious smile on his face and he met you with laughter that was impossible to resist. I might have ignored Amanda once but never Tex.

My attraction to Tex centred on a long-standing rumour that he owned one and possibly two of Phar Lap's shoes, as in horse shoes. To most of us Phar Lap, winner of the 1930 Melbourne Cup, is still regarded as Australia's greatest racehorse. More than once I asked Tex if he indeed had the shoes, could I please see them? He never gave me an outright No or a Yes and by the same token my questioning did not take the happiness from his face. You couldn't help but like the bloke although he always left me wondering. I still don't know. I believe two shoes have come to light and been sold over the years but even so that leaves the other two. Did Tex take them with him when he left the barrier for the last time?

Everyone wanted a part of Phar Lap. In the Melbourne Museum I have seen Phar Lap's hide on display but not his heart which rests in the National Museum in Canberra. The land of his birth, New Zealand, is home to his skeleton in Wellington's Museum of New Zealand.

For some reason I developed a strong interest in thoroughbred horse racing, not so much the betting on racehorses but the breeding of them and their bloodlines. That interest could hardly have been hereditary as my parents never even mentioned the word horse although my grandfather Stanley did run horses at picnic race meetings. His horse Sunaki won the Club Plate at the Holbrook Amateur Picnic Race Club. The trophy, which I tend to treasure, was a silver cup with the words and a drawing of a handsome horse all engraved by hand and the cup being pure silver, as confirmed for me by a jeweller. As he said, they don't make them like that anymore, that being in 1927.

During those Mudgee days I did follow the racehorses but only punted what I could afford to lose. I came across a racehorse from Forbes which took my fancy. He was Dawn Boy, a sprinter. In fact he was an out and out sprinter. Well I thought so but perhaps I didn't know so much as I preferred stayers but I had a liking for this horse as he came from the country and he was every now and again going to Sydney and having a crack at the big boys. I thought he was improving all the time and he began to win Sydney races.

He came back from a spell to begin his next campaign and won his first two starts. I was in the money and at his next start I outlaid my biggest bet ever. I broke my own rule. That was the bet that I could not afford to lose and the horse and I went down by a short half-head. It was a photo finish but more to the point it was a lifelong lesson. Apart from that my punting was alright and I decided to do something else in the world of horse-racing. By no means would I ever be able to afford to buy a racehorse but I brought my knowledge of breeding into play and I bought a one-fortieth share in a thoroughbred stallion.

My selection was an Irish stallion newly arrived in Australia by the name of King of Babylon. The horse stood at Woodlands Stud at Denman in the Hunter Valley and I bought my one share, that

Chapter Two *Panda*

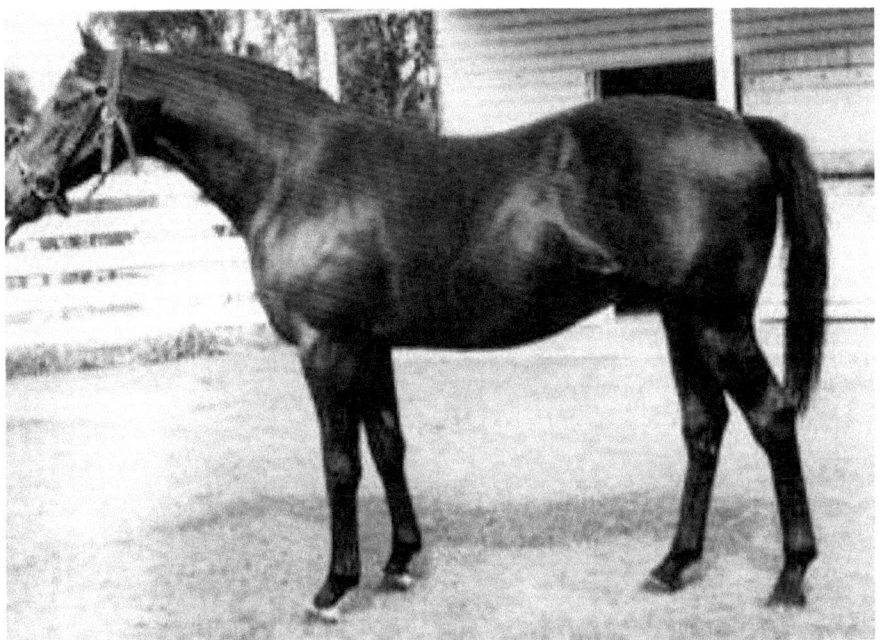

King of Babylon, the thoroughbred stallion Bill invested in.

is one fortieth of the horse, for $1,400, the going rate at the time because the horse was new to the industry. He had moderate but immediate success at stud and then one of his sons, Beau Babylon, defeated the then unbeaten champion Vain in the Sires Produce Stakes at Randwick. That created demand for King of Babylon's services at stud and I put my share up for sale at Inglis's auctions of thoroughbreds. My share sold for $5,600 and I mention this matter that is trivia to others today because that price set the Australian record for a share sold in a thoroughbred stallion at public auction. It appears trivial because today, in 2025, the thoroughbred stallion, Wootton Bassett, commands a service fee of $385,000 including GST. Hopefully the service is successful as the mare's owner otherwise goes without, not having a financial share in the stallion.

The rutile mining multimillionaire Lloyd Foyster lived in Mudgee on his renowned thoroughbred Gooree Stud and I came to know him quite well. Lloyd raced good horses and he also bred some, such as Ming Dynasty which won the Caulfield Cup. When his horse Gooree King was entered in the 1968 Cox Plate, Australia's premier weight-for-age race, Lloyd thought he could win the prestigious race. I suggested that Rajah Sahib would win and Lloyd said I should put my money where my mouth is, on a side bet between the two of us. I had not expected him to react like that and there was no way I could match a bet with him. Eventually he offered me a wager of $40. That is nothing today but the Australian Bureau of Statistics (ABS) states that in 1969 the average weekly wage in Australia was $42.65, which backs up my saying $40 was the weekly average in 1968. In May, 2024, the Australian Bureau of Statistics stated the average weekly ordinary time earnings for full time work for adults was $1,923.40. Today that equates to $2,000. So it was a massive one-off wager for me. Lloyd and I each gave $40 to Keith Cummins and he put the money in his safe in the Occidental Hotel that he owned in good old Mudgee. Rajah Sahib won the Cox Plate.

One day I was at Canterbury racetrack in Sydney with Lloyd as he had several horses in work out there. Typically it was early morning and Bart Cummings came along to talk with Lloyd about the horses he was training for him. Bart Cummings won twelve Melbourne Cups and is generally regarded as one of the three best racehorse trainers ever to grace the Australian turf. Lloyd introduced me to Bart but I mostly just listened to their conversation. A few days later I was at Sydney airport and Roy Higgins walked up to me and introduced himself. I was amazed as Roy was the champion jockey in Melbourne at the time and arguably the best in Australia. I recognized him immediately but I was surely a stranger to him so why would he be offering his services to me? The penny dropped when Roy told me he had seen me the other day talking with Bart and he made the mistake of taking me for being one of Bart's wealthy racehorse owners.

Over time I became friends with John Marskell, probably as good a judge of cattle as you would ever want to have on your side. I heard his reputation from reputable stockmen and agents and eventually I met him. Like Dooley Wallace at Wingadee we hit it off straight away. One day he offered to help me along by finding a mob of steers I might like to buy at a value price. I had a paddock of feed oats on hand at the time and accepted the proposition.

The cattle were delivered and I took particular care to ensure nothing untoward happened to them. After four months they had increased their weight and condition so I sold them for a net thirty per cent profit.

That was a good result but at the same time the wool market and therefore the sheep market was collapsing. It would soon be buoyed by the Wool Reserve Price Scheme which was an artificial Government supported higher price to keep sheepmen and dealers in the game. Being unrealistic and not a true market price it eventually ran its course and collapsed. I didn't hang around for that to come to fruition.

I decided I had to strike out elsewhere and I did what is even more popular today. I would have a crack at the mining business but without the qualifications required to be an engineer, a geologist or machinery operator I would need to start at the bottom and work my way up. Before setting off it was necessary to ensure my block of land did not go backwards in my absence and I had no idea how long that would be but I had a plan. I explained the situation to John Marskell and the result was that he leased the land from me. He would run cattle on the block up to an agreed maximum number of head so as not to abuse or run the place down. I didn't have to go through the finer points as I was positive I knew him well enough by now to trust him but to satisfy myself I did and he understood my concerns. I have always preferred to have matters sorted out upfront rather than be disputing disruptions later on. John would pay me every three months and that would cover the Council rates, the Pasture Protection Board fees and contribute to the mortgage.

I had one final matter to deal with before I left for the unknown. Where I would end up was not an issue by itself but if something went wrong then I could have a problem. I wondered what might be so unexpected that it would set me back more than a degree or two. It could be medical but I thought dental would be worse if I was in a remote and distant area. I decided to have my wisdom teeth removed. We don't all have wisdom teeth but for those of us that do there is the potential for the wisdom teeth to not have enough space to fully come forth, which means they can become impacted against other teeth or even the bone, leading to pain, swelling and infection. Hard to overcome when riding across the steppes of Mongolia, sailing a wooden boat to the Orkney islands, let alone to Antarctica or camping in the Pantanal in Brazil and the like as I would go on to do. Mere movement of the wisdom teeth can also push against other teeth causing misalignment and bite problems as well as create flaps of gum tissue that trap food and bacteria and cause decay due to the difficulty of cleaning the blighters.

Not everyone's cup of tea but I would drink from that cup whatever the taste. A Mudgee dentist extracted my four wisdom teeth in the one day. I did not feel good for two days and then I was alright. I'm pleased to say that I have not had a problem in their vacated area since and am happy to be able to run my tongue around where they once resided and feel the vacant healthy space, irrespective of the size of my mouth, whatever that might be.

CHAPTER THREE

Koolan Island

Cast off the bowlines, sail away from the safe harbour, catch the trade winds in your sails. Explore, Dream, Discover.

I made my farewells, travelled to Sydney and then with the luck of the devil I bumped into Doug Pinnington, whom I had been at school with. He was about to return to Melbourne and he kindly invited me to go with him, in his car, which happened to be a Porsche 356B. That was a drive and a half. Thank you Doug. I met up with another good friend, Craig Potts, in Melbourne but as his girlfriend had moved in he had no room to accommodate me. I was meant to be heading for Perth but Craig contacted generous Marcie and sight unseen but on Craig's recommendation she took me in. I was lucky as Marcie was a lot of fun and great company but after ten days I realised I should be moving on.

Without the distractions of Melbourne I was back to carrying out my plan. I found a trucking company that didn't mind a hitchhiker now and again and I went by truck all the way, across the Nullabor and on to Perth. I took a room on the city's main street, St. Georges Terrace. In case you notice the apostrophe is lacking the authorities

Chapter Three *Koolan Island*

removed it from St. George's in the 1980s.

The following morning was Monday and I sprang into action. More than 470 mining companies have registered offices in Perth and most of the majors appear to be on St. Georges Terrace. I learned that Canada is the country that hosts the largest number of mining companies in the world. There were more than enough for me on St. Georges Terrace and armed with their address courtesy of the phone book I set out to systematically work my way door knocking along both sides of the street.

I adhered to my plan for three days with barely an inkling of interest. By Thursday morning a little of the bounce may have gone out of my step but the weather was fine and I had no excuse to linger so I sallied forth. The same result left me feeling a little downtrodden as I trudged back to my lodgings.

To my surprise there was a phone message for me that evening, one that asked me to call in to the office of Dampier Mining on Friday morning. I was on the doorstep before they opened up and taken into an office where I was interviewed. The man then offered me a position in a mining camp in the Kimberley. I accepted and he told me to be at the airport that night, ready to go. No beating about the bush from either of us. Suddenly my world had turned around and I had time on my hands.

No longer having to hurry from one office to another I strolled out on to St. Georges Terrace and ambled, enjoying the sights of pristine Perth. It used to be said that as you went around Australia from Darwin to Brisbane, on to Sydney, Melbourne and Hobart and as attractive as Adelaide is that by the time you reached Perth you truly were in the prettiest and cleanest city in the land.

It didn't take long to pack up my meagre belongings and make an early start out to the airport. The night-time transport was more of a cargo plane than the usual passenger version but that didn't faze me as I was eager to start the 2,000 km flight north to Derby. There were certainly no flight attendants.

In due course we passed over several significant mining camps in the Pilbara as evidenced by their lights and in one case a large but seemingly controlled fire. As the night was otherwise pitch black those contrasting illuminations stood out. A few hours later we landed at Port Headland where freight was unloaded and several men left the plane.

We flew on and on and as dawn began to break I looked out the window and saw the sunrise. Not that it bothered me but I did not sleep that night, perhaps because I might miss something. The plane began its descent into Derby. Having landed no time was wasted unloading the remaining cargo while an airport worker told the other fellow, Darren, and I to wait nearby. While doing so I saw the sun come up, for the second time that morning. I have not experienced two sunrises on the same day since and I am without doubt a morning person. I enjoy getting up early and making the most of what I consider to be the best part of the day when it and I are both fresh. Early to bed, early to rise.

The airport man took Darren and I over to a four-seater plane and we climbed in behind the pilot who took off immediately. I have always preferred small planes to the larger ones, as might a traveller compared to a passenger.

We lifted up into the air and were away, flying over Yampi Sound and then King Sound on a north-west heading for the Buccaneer

Chapter Three *Koolan Island*

Archipelago in the Indian Ocean. After 130 km one of several islands came into view. We were confronted by a 190 metre high black sheer cliff rising out of the ocean like the Devil's staff. Our pilot dipped the nose of the plane and dropped down towards the cliff top, the very edge of which was the beginning of the runway landing strip. That could have been a little nerve-wracking for some. The pilot would not want to misjudge the angle, the distance, or the strength of the wind that is occasionally reinforced by the energy coming off the water below. Our man must have been good because he seemed to skim over the rim of the cliff and then we were on the runway. I though it exciting but Darren didn't look too pleased.

The plane rolled to a stop and we jumped out. The surroundings were a blaze of colour, the ground was either jet black such as the cliff face or a strong red, both indicative of their iron ore content. Bright green vegetation was splashed amongst the ore while the ocean below was not blue or green but that soft, gorgeous turquoise. Blue was to be found in the umbrella of the sky along with the gold of the sun for this was the dry season. This was Koolan Island and I fell in love with it at first sight.

I'm out of here, exclaimed a shocked Darren. He did not share my optimistic and happy feelings, no way. I don't know what Darren expected but he was instantly hostile to his surroundings and turned around to get back on the plane. He was too late. Having jettisoned his two passengers and not cut the engine the pilot had turned his plane around and as Darren waved to him to stop the pilot was already racing down the airstrip. He disappeared briefly after crossing the rim of the cliff and then he was climbing into the distance. Gone.

Darren was quite agitated. He was not a happy camper. I have no idea what he expected but immediate repatriation was not offered. He was told he could leave at the same time next morning when the plane made its daily flight but it would cost him a lot of money. Like other remote areas the way it works is that the company pays the costs of your return air fares from Perth but if you leave the island before you have worked there for six months you pay the full fares.

We were driven into the township where we were split up and I never saw Darren again. I was immediately taken to the doctor for a medical although I thought that might have been done beforehand, in Perth. I passed that and the next stop was a long building on stilts on the top of the island. I climbed the steps at the front of the structure to a verandah before entering the building proper. A corridor stretched away in the distance and on each side were single rooms for the men. I was allocated one of them and apart from being of more recent construction they weren't any different from the basic run of the mill rooms the jackaroos enjoyed at Wingadee Station and more to the point in this tropical setting there was no air conditioning.

Koolan was an eight km long and two and a half km wide island composed mostly of high grade iron ore and some of that was fines. While much of the ore was solid and had to be crushed a good percentage of it was known as fines, ore that is more valuable because it does not require crushing and therefore saves on costs. The quality of iron ore is invaluable and therefore graded.

Iron ore with an Fe content of less than 58 per cent is considered low grade while an Fe content of between 58 per cent and 65 per cent is ranked as medium. Anything above 65 per cent is regarded as high grade. Until the Koolan Island mine was temporarily closed in 1994 sixty-eight million tonnes of high-grade haematite iron ore averaging sixty-seven per cent iron had been extracted. It was a magnificent asset for Dampier Mining which in turn was owned and developed by BHP.

I have heard it said that courtesy of the island's picture-perfect setting and open-cut mining those qualities are used by employment companies to attract workers. However they don't mention the summer humidity that drives some people troppo and the mind-set needed to adapt to another way of life. Management always stated that jobs were available for Aboriginal people from the mainland but while I was there only two men took up that offer, making them one per cent of the workforce.

The next morning I was introduced to Blue, the chief electrician, the boss of the sparkies, he who must be obeyed. He was in his mid-forties, tall, lean and an absolute expert in his field. Blue of course had red hair and I never heard his real name but I was to be his off-sider, a tradesman's apprentice. I told him I could turn a switch on and off but that was all I knew about electricity and I did not want to electrocute anyone, let alone myself. He told me not to worry, all I had to do was carry his bag and do exactly what he said.

Blue and I got along famously. The hours were long but not difficult so when I learned that anything large or heavy came to the island not by plane but by ship and had to be manually unloaded I applied for that job as well. The ships had to be unloaded at night because everyone was doing their regular job during the day, unless they worked in the quarry and I will soon cover that.

They were Western Australia State ships and they sailed from

Fremantle to Darwin calling at remote places in between. Some of the water they carried as ballast was off-loaded for the island's use as we had no regular water supply. I unloaded sides of beef carrying them on my shoulder and back and all manner of cartons and bags of food and other supplies. The unloading went on all through the night and there were times when including my job with Blue during the day that I worked twenty-seven hours straight. The money was good anyway but by doing two jobs my bank account at the island post office reached heights never before scaled. The Australian Taxation Office provided a substantial tax exemption for people working in certain remote areas and Koolan Island qualified on that score.

There were times when Blue's work took us into the quarry which was where the mining operations were conducted. I saw the rigs drilling down through the orebody, the powder monkeys filling the completed holes with explosives and blowing them up at four o'clock every afternoon, the gigantic shovels loading the broken ore into the Haulpak or dump trucks which delivered the ore into the heavy duty crusher whose sides then came together and crushed boulders of iron ore until they were mostly pieces to be held in one's hand let alone those that were the fines and did not need the crushing. I followed the crusher and its contents down through the bowels of the earth until the ore emerged and came out into the sunlight on a conveyor belt which ran along the dock beside the natural deep water harbour where large iron ore carriers from Japan were able to come alongside without any dredging, delay or interference. An efficient system of production and delivery all in one.

Straight away I knew this was where I wanted to be, in the quarry,

Chapter Three *Koolan Island*

all the time. There were two hundred men on the island, thirty of them worked in the office while most of the other one hundred and seventy men did their thing in the quarry. I told Blue I had enjoyed my time with him and I appreciated that he took me under his wing but would he help me gain a transfer to the quarry? He did not hesitate and a few days later he introduced me to Len 'Sinbad' Sailor, the boss of the quarry.

Sinbad asked what might I be interested in, such as truck driving, explosives, machinery work and I said operating a drilling rig. So I started off as an offsider on a small rig. Due to the specialized and perhaps more dangerous occupations the men in the quarry only worked ten hours a day, six days a week and were not allowed overtime. However they had Sunday off and that was also the day when the day shift became the night shift for the next week and vice versa. In the quarry we did one week of days followed by one week of nights.

Sunday was also special for the meal of the week. Everyone looked forward to Sunday lunch. It was a rare few hours when you could meet the blokes from the other shift and come to know them. There were three courses, each one a meal on its own with the highlight being roast pink chicken that the Chinese cook and his team produced for two hundred ravenous men. We never knew how or why the outer skin was pink but it was delicious and always consumed. There were soups, superb vegetables, salads and fruit kept as fresh as possible, desserts, ice creams, cakes and more.

I settled in to my role of drilling. You don't want to be making mistakes with machinery, especially when someone else is entrusting it to you so I went steady but learning as best I could.

I worked my way up and eventually was placed in charge of the biggest and most valuable drilling rig on the island.

I had a Bucyrus-Erie drilling rig and it had just been imported from America at a cost of US $250,000, which was a substantial amount some fifty-four years ago. American Bureau of Statistics figures show inflation of the dollar for that time to be 3.98 per cent per year so that today the rig would cost $1,948,543. When converted to the Australian dollar it comes in over A $3,000,000. A few years ago Caterpillar bought Bucyrus-Erie which had been in production for 127 years. Caterpillar wanted it to gain a hold in

Bill drilling on Koolan Island

the manufacturing of mining equipment, not by working for it and being productive but simply by buying it.

It was far superior to the two-man rigs on the island and whilst it was relatively big I was able to walk it slowly but surely on its tank-type tracks. I had exterior controls at the front so that I could almost stand over the hole I was drilling and add or change new rods as required. I could also use the controls in the cabin for walking the rig or avoiding bad weather but keep operating. It was necessary to learn by touch and sound what grade of ore-body I was drilling through as the terrain varied from ore that could be soft as in all fines, to good going to extremely hard ore or mullock to drill through. Mullock is the non-ore such as other rock, soil and unwanted material.

I was mindful of the men back in the sheds who had to sharpen the drill bits as that job required expertise and I doubt they appreciated any driller simply going hell for leather and making their job harder than it should be. Anyway that rarely happened as Sinbad came around now and again to see how we were progressing. He was a long-time Koolan resident and knew his job. He had a good manner about him and I would rate him in terms of severity as a moderate overseer, an understanding overseer. I think everyone responded to and liked Sinbad and it made for an efficient workforce.

There was an unwritten rule that if an employee hit another worker the instigator would lose his job. Today I see footballers hit their opponents in the head with a deliberate swinging arm or a callous shoulder charge and if they are sent off it is only for ten minutes or they pay a miniscule fine afterwards, while their victim no doubt will suffer in the years *ahead*. If the offenders lost their football job and were fired the foul play would presumably stop but much of society these days has become soft, it is too much about money in the form of advertising and entertainment. No doubt adherence to the Koolan rule was instrumental in men from all walks of life and from many countries keeping the peace. There were discrete moments when the rule was broken but it was a minor infringement so nothing was said and order restored. I will confess that at the end of a hot day a few of us played up. I copped a beauty on the jaw but gained the satisfaction of knowing I do not have a glass jaw.

The island had a bar and that was too obvious and stupid a place to do the wrong thing so you could always enjoy a quiet and peaceful drink there. Like many of the other fellows I was enticed by the money flowing into my bank account so I swore off alcohol for at least the first six months and I stuck to it. When we came off night shift we had breakfast, a shower and went to our rooms to sleep. That was alright in the winter but when the summer sun and its friend, humidity, heated up it was difficult to sleep past high noon and most blokes were to be found elsewhere in the shade of the outside surroundings.

A few of the men were of the dubious type and there was no doubt several were on the run from the law. You can't run much further past Koolan Island. The time came when the police received word that Ronnie Biggs was in the Northern Territory. Biggs was one of the seventeen men who had been part of the gang that committed the Great Train Robbery in England in 1963. They robbed the Royal Mail train travelling overnight from Glasgow to London and escaped with £2.61 million or a little over A$5 million. Today that amount has a value of A $136 million and while the gang was caught most of that money has not been recovered. After two years in prison Ronnie Biggs escaped and a world-wide hunt led to Australia. The police closed in on Darwin and soon the publican at Katherine, 320 km south of Darwin, was quoted as saying that in the past week 200 men had passed through his Katherine pub and were heading west. That would have taken them directly to Kununurra and into the Kimberley. Some of our blokes were said to be nervous but they had no way of leaving without drawing attention to themselves, so they stayed.

On the other hand there were the different types. One was Dennis, I forget his surname, but he came from Mareeba, up above Cairns. He had charge of one of the smaller drilling rigs and he was your typical knock-about larrikin and a lot of fun. I was in Mareeba a few years ago and tried to find him but he could have been anywhere. One night, on my shift, he had his rig working smoothly in good going. He was probably tired after not sleeping during a hot afternoon but I have to say he did the wrong thing. He sat down by the rig with his legs stretched out in front of him and was soon fast asleep. As far as I know he never heard the Landrover come by but he felt the pain when Sinbad, not expecting such slackness from anyone, accidently ran over Dennis in the dark and broke both his legs. That was tough.

Another driller and also a runner was Big John. He had by far the best physique on the island and he was as gentle as a lamb. Nothing provoked him and I suppose no one wanted to provoke him. Apart from that the thing I never forget about him was where he came from. His home town was Nuneaton, where once upon a time there had been a prominent nunnery and that name just sticks in my mind. Nuneaton is in Warwickshire and close to being in the centre of England.

I have to mention the best blokes without doubt. They were six New Zealanders and Duncan, Terry and the others were the most friendly, easy-going, sensible and diligent, if that's the right word, work-mates and fellow quarrymen around. It was a pleasure to be accepted into their company.

Jin Ponsonby became a good friend although we didn't catch up that often as Jim worked in the office. Prior to that he had been on Mt. House Station, one of the Kimberley's premier and long established cattle stations, widely referred to as Mount House. The station is 245 km north of Hall's Creek and can be reached via the Gibb River road. Its 566,000 hectares support the Grey Brahman cattle herd of media owner, Mr. Kerry Stokes, who purchased the property in 2016. In 1923 its inaccessible location saw a pedal wireless set to be used by Mount House and surrounding stations installed and paid for by the Lottery Commission.

Jim was a close friend of Ed who was also in the office and had been on the island for years. During that time Ed built a boat, one sound enough that he could take to sea, with a good-sized cabin, capable engine and well equipped with electronic communication, navigation and safety features. There was a long week-end coming up and they invited me to accompany them for the three days at sea. I was stunned to be asked and could not accept quickly enough.

I do not know precisely where we went but we headed out into the Indian Ocean as far as we could in that time. I felt the freedom of being out there, it was magical. We did not see anyone and when we came to a lovely little island with a welcoming beach we took the boat in and then ran like children through the shallows of the surf, kicking up spray and laughing. Human footprints and animal tracks can last a long time in those undisturbed circumstances. I was later told that by the Coastguard, when they make their regular flights over the area looking for signs of illegal visitors, to Australia. We felt it quite likely no one had ever set foot on the golden sands of that island. Not even Indonesian fishermen.

The other highlight was fishing from the boat. Our catch included several Spanish Mackerel and Sea Perch which are good eating but the excitement was when I knew I had something big or heavy on the line. As I struggled to bring it to the boat imagine our surprise when Jim and I realised I had caught a shark. For some ridiculous reason we tried to bring it on board and actually had half of it out of the water and resting on the gunwale. It was at least a metre and a half in length and we then hesitated as if we did bring it on board it would be flapping around with those dangerous jaws. Before Ed had something to say about having a shark boat I cut the line and gave it a careful shove backwards.

Well after I had completed my self-imposed six-month alcohol ban Alf and I decided to have a week in Broome. Alf had served in the German Army for a number of years and although he was a few years older than myself we found it easy to converse. I could answer his questions about Australia and he talked to me of Germany and Europe. By now I had met men in the camp from the former country of Yugoslavia which nowadays is represented by Croatia, Macedonia, Serbia, Slovenia, Montenegro and Bosnia Herzegovina. Several of them were older and had endured World War Two which had left its mark on them, making them cautious to say the least. I found that by being polite and patient with them they came around and would open up after a while.

Alf had left his car, a VW, in the Perth airport. He flew from Derby to Perth, picked up his car and drove up to Broome. He never mentioned what the parking fee was and I didn't ask but I suspect back then it wasn't a big deal like it might be in some airports today, such as Sydney which apparently has the highest airport parking charges in the world. Meanwhile I flew to Derby and took a bus for the 220 km trip south-west to Broome and as I got off the bus, Alf, with typical Teutonic timing, arrived alongside.

Broome only had one pub in those days, the Roebuck Hotel, and that is where we headed to. Not to stay but to enjoy those relaxing beers. With the help of a newspaper I studied the form of the horses racing in Perth, which was nigh on 2,000 km away and placed my bets with an SP or starting price bookmaker who was to be found in an alcove by the bar of the hotel. I wasn't expecting much with my punting as I was out of touch in several ways but a horse named Isuelt took my fancy in one of the main races and I backed it at twenty to one. It won the race as otherwise I wouldn't be telling you this and after being out of racing for a long time the winning feeling was magnified.

That Saturday afternoon was interesting for another reason. Alf and I were sitting up on our bar stools, a light breeze wafting in off the nearby beach through the open doors when I felt a gentle tap on the shoulder. I turned and looked straight into the face of an Aboriginal girl, full blood and perhaps eighteen years of age. She might have looked appealing if her lovely large eyes had not been weeping courtesy of some unpleasant-looking sticky substance which slowly trickled down her cheeks. That attracted flies which used them as ladders to climb up and down her face, poor girl. She seemed not to bother about them but when she made it obvious that she was offering herself to me they did not help her cause. I declined but nodded in Alf's direction as there is a lot to experience in Australia and you never know but he preferred the beer.

Every night we left the pub not long after dark and drove along the beach until we found a secure place to camp for the night. Back then Derby was the civilized one and Broome was on the wild side. There were groups of miners such as Alf and I, other men who worked in the oil and gas industry, the road gangers who repaired and maintained the rough network of rural roads which copped a hiding in the Wet, the Aboriginals, the station hands and other rural workers and the loners who were there for silent reasons.

Enough of them got into fights as the nights wore on so that by Friday the convention was that the king white man of the week would fight the king black man of the week for the title of man of the week. Neither Alf nor I were interested in fighting and more to the point we wanted to stay fit and healthy and keep our well-paid jobs. So we left them to it.

One of our drilling team was Don and I don't remember his surname but he was the size of Big John. However Don was fifteen years older, much heavier and past his fighting prime. For some years he had played first grade AFL for the Melbourne club Fitzroy. One look at the scarred and battle enlarged knuckles of his hands confirmed he had been in the thick of the action for a long time. I have only been to one AFL (VFL) game and that was to watch the mercurial goal-kicker Peter Hudson playing for Hawthorn but I think Don might have played in the ruck for I once heard a commentator say if you win the ruck you win the game.

After Alf and I returned to camp Don took a room in the Roebuck

Hotel and later retired for the night. He was woken by the sound of a ruckus in the corridor and then his door came off the hinges as two men fell into his room, fighting furiously. They punched each other oblivious to their surrounds and still trading blows staggered out into the corridor and onwards into the night. Don said he placed the ineffective door as best he could and then went back to sleep.

I gradually came to know more of the other men in the camp and was interested in those who came from behind the Iron Curtain. To escape from the heavy hand of their Soviet Union overseers those men had risked their very lives to reach freedom in western countries. Quite a few had come from Poland, Hungary, Czechoslovakia and Romania. They defied armed shoot-on-sight border guards and their dogs. One man had made a type of sheeting that was impervious to fuel soaking through it. He tied it up to his neck and with help he was lowered into a fuel tanker in which he could stand with his neck and head protruding above the swirling fuel. For hours he defied the fumes let alone he kept his balance until the truck crossed the border of a non-Soviet country, to freedom.

When the night shift finished work, tidied up for the next man and had a decent wash we climbed aboard the open back of the truck. The fellows on the sides had something to hang on to but those who found themselves standing in the middle only had a raised bar down the centre and had an unsteady ride back to the town and the kitchen. About halfway home we would pass another truck bringing the day shift to the quarry and by now knowing most of them we would offer some raucous advice for their next ten hours, all in good fun.

More than once someone on night shift had come across a snake and been able to take it alive. As we approached the day shift truck and having been allocated a helpful position on our truck, he would briefly swing the snake above his head and with good timing let go of the reptile so that it flew through the air and usually landed in the middle of the day shift crew. They didn't forget that for a while as we laughingly left them to it.

The island was renowned for one snake in particular and we did not pick that one up let alone attempt to throw it and that was the death adder. Research will tell you that the common death adder is found only around Sydney. That may well be so but it also says the Kimberley death adder was found in 1985 and 2015, in the Kimberley. Well we had them on Koolan in the early 1970s. They are small but solid or stocky, perhaps fifty to seventy cm in length, the skin colour ranges from orange to a strong brown with bands of dark brown to black. The tip of the tail is another colour and the death adder twitches it to attract a victim. They are happy to lie in wait for a long time for their prey, as does the Indian tiger, and they are said to have the longest fangs of any Australian snake. Some sixty per cent of bites to humans prove fatal. A point of interest says that the

Death Adder, Koolan Island

death adder is actually deaf and at some stage it may have been known as the deaf adder.

To ensure we gained some of our fitness away from work a dozen or so of us took to cross-country running around the top of the island. This afforded us wonderful panoramas of the ocean below but when the long-time island residents told us the Kimberley death adder has the patience of Job to ensure a kill we kept to the one running path that we carved out around the island. By doing that route repeatedly we widened the track which we hoped gave us an earlier and better chance to see the snake in time and to avoid its ambush. However the old hands then said the adders often cover themselves with leaves.

Over the years those veteran miners had hacked out a golf course on the island and whilst it was somewhat rough and ready it was all credit to them for effort. The highlight of the course was the par 7, sixth hole which was 786 metres long and for decades it was the world distance record. It was incorporated into the airstrip's runway. I like golf but I probably prefer cricket and so when it was suggested we challenge the golfers to a game of cricket I put my hand up to be in that. After a couple of practice sessions an Indian gentleman and I were selected to open the batting and whilst we set a reasonable opening score the golfers who had their eye in by way of regular golf gave us a beating.

About early October, if memory serves me right, when we were on day shift we would sit out on the verandah in the evening and looking out to sea, to the north-west, way off in the distance and over the ocean we could make out faint flashes of lightning on the far horizon. From then on every night the lightning, imperceptibly at first, grew in size and brightness. It was the beginning of the annual

Chapter Three   *Koolan Island*

Wet season. By November there was no doubt about it and at the end of that month thunder joined in. Early December the humidity was making itself felt and two weeks later, as others said, you could sit out on the verandah and read a book courtesy of the lightning bolts. As a single flash of lightning in the night shows up in an instant every detail of the landscape you might imagine the revelation arising from an unending barrage of such illuminations. They were relentless and it did feel as though we were being attacked. On or about Christmas Day each year the heavens usually opened up and eased the pressure by dropping merciful rain upon us. I do recall being caught out in the open when a cyclonic wind struck. I lowered the rig's tower in time but had no way of avoiding it and the deluge of rain. I couldn't even get inside the cabin in time so I crawled under the rig away from the wind as much as possible and hung on for dear life.

Before the seasonal change took place three of us flew back to Derby, hired a small plane and flew to Kununurra for five days R & R. It was a great flight across the Kimberley, pretty much from the south-west to the north-east. From Derby we passed over the aggregation of Mount House and Genroy Stations, the Gibb River road and the Karanjie Track, which was used as a stock route and it has access to El Questro Station and from there some of the extraordinary outback scenery that came to life in the film, *Australia*. Next we diverted a little more to the east and came to Lake Argyle and then flew north to the Ord River dam and on to Kununurra.

While I was on Koolan Island I regularly heard talk of Argyle and its kimberlite pipes, the narrow, cylindrical bodies in the crust of the earth that hold diamonds. Years before it was formally announced that production of diamonds would occur people in our

Argyle mine diamond, Kimberley, Western Australia

part of the world took it for granted. I don't know much of the mine's development except that a large number of rare pink diamonds were found during the life of the mine from 1983 to 2020.

We stayed in a Kununurra motel, hired a car and didn't have to drive far to witness the magnificent scenery that abounds wherever one goes. Apart from checking out the Ord River which was even then making headlines for its contribution to irrigation, low hills formed the background for the ever-increasing varieties of crops which created a dazzling patchwork of colour for us to absorb. The agriculture was larger than life although initially there were failures. With an abundance of water rice was highly favoured and indeed good crops of rice were produced, much to the delight of the countless numbers of unexpected geese which flew in and devoured them.

Today the Ord River produces watermelon, citrus, rock-melon, mango and pumpkin crops, maize, sorghum, millet, chickpea, sunflower and I believe sandalwood. I know of a farmer a little north of Dubbo who recently sold one of his properties for $40 million plus and is now going to the Ord River to develop country there to grow irrigated cotton and corn. We all enjoyed Kununurra and the Ord and it is another reason I recommend the Kimberley. Dare I say it but you haven't lived a full life until you have a little dirt on your hands.

Before we took off I asked the pilot if we could bypass Derby and return to the island by a different course i.e. to fly due west but with a bit of north until we hit the Indian Ocean about Camden Sound, where the humpback whales go for their calving, and then follow the coastline south to Koolan.

He was happy to do that and my friends were in full agreement. I realised we were too late for that season's calving but the idea of island hopping appealed to the boys. In fact we scored a bonus in that department. The pilot took the plane down to wave height and as the sea was relatively calm we were flying at what looked to be no more than a metre off the water. To prove the point in the future I took a few photos as we approached a low-lying island and when I show those photos to people nowadays they assume I took the photos from a zodiac or a small boat.

A few weeks later Sinbad came to me and said he would like me to go across to Cockatoo Island and drill for water. Cockatoo is sixteen km from Koolan and Dampier Mining also owned it on account of its iron ore. I was happy to go and walked the drilling rig down to the dock where I then trundled it on to a landing barge and we set sail but very slowly. The voyage went well but when I took the rig ashore it was a steep climb up to the town area. That was fine. It just meant I had to go slowly and carefully. I noted Sinbad had not asked

Darryl the operator on the other shift to take the rig so I took that as a positive from the overseer. As good a man as he was he was not known for handing out bouquets.

For several weeks I drilled and I drilled but did not detect a drop of water. However it was a lovely island and the pace of life seemed ever so slow and relaxed. After Koolan it seemed like a holiday camp. I suddenly realised I had been living for years by now according to the work ethics and self-discipline of Wingadee Station and Koolan Island and looking back I am satisfied my life continued along those lines. The State ship called in and if you needed something, anything, it was damned expensive. I will give you an interesting example. A postage stamp then was ten cents, anywhere in Australia. Except on Cockatoo where it cost twelve cents. Can you imagine that. Someone charged freight on a stamp. Well I guess it had to travel as far as anything else.

The turquoise water was edged by a golden sand beach bounded by luxuriant trees. You would go a long way to find another of Mother Nature's such secluded treasures. And there was barely a footprint. Why? The only human handiwork to be seen was the clearly marked sign that warned one and all not to enter the water. It was occupied.

That water and its approaches were mined with saltwater crocodiles, stonefish, blue-ringed octopus and sharks courtesy of their feeding grounds amongst the nearby mangroves. The common denominator was that each of them in their own way could kill you.

Long after I left Cockatoo Island the lease was bought by the entrepreneur Alan Bond who developed much of it into a world class hideaway resort. People called the beach, Bondy Beach, his wive had the villas painted pink and an infinity pool was installed one hundred metres up in the air and looking out over the pristine waters.

Chapter Three *Koolan Island*

Alan Bond is remembered for many things such as winning the America's Cup, the first time in 132 years a foreign competitor had achieved that holy grail, being joint Australian of the Year with Galarrwuy Yunupingu in 1978, founding Bond University on the Gold Coast, paying Kerry Packer one billion dollars for Channel Nine television and when his business failures mounted selling it back to Mr. Packer for $250 million and later being declared bankrupt. He was then sentenced to seven years in prison for committing fraud. I think he served four years inside.

I loved the Kimberley, Koolan and Cockatoo Islands and twenty five years later I would return there as a volunteer crewman to assist two Canadian marine biologists aboard a catamaran to track, identify and record 600 humpback whales in fourteen days while heading north of Broome to their Camden Sound calving grounds. When I eventually was recalled to Koolan I told Sinbad I would shortly be leaving. I had become intrigued by the men I had met from around the world and I wanted to see for myself their distant lands.

P.S. Long after I left Koolan Island the drilling was down to ocean level and the island sold. The new owners drilled below ocean level and before they sold they blasted a hole in the side of the quarry and flooded it with sea water—so no one could come along and injure themselves. Then it was purchased again, the massive crater somehow drained and the hole plugged to keep the Indian Ocean out. Mining started up once more and when it is finally closed down at the end of 2026 the drilling etc will finish at 200 metres below sea level.

CHAPTER FOUR

Shota Rustaveli

Russian proverb; *Don't go to someone else's monastery with your own rulebook.*

As far as I knew everyone came to or left Koolan Island by plane. I asked Sinbad if I could take my leave courtesy of the State shipping line. He not only approved my request but organized it for me. Thank you Sinbad, wherever you may be.

I said my farewells and boarded the ship. Apart from the ongoing cargo were nine passengers, one of them a girl about my age travelling by herself. I was a little uncomfortable with her for the first couple of days as I had not been in the company of women for ages. By the time we dropped anchor in Wyndham which is 475 km further on, I was beginning to feel comfortable coming back into society. I met a few girls in my time and they were all good company but two were special. I am not going to say anything about them as they were close and in a friendly way they still are. I am pleased to say that as far as I know I never left a girl on bad terms.

Thinking about that, the reason may not have been down to any good conduct on my part but because I never lived with a girl as did most of my friends. I was usually in a remote area or one where unmarried women were not permitted or I was travelling and as wonderful as women are they can slow if not tie one down. I did enjoy being free to come and go as I pleased. That probably seems selfish.

Wyndham is 3,315 km north of Perth and came into being as a service area when gold was found at inland Hall's Creek on Christmas Day, 1885, by prospector Charlie Hall. They say he was followed by up to 15,000 others in what must have been one of the most testing of all gold mining areas. In later years Wyndham was known for its large meat works and today it functions as a significant port. During World War Two the Japanese bombed Wyndham four times. If you like summer humidity you will be right at home there.

We moved on to Darwin, some 973 km by road but only 331 nautical miles or 613 km on the high seas. I found a handy place to stay for five or six days and began by walking the streets to take in the atmosphere and become used to being amongst so many strangers again. A colourful Buddhist temple attracted me and as a consequence in the years to come I believe I went to at least one such temple in all the predominantly Buddhist countries in the world.

Marrakai Plains or Station lies mostly eighty km east of Darwin, bounded by the Mary River to its east, the Adelaide River to the west and it extends all the way north to Van Diemen Gulf. I joined a full day safari going there to shoot buffalo with a camera. The lush scenery is suitable for the wallowing buffalo which grow large and heavy. They probably find that part of Australia as good as anywhere in south- east Asia from where they were imported as food supply for the men constructing The Overland Telegraph Line. Like a lot of international visitors they didn't leave. I bought a set of buffalo horns and had to carry them around for quite some time but they were worth it as I still have them. I would have them in the house but I am married now and she confines my horns to the shed. As I suspected women tend to take over.

The next part of my plan was to go home via Alice Springs, 1,500 km to the south. I settled for the bus so I could sit back and take in some of the Northen Territory while travelling. At the half-way mark we stopped at the small town of Elliott, which is on the edge of one of the Territory's best-known properties, Newcastle Waters Station. Elliott began life as a World War Two Australian Army camp and is named after Captain Snow Elliott. I found it to be one of the hottest places in Australia but of no great concern as it is far enough south to be dry heat, not humid. I thought the little town had good atmosphere. I liked being there.

Continuing on we reached the Alice and I checked into a boarding house on the far side of the Todd River run by a lovely lady by the name of Caroline. I clearly recall she had a kind nature and kept a good house. It seems to me that from a distance many people have the initial impression that the Alice is a desert or in desert country. The reality is far from that. Alice Springs residents are proud of their green surrounds. Apart from plentiful and bountiful trees most home sites are alive with green lawns, plants and flower beds. There is a price to pay for that as the average yearly rainfall is a mere 290 mm which falls mostly in December and January.

Alice's water comes from underground aquifers and after being pumped to the surface it is treated for human consumption and stored in tanks. The Amadeus Basin is believed to contain enough water to supply Alice Springs for 300 years so it is interesting to learn that the Basin also contains all the oil, which is not much, and all the natural gas, which should be huge if the Beetaloo gas operation in the Northern Territory is permitted to go ahead.

I am told that Alice Springs or Mildura residents have the highest water consumption rates in Australia. Back in 2017 the average annual water and sewerage bill for Alice was $1,950, consisting of $800 for sewerage, $300 for having the connection or supply and $850 for the consumed water. I was in Alice in 2021 and the average annual cost had reached $2,000. Water supplies interest me. All that results in Alice Springs looking remarkably green but it should be noted that the residents use fifty-six per cent of the water on their gardens. The next highest uses are for showers and also leaks, each at eleven per cent.

The Alice Springs Telegraph Station is four km north of the town. The Overland Telegraph Line (OTL) consisted of twelve telegraph stations established from Port Augusta to Darwin, a distance of 3,000 km tracking through barely chartered and harsh land in 1871/72. The purpose was to connect a telegraph line to a submarine cable from Darwin to Singapore and from there by various ways and means to England so that Australia's communication with the world would be speeded up and modernized.

The Alice Springs Telegraph Station served its purpose for sixty years and was regarded as the leading repeater station of the OTL. The buildings have been restored to their past glory and contribute first-hand knowledge of how white settlers and the local Aboriginal tribe, the Arrernte people, lived in those days.

I spent much of one day at the Alice Springs Telegraph Station, admiring the crafted and substantial stone buildings which consist of the actual telegraph office, station master's residence, a kitchen, blacksmith's residence, harness room and wagon shed. I know from past research that the colonial kitchens were kept separate from the house because many of them caught fire.

Weather-wise it was a glorious day but above that there was a good feeling in the air as I left the stone structures and I felt somewhat entranced as I stepped out on to a surprisingly soft green lawn that flowed down the slope to the Alice Springs waterhole. Halfway down I came to a monument, a plaque, set in stone and I stopped to read it. The words declared that the OTL surveyor William Whitfield Mills had found and named the waterhole on 11th March, 1871. For some reason the thought crossed my mind that Mr. Mills could hardly have expected such recognition to be awarded him at that time or afterwards while he and his men pressed on towards Darwin and the eventual completion of the OTL. Was ever an Australian town so well named?

The waterhole itself is not derived as first thought from a spring. When the rains come the water is collected and held on large slabs of granite rock and when more rain is not forthcoming the river water does dry up. Strange to say but when I left the waterhole a calm wave of contentment and serenity washed over and then came away with me.

Most of the best sites to see around Alice are where you would expect them to be, outside the town and well worth every kilometre. You have probably been to the Centre of Australia but I will take the opportunity to mention another one close to town. That is the Desert Park which is surely for all ages and all people, no matter where you

Chapter Four   Shota Rustaveli

hail from. In the 1970s it was known as a wildlife park. In today's apparently enlightened age it is proclaimed as an environmental education centre and wildlife park.

One of those more distant places I wanted to see was Ayers Rock, which in 1995 had its name changed to Uluru in favour of the traditional owners the Pitjantjatjara people also known as the Anangu. In the early 1970s the 463 km long road from Alice was still dirt and not sealed until 1987. People spoke of the surface as corrugated bone-rattling sufferance. As I had not touched my Koolan Island earnings I decided to treat myself and fly. I bought a ticket on a ten-seater Beechcraft Queen Air and keenly anticipated the flight.

I had to wait a few days for the flight but I met Lily, an interesting young woman from Adelaide who showed me around Alice in the meantime. On the day a taxi picked me up from the boarding house and then stopped at a motel to collect two American visitors, a U.S. Senator and his wife, before taking us to the airport. The other passengers were a couple with their baby son and a middle-aged man, plus the sole pilot. Seven people on the ten-seater plus pilot plane. A little larger than I prefer but near enough. At about 7.20 a.m. we were all but aboard the plane when I turned around and walked back through the terminal. I can only tell you what happened in the simplest of terms for that is all I know. Some things I cannot explain although this would be the first in that category for myself.

As I had moved toward the plane there was a repetitive message permeating my head and it told me to *leave the airport, get away from the plane*. It sounded like a voice, as though someone was speaking to me. Only my fellow passengers were close by and I didn't believe

The actual Beechcraft Queen Air plane, VH-CMI, which Bill walked away from moments before it crashed in Alice Springs

they were at that moment talking to me. The message was repeated until I turned away and walked back through the terminal and outside as in a trance. I spoke only to a taxi driver whom I asked to take me back to the boarding house.

I silently made my way into the lounge room and sat in a chair, where I experienced what I have heard some people describe as looking at themselves from outside their bodies. It was about three minutes later that I was disturbed from my blank mind when I heard the phone on the wall ring. I didn't lift my head to it until I realised Caroline, the lady of the house had entered the room and was now talking to someone.

As I looked up she was staring at me in a slow surprised manner and saying, *Yes, he's here.* She finished her conversation and came over to me. Rather gently she asked why I didn't go on the plane as planned. I wasn't quite sure how to answer that except to vaguely say someone told me not to go on the plane. I later calculated that I had previously flown on about forty planes and never thought twice about that except that I have a preference for small planes. My flights now number in the hundreds and that day's foretelling and internal refusal to fly have not been repeated.

From what Caroline told me the plane took off with the pilot and the six remaining passengers. It was still in sight of the Alice Springs airport tower when the end of the starboard wing along with the starboard engine caught fire and fell off. The plane crashed to the ground and all aboard died instantly. On the occasions when I reflect on it, I naturally think of those who died and then wonder why I did not. I have not gone on to develop a medical cure or necessarily make life better for others. I dare say other people have had similar experiences but that apparent haphazard aspect of our time on earth makes me curious as to why it sometimes evolves in such a Russian roulette manner. At times I feel a little guilty still being here, more than fifty years on.

Years later I was in Alice doing a live interview on ABC radio and a man who heard me speak of that incident tracked me down. He was a pilot and had flown the previous flight. He then refused to fly the plane, saying that although he could not then pinpoint the problem, that something was wrong with the plane. He later learned and told me that the plane's main bearing in the engine was slipping. That slippage caused the keeper to stop and when it seized it broke the crankshaft. This resulted in half of the engine not running and consequently it was pouring fuel into the augmenter tubes, of which I gather four of them extracted exhaust gases and the remaining two allowed fresh air to enter and keep the engine cool. My understanding as a layman may be inaccurate. Consequently the engine became hotter and fire broke out. When the flames reached the flaps they ignited the magnesium component therein and magnesium fire is extremely difficult to extinguish. Water can rarely do that. Subsequent investigation showed the unfortunate pilot had used two basic fire extinguishers but it is generally accepted under such circumstances a pilot has no more than three minutes to put his plane on the ground, a near impossible manoeuvre.

Over the years since then I have heard several people talk of knowing someone who experienced a premonition so I might mention a more extraordinary occurrence than mine, which was an immediate happening, where I was warned at the last moment, as compared to something that will occur in the future. I shall attach a photo of the actual plane, VH-CMI, the one that I walked away from moments before it burned and crashed.

Esther Hart and her husband, Benjamin, along with their seven-year old daughter, Eva, had decided to emigrate from England to Canada for a better life. In 1912 they booked a berth on a regular passenger liner to take them to New York. However a coal miners' strike in Britain meant their ship was one of many deprived of its fuel. At the time the newest, largest and most luxurious ship of all time, *RMS Titanic*, was due to make its maiden five-day voyage from Southampton to New York. The ship's owner, the wealthy American J. P. Morgan, ensured enough coal was siphoned off to the *Titanic* so as not to impede its much-publicized departure. This resulted in a number of passengers booked on ships which had been deprived of their coal being transferred to suitable berths on *Titanic*, amongst them the Hart family.

They travelled by train to Southampton to board the ship but on their arrival and as they climbed the gangplank, Esther, for the first and only time in her life experienced a premonition of impending disaster. She said to Benjamin, *That ship will not make it to the other side.* She told Benjamin she did not want to board the *Titanic*. Benjamin was not of the same mind, being only too happy to have been upgraded to the *Titanic* at no further cost and where their second-class cabin was outfitted as well as a first-class cabin on any other liner. Eva said it was the first time she saw her mother cry, such was her conviction. They boarded the *Titanic* and each night Esther stayed up, never going to sleep but fully dressed and prepared for come what may, reading and writing while Benjamin and Eva slept in their four-bed cabin. When her husband and daughter went out for breakfast and to explore the magnificent floating hotel during the day, Esther slept.

At 11.40 p.m. on the fateful night of 14 April, 1912, Esther heard a bump. She woke Benjamin and sent him out to investigate. On his return he immediately took Esther, who was dressed and ready for such a disaster, and Eva, up on to the deck as the *Titanic* had a sixty-metre gash along its side after hitting an iceberg. The so-called unsinkable ship was taking in water and all too quickly she sank, four kilometres down. There was barely time for Esther and Eva to be placed in a lifeboat. They survived but Benjamin went down with the ship. Esther had earlier finished writing a letter to her mother and it was placed in Benjamin's coat which he gave to Esther to keep her warm in lifeboat Fourteen. In 2014 that letter was sold for £119,000 or close to A 250,000, today. It was the last written communication from *RMS Titanic*.

The boarding house phone began to ring frequently with strangers, media perhaps, requesting to talk to me. I had nothing worthy to say and declined them all. Taking my leave of Caroline I walked down town to escape the unwanted attention but within minutes I noticed people in the street pointing at me and heard remarks about myself. They were not unpleasant but they made me the centre of attention and I was uncomfortable with that. In the current circumstances where people had died there was nothing positive I could add and I certainly did not want to talk about myself.

As I walked along Todd Street I came to the John Flynn Church and quickly stepped inside. No one followed me so it was my sanctuary for the next two hours as I tried to make sense of what had happened. It was cool in the great man's building as I seated myself in one of the empty pews and mentally began to absorb my situation. Nevertheless, no revelations flashed before me and although my head cleared I was none the wiser, bar one thing. Until I thought back to the previous day at the Alice Springs Telegraph Station, when and where I had been enamoured by the setting as had never occurred to me before. I felt affected by that and then it entered my head that the subliminal warning I had received to abandon the airport and the plane had come from there. In fact I could now feel the direct connection although at that stage of my life I knew little of Alice Springs and nothing of Mr. Mills.

Yet the reality was my conviction, that Mills, as absurd as it may sound at this point, or later, had communicated that ethereal bond from himself, across intervening years to my unplanned physical presence, such as a supposed genie might do for a fortunate wanderer. Rather ridiculous isn't it? Yet for whatever reason it, or he, saved me from an early demise.

Two days later I landed at Adelaide airport to find a crowd of people pushing forward against a barrier, to see me. The previous day the crash was on the front page of several newspapers and Lily, the girl who had earlier shown me around Alice Springs called out, *I knew it was you.* I wasn't sure what she implied by that but she seemed caring about it.

I had no need to return via Melbourne at this stage so I took the more direct route, heading east and did my usual thing and hitched a ride with a truck driver going the 500 km to Swan Hill. I found it to be a pleasant town, probably a city by now. The good weather influenced me to stay a couple of days. The town is situated on the Murray River which is the border between Victoria and NSW. Burke and Wills passed that way in 1860 and must have also been tempted to stop over as they took the time to plant a Moreton Bay fig tree which is now twenty-seven metres high with a spread of forty-four metres. I still remember sitting at tables and chairs talking with the locals in ideal sunshine by the river. A warm memory.

One more truck took me the 850 km to Sydney, more or less. The driver was going as far as Liverpool and from there I was able to take a train into Sydney proper, to Central Station and then another train across the Blue Mountains to Mudgee.

I went to see my parents and talked of my time away. When I specifically mentioned the Alice Springs Telegraph Station, with emphasis on the calmness and serenity I felt as I read the Mills monument and walked on to the waterhole itself, my father for once told me something worthwhile. His words would later lead me to write a non-fiction 162,000 word book, *Skirmish Hill*, with William Whitfield Mills as the central character in the Australian outback. I am proud to say that the man regarded as Australia's greatest living historian, Professor Geoffrey Blainey AC, read the book and endorsed it on the cover with his words, *Many readers new to Australian history will enjoy your unconventional book.*

My father said, *Mills was your great-grandfather.* That meant of course that Mills was also my father's grandfather and never a word had been spoken about the fact. I think I felt both surprise and shock. Of course my father had never been in the habit of genuinely conversing with me but I asked why had he not told me before, at any time? He gave the off-hand if not rather crass remark that Mills was the black sheep of the family. That did not jell with the contentment and serenity I had experienced at the waterhole and Mills's association. I was now more strongly of the belief that Mills had made contact with me.

My father probably regretted saying that for my later research, and I can dig like a ferret, would put the lie to his unfortunate comment. I might sound bitter about that but the fact is that he had chosen to live a lie for all of his eighty-four years, only revealing the truth of his own face to the world, via my mother and I, when he was literally on his death bed. Dear oh dear. I wasn't at the family home too often but I did experience my father's strange behaviour when certain strangers contacted him. If they phoned and identified themselves with the family name of Stanford he straight away hung up the phone. If they came to the house, knocked on the door and proclaimed themselves to be of the Stanford clan and wishing to speak to him about family connections he told them to go away and shut the door in their face. My mother said over the years she witnessed that more than half a dozen times with no explanation given. They say every family has its secrets and that may be so. Over time I strangely felt sorry for him.

On a cheerier note I went off to see my block of land and then John Marskell, who was still leasing the country for his cattle. Both were doing well and John was keen to keep going with the business-like but amicable arrangement we had in place.

I was restless but made my way to Sydney where I stayed with a friend, Mike Stening. He rented a four-bedroom house at Castlecrag and at the time sub-let two rooms, one to a German businessman and the other to a Malaysian student. Mike was so good as to let me have the other room for free. I gained employment, for a while, with a billiard table manufacturing company. Each table was a work of art courtesy of exemplary craftsmanship but it wasn't for me.

I then tried my hand at selling medical equipment but my heart was not in that, pardon the pun. I stayed longer with a real estate/land developer selling newly built apartments on the northern beaches but with no disrespect to those three enterprises I was probably bored.

One day I was reading a newspaper which carried a small advertisement for a Russian ship that would be sailing from Sydney to Southampton and that immediately took my interest. It was a 20,000 tonne passenger ship, the *Shota Rustaveli*, which to some passengers came to be known as the Rusty Bucket. I paid for a bunk in a men's four berth cabin.

The fare was about $400, I can't be certain but it was well worth it because the six-week voyage was exceptional value. We stopped off for a couple of days in each of Auckland, Papeete/Tahiti and Panama before passing through the Panama Canal. The meals and the gymnasium were great, the film theatre selections were excellent, the bar was generous and I had no problems with my three cabin mates. We were exceedingly lucky with the weather. I am a land lubber but sea sickness has never worried me and in addition I do not recall having one bad day from the point of view of the weather. The other positive was that not only did I make friends among the crew but because I did I was able to speak close to 200 words of Russian by the time we sailed into Southampton. I suppose nowadays most people fly, except for cruises, as the overall cost of competitive airfares has come down.

I only drank cans of beer but they were priced at ten cents a can while you could buy a bottle of Scotch for A $1.80 or Bourbon for A $ 2.10. I heard from a man who a couple of years later sailed on the return voyage to Sydney. At 11.15 p.m. on the last night at sea the *Shota Rustaveli* was twelve hours from berthing in Sydney when he and his friends in the bar noticed that the ship had stopped.

The men went outside and in the light of arc lamps hanging over the side of the ship they saw a Russian submarine close by on the surface on the starboard side. The submarine was also stopped and one of the *Shota Rustaveli's* boats was taking four of the ship's crew to the submarine, along with crates of cargo. The ship and the submarine parted company at midnight.

The next day he learned that the four departees were two of the bar staff and two stewardesses who had become too friendly with some of the passengers. That interested me as I shall soon relate. The *Shota Rustaveli* sailed through the Heads at 12.30 p.m. and berthed at Pyrmont at 1.30 p.m. However no one was allowed to go ashore.

It turned out that the ship was short one passenger. A threesome of two men and one woman were drunk, even at that hour of the day. One of the men had asked the woman to marry him but she declined because the other man had already popped the question and as he had asked for her hand first, she had accepted him. So the jilted man had thrown himself off the ship, about the time it went past Bradley's Head. The alarm was sounded and a search made. As it happened he was found alive and the numbers being restored the other passengers were permitted to disembark, after 4 p.m.

When we arrived in Auckland I made a point of going to Mount Eden football stadium to put a hex on the New Zealand All Blacks who are all but invincible when they play there. Obviously I am not good at that line of attack as the last time the Australian Wallabies defeated New Zealand at Eden Park was in 1986, winning 22-9.

Papeete is the capital of French Polynesia in Tahiti and must be one of the most beautiful parts of the world. It is so colourful that many of its best beaches have black sand which does not detract from the tropical environment. Could have stayed there a while longer.

The place that I explored the most and was intrigued by was without a doubt Panama City. This was the first historical part of the world for me and so I set out to explore Panama Viejo which was the original Panama City. I took a bus out to what remained of the then Spanish city that was destroyed in a well-planned and determined campaign by the Welsh pirate and later privateer Henry Morgan in 1671. Morgan led a strong force of 1,860 English and French buccaneers along with Dutch, free blacks, Portuguese and a few renegade Spanish.

After leaving men to hold captured forts on the overland journey to Panama he attacked the city with 1,400 fighting men and as soon as they had plundered the Spanish treasure they burned the city to the ground. The Archaeological Site of Panama Viejo holds the remains of

Matavi Bay, Tahiti, painted by William Hodges who accompanied Captain Cook on his second expedition 1772-1775

the Spanish settlement's urban centre that was founded in 1519 and that was what I explored for that was not rebuilt. In 1673 the town was officially transferred to a peninsular eight km to the south-west and it is that area that became today's modern Panama City. I was free to clamber over the ruins as many would have done and marvel at the meticulously planned pirate raid and the brutal outcome.

Driving back into the modern city took us through the suburbs of Panama City and not that I have been everywhere but I don't recall seeing a city in which suburban houses have more colourful trees, plants and flowers in their gardens. The climate and the soil at Latitude 8.98 North and Longitude 79.51 West might be more receptive to that side of Mother Nature than elsewhere.

The following day I went downtown, into the heart of Panama City and by myself again. I came to a central street and looking around saw that one hundred metres further along there was a prominent intersection for vehicles and pedestrians. Before I reached the corner I stopped by a platoon of soldiers on the footpath who were being addressed by an officer as they stood around him. I always remember him for his physical appearance. No more than average height and less than average weight but by his aura well above average authority, his close-cropped hair matched the taut lines of his skin which was stretched tight across an early thirties aged frame of lean sinew and muscle. I noted his eyes for they were clear, without a hint of lines, of someone who thrives on their being conditioned to excel. His men hung on every word as if to draw experience and resilience from their commander. He had the presence of one who surpasses adversity and you want to be with him.

I stopped at the corner with no immediate intention of crossing the road until I had felt the beating heart of this historic and colourful city. I must have touched a nerve for I received more than I had anticipated. The first man to confront me asked what sort of woman did I want? I said I'm ok but he might have thought I meant I'm ok with whatever he had on offer for he proceeded to describe in great detail the women he has in his stable.

When I turned them down, all of them, he said perhaps I am more inclined to go with the boys or do I prefer men. I straightened him out on that one but he was persistent and suggested I might have a liking for some animal interaction. I know he offered to include a donkey but he had me shuddering when he suggested I try the horse. When the pest finally left his place was instantly taken by others of the same brigade, all like a Health Fund, asking much the same price but with different benefits. I only stayed there to hear

Building a lock of the Panama Canal, 1912

the extraordinary offers that I did not expect to come my way again, well hopefully not.

All the while there were worse characters offering me drugs galore. I don't hold with drugs unless they are to ease people's pain and while I loathe drug dealers neither am I impressed by people who take drugs. I see drug takers as weak, lacking in self-discipline, of dubious qualities and disappointing. Only this morning the radio news announced that in the past twelve months NSW police conducted 200,000 road-side drug tests and they are shocked by the number that proved positive to drugs. They drive amongst us. For the first eleven months of 2024 the money spent on illegal drugs around the world is estimated at US $363,473,810,047 and that does not include the attached devastation of suicides, robberies, medical treatments, killings, divorces, child abuse, financial losses and traumas. If illegal drugs could somehow be eliminated hopefully that money could be used for the benefit and progress of mankind and the world we are beholden to.

The next day the ship was scheduled to pass through the Panama Canal and I was looking forward to seeing how that is done. It takes about eleven hours to traverse the eighty-two km and we were lucky that we set off early in the morning so we could witness the passage. Before the canal was built ships had to sail around Cape Horn at the bottom of South America. It is not too bad going from west to east but rounding the Horn from the east means battling the strong westerly winds and the fast-moving current coming from the Pacific Ocean to enter the Drake Passage, let alone the many storms. As a result there are some 700 ships resting below Cape Horn. The canal would save lives and time.

France began construction of the canal in1881 but failed due to engineering problems and the thousands of workers who died of malaria. In 1904 America took over and after virtually eradicating the malaria problem brought in equipment that was far superior to what had been available to the French. The machinery included no less than one hundred and two large, railway-mounted steam shovels, seventy-seven of which were made by Bucyrus-Erie. You might recall that my drilling rig on Koolan Island was a Bucyrus-Erie. America's President Roosevelt was photographed on the canal in one of the Bucyrus-Erie machines. They were accompanied by enormous steam-powered cranes, concrete mixers, pneumatic drills, giant hydraulic rock crushers and dredges incorporating the latest American technology.

We started off by entering one of the three lanes to take us through the canal and each lane has three locks at the start and three more at the end of the canal. Each of the first three locks raised the *Shota Rustaveli* until we came to Gatun Lake which was created by damming the Chagres River. Gatun Lake is a freshwater artificial lake that is twenty-six metres above sea level, occupies about 470 sq. km and took us thirty-three km on our journey. The lake provides the required average of 200,000,000 litres of freshwater that is used in the passing of a single ship.

Using seawater was a limited option as it would have been expensive to always be pumping and the salt in seawater would probably damage the canal's sluice gate mechanism. Also the seawater could damage the aquifers and the canal's water treatment plants don't run to desalination operations.

As we slowly progressed we had ample time to take in the passing scenery which is different from most voyagers' surrounds. What you have is impassable rainforest around the lake and that is regarded as the best defence of the Panama Canal. The rainforest has maintained a barrier all but unscathed by human interference. This has resulted in Central American animal and plant species being undisturbed in their natural habitat.

At the end of Gatun Lake we descended the three locks which saw us enter the Caribbean Sea before continuing on to the Atlantic Ocean. In a good year about 14,000 ships pass through the Panama Canal or thirty-eight a day. America is the largest user with its imports and exports accounting for seventy-three per cent of the traffic and forty per cent of all American containers pass through the canal each year, for about US $270 billion in cargo. Since 2023 drought has lowered the level of available water and there are now limits on how many ships can pass through. Some ship owners pay millions to jump the queue.

From then on the *Shota Rustaveli* did not stop until we came to Southampton and while it is good to go ashore I believe we all enjoyed settling back on deck each day or wandering into the theatre, the gym or the bar without having to think about anything for another three weeks of blissful sunshine and cool ocean breezes.

During that period of nautical hardship I became friends with several of the Russian crew, especially Valentina, Lara and Dimitri who all helped me with the Russian language. When we were about to dock in Southampton Lara invited me to visit her and her family in Moldova, a Soviet Union republic on Ukraine's western border. I told her I would make every effort to be there and thanked her.

I said goodbye to many people whom I would never see again but I had enjoyed their company. As soon as I was on dry land I took the train to London and went to a pub, not so much for a drink but to meet a stranger. It is a long story but I had met a man at Randwick races before I left Sydney at a bar at the rear of the Members stand. I was walking past the open-air bar when he looked at me and smiling, said hello. He was Stan Trothe, a generation older than me but I returned his acknowledgement and within minutes we were forever friends. He came from Nyngan and now owned the New Brighton Hotel at Manly. He and his pub were in good company and good competition as it was on the Corso at Manly just a few doors from the Steyne Hotel.

Stan later introduced me to his son Adrian and when I mentioned I was heading off to England Adrian told me of his friend Warren Lewis who was due to arrive there in a few weeks. He gave me

Warren's contact details should I want to meet him. I had time to contact Warren before I left and we agreed to meet as soon as I arrived, so I was glad to realise the voyage kept its schedule. That evening I entered the London pub and as Warren had been waiting for me he correctly made the first contact.

I was in luck for Warren and another bloke were sharing a three-bedroom house that backed onto the railway line in Barron's Court. The place was old and small but with a room to myself and on my first night in the big city I was well pleased. The other two said I could have the third room for one third the rent and everyone was happy. Memory tells me the one-third rent for a week was £5. There are two rail lines servicing Barron's Court, the District line which is five metres below ground going into the centre of London and the Picadilly Line which is twenty metres underground for its entire length. Leaving Barron's Court and heading further west the District line becomes above ground and that is how we were next to the rail line which for me was so different I actually enjoyed seeing the trains so much I didn't notice the noise.

I won't dwell too much on all the tourist things we saw and did as good as they were for you probably know as much about them as I do but I will say most of them were fascinating, such as the British Museum. Actually I will briefly mention sporting activities that I was interested in. We went to Lords cricket ground to see Australia play England. Dennis Lillee opened the bowling as usual for Australia but it was his opening bowling partner, Bob Massie who took the honours, with 8-84 in the first innings and 8-53 in the second.

Later I went to Leeds to see England play New Zealand and that was interesting, to see the spectators more than the players. Each day the crowd of about 30,000 were mostly Yorkshire men. I could not help but notice nearly every man wore a cloth cap and well-worn coat, some with padded elbows as they leaned slightly forward in silent judgement broken only by polite applause when the game was well-played. I found the crowd enthralling and obviously the result of a by-gone age without excessive noise or advertising.

I was also at The Oval in London to see the West Indies play England. In the Windies first innings Clive Lloyd scored 132 and with Alvin Kallicharran who scored 80 they put on 200 runs in 200 minutes. In the second innings Kallicharran scored another 80 with both his innings being pure class. That team also contained Rohan Kanhai and Gary Sobers who both scored 150 run centuries at Lords and Roy Fredericks and Lance Gibbs. At The Oval I sat on the bare wooden planks of the ancient bleachers amongst the poorer West Indian supporters. At one stage some of them said to me I must be Australian. I was drinking cans of Fosters.

Speaking of things Australian I heard that the Australian steeplechaser horse, Crisp, was to run in the 127th Grand National at Aintree, Liverpool. I had never attended a steeplechase but I knew Crisp was a worthy entrant and went to support him in the race over seven km. He had the topweight by far of the thirty-four starters. Only seventeen would have the stamina and ability to finish the race. Crisp gave it his all but was run down by Red Rum who carried far less weight and would go on to win the Grand National three times. He caught Crisp two strides from the finish line in race record time with the third horse twenty-five lengths back.

I also attended international Rugby Union at Twickenham and the Queens Club tennis finals.

Warren had been working in Papua New Guinea as a bulldozer operator and like myself he was keen to travel around Europe. We met two interesting girls, both nurses working in London. Shona was from New Zealand and Michelle from Rhodesia and they said they were looking to travel. As I recall Rhodesia's Zambezi river became the border between Zambia to the north and Zimbabwe to the south of the river. They were happy to go along with us so we each put in £200 and bought an old VW Kombi van. On the side of the van was an outline of a large map of Australia and in the centre of Australia was a magnificent red kangaroo. Most people admired it but it meant we would be known, for better or worse.

We discussed where we might go and there was a general feeling to go with the wind and see what happens. A few days later the girls came back from work and said they are obliged to complete the contracts they have with their hospital, especially if they later want to work there again. Warren and I thought that puts a spanner in the works as they own half the vehicle. I said to Warren we can pay them out and go our own way. I asked if he would like a drive to Russia. No problem with that he reckoned.

We discussed the situation again and Shona and Michelle said if we go to Russia they would be finished about then and would meet us afterwards in Istanbul, Turkey. They trusted us with the Kombi and didn't believe we would do a runner on them and we assured them we would look after their share of the investment and would meet them in the Istanbul camp site on the pre-arranged date. Great! We would not drive in a straight line from London to Odessa but do sight-seeing along the way and I estimated it would be a 3,500 km drive.

Chapter Four   *Shota Rustaveli*

With plans now in hand for the four of us Warren and I went shopping. We bought torches, batteries, matches, sleeping bags and ground sheets, knives, a portable stove, rope, maps, spare oil, tool kit, basic medicine kit, basic crockery and cutlery, detergent, washing powder, soap, towels, tea towels, toothpaste, an Italian dictionary, a Russian dictionary and food. Food was our biggest expense and our biggest saving for we intended to camp out as much as possible and we did. We found a dry food warehouse that allowed us to purchase what we liked and in quantities that suited our needs. We did not know it at the time but we would be on the road for ten months so as it turned out we were modestly prudent in our planning. We also checked the tyres plus the spare and the jack and had the vehicle serviced. When we were finished more than half the vast space of the Kombi was taken up by cartons, boxes and packets of dry food.

Warren and I took our leave of the girls, drove to Dover, where we explored the castle and then crossed the English Channel by ferry. In Paris we met easily the dirtiest camp site we would encounter anywhere in Europe. Sad but true. Paris itself made up for it and as in London we made the most of the charming city. I remember walking past the office of the Department of Agriculture and nearly went in there to tell them what I thought of France putting restrictions on the import of Australian beef by way of applying quotas but I held my tongue. There was an oversupply of beef in Europe.

From Paris our next stop was Strasbourg, well to the east of Paris and an attractive city on the Rhine River. It is near the border of Germany and is the formal home of the European Parliament. We then turned south to Basel and Zurich in Switzerland for a while before arriving in Innsbruck, Austria. After Paris I immediately had a real liking for Innsbruck and later would return. I loved the architecture of Innsbruck, the layout of the city and the snow covered mountains that surround it. The Winter Olympic Games have been held there twice as have the Winter Paralympics. I am more of a summer person than a winter follower but Innsbruck had me enthralled and I may not be only the only person attracted to it. It might have changed but residential housing there did cost more than in world-wide well-regarded Vienna although I believe both are topped by Salzburg for Austrian house prices.

Innsbruck allowed us easy access to the Brenner Pass road and we followed that through the Alps which was a glorious drive. Several times Warren and I stopped to take in the majestic scenery and the refreshing mountain air, the likes of which we do not experience in mainland Australia.

We were headed for Italy to see my sister Wendy and her Italian husband Mario at their home in Bocca di Magra----Mouth of the River. The small town is situated on the Italian Riviera on a spit of land that borders the river before it flows out into the Mediterranean. Vehicles are prevented from entering the town by a barrier on its outskirts. Visitors have to walk from there on and it adds to the attraction. In the distance are the snow topped Carrara mountains within which are stored much of the best marble in the world. Mario's restaurant and other premises extend to the river bank which enables yacht owners to sail in, tie up and walk through the garden leading to the dining area. Very stylish.

Over the next few weeks we were taken to Milan which is noticeably a city of style and class. Indeed it is Italy's wealthiest city and dominant in numerous facets of national and international business in addition to being a cultural centre. It is regarded as one of the world's four fashion capitals and is the headquarters of Versace, Zegna, Valentino, Prada, Loro Pana and Armani. The city will host the 2026 Winter Olympics and the Paralympics.

Wendy, a culture vulture, also guided us to Florence and of course that was an exceptional eye-opener, a city that everyone should be privileged to attend. We stopped off in Pisa, climbed to the top of the Leaning Tower and carefully walked around the outside. Mario took us to Forte de Marmi, the upmarket holiday and playground for the more well-heeled and more to my liking to the Carrara mountains

Bill and Warren with Mario at Forte di Marmi

Italy's Carrara mountain where Michelangelo obtained his marble supply

In days gone by this was how the marble was transported

to see the workmen cutting out large slabs of marble. Michelangelo made repeated trips to Carrara to procure his preferred marble.

Warren and I took ourselves off to Monaco and played the

Monte Carlo casino where we lost more than we won. A strange thing happened there, not that we lost money but an elderly lady somehow enticed not one but both of us from the casino to her impeccably furnished home. At first we were impressed by the luxurious trappings she had surrounded herself with but gradually we came to the nervous understanding that an eighty year old woman was endeavouring to seduce two blokes in their twenties. Talk about toy boys.

The speed with which we left resulted in us jumping into the Kombi van and heading for the nearby Monaco Grand Prix race track. We took our adrenalin out on the track, hurtling the Kombi around the narrow bends and cranking it up to warp speed in the straight. Now that was real fun. Another day we were in Nice, soaking up the atmosphere of some of the rich and famous. Back in Bocca Di Magra I had seen Catherine Deneuve several times as she was staying nearby. The New York Times rated her as one of the greatest actors of the past century. She appeared in films that attracted a total of nearly ninety-nine million patrons in theatres, the highest admission numbers in France where she became the official face of Marianne, France's national symbol of liberty.

We met another film star, Franco Nero, several times as he was also staying in Bocca. Franco was an Italian heart-throb, the Brad Pitt of Italy and probably of Europe. He gained his break when he was given the lead role in the spaghetti western, *Django*. All up he made 200 films in which he had leading or supporting roles. They included *The Bible: In the Beginning, Camelot, The Day of the Owl, The Mercenary, Force 10 from Navarone, Enter the Ninja, Die Hard 2, The Pope's Exorcist, John Wick: Chapter 2*. Franco married Vanessa

Italian film star Franco Nero and Warren

Redgrave, they live comfortably in London and she still does the voice-over for *Call the Midwife*.

I went to Genoa but for an entirely different matter. I had a tooth problem and Wendy said the best dentist was to be found in that city. After the nurse had placed me in the chair the dentist entered and inspected my teeth, before suddenly rushing from the room. Strewth, what was the problem. The dentist returned with no less than four colleagues, told me to open my mouth and invited the four to look inside. What was going on? I needed my dictionary. Back in Australia I had enough dental work done and the Italian dentist was so impressed by the quality of that dental artistry he insisted his associates should see such skill for themselves. Perhaps my missing wisdom teeth took them by surprise.

One day I was bitten by a dog in the street. Normally that wouldn't bother me unduly as I have been bitten before by a stranger's dog that was in the back of a utility in Australia, where we do not have rabies although we do have fruit bats and flying foxes in Australia which carry a virus that is closely related to rabies and that can be fatal to humans. Acting as a guard dog he attacked me even though he was on a chain, a long chain. I was then told that rabies was everywhere in Italy at the time and the required, even mandated, treatment for recovery was twenty-eight daily injections in the stomach. I did not fancy that and decided to take my chances by not going to a doctor.

Fortunately I did not commence to foam at the mouth or display one of the many signs of rabies and I got away with it. The time it takes for the symptoms to appear depends on how long the virus takes to travel from the bite area to the brain. Since 2013 Italy has been free of rabies but I suggest anyone going to Asia should be aware that each year 35,000 plus people die there of rabies. India is the most affected country with sixty per cent of rabies deaths being in that country and with thirty -five per cent of rabies deaths globally. I have twice travelled in depth across India, on our honeymoon and for the forty-fifth anniversary of that auspicious occasion but at age eighty I am not going back for a third time.

I once spent some time in Ethiopia's Simien Mountains, known as the Roof of Africa as they rise to 4,600 metres. Rabies there has decimated the ranks of the Ethiopian wolf to the extent that nowadays no more than 500 exist and so we did not find that species of wolf. While later horse-riding across western Mongolia for three weeks we did find ourselves in plague country. Marmots are of the squirrel family but to us look more like large rabbits, weighing up to ten kg. They hibernate during winter and only in Mongolia are they considered a delicacy. We rode into territory where plague was affecting them as can easily be detected when their faces swell up as if they have been infected by myxomatosis. When that passes the Mongolians resume eating them. We quickly rode on.

From beautiful Bocca di Magra we drove south to Rome which everyone knows about so I won't dwell on that except for two things. At the main railway station we met up with sixty to seventy Roma people who are also known as gypsies and very colourful they are. Some of them were travelling in their wagons. They are said to have originated in southern India.

The Roma or Gypsies in their covered wagons, Rome

The other item that may not attract people's attention so much as mine are the catacombs. I was not seeking them out but was interested when I heard about them. In Roman times the deceased were not allowed to be buried within the city. So the custom was to cremate the body and place the remains in an urn which would be stored away in a columbarium, that being a large purpose built construction above ground but sometimes partly below ground. From 100 BC to 450 AD Rome was the world's largest city and I believe it was the first to have a population of one million people, which no doubt sustained the Roman army and its empire for so long against its numerous enemies.

The growth in numbers was aided by the Roman practice of awarding citizenship to those of other lands who fought for Rome, as Vladimir Putin is now doing in Russia. Once foreign mercenaries had been in the Roman army for fifteen years they became Roman citizens but Putin is so scared of antagonizing people in Moscow and his home town of St Petersburg by inducting them into the Russian army that he is offering Russian citizenship to foreigners if they serve in the military for just six months. If you trust him. Not that he can be believed on anything. In Rome the growing population created a shortage of land outside the city for burials at the same time as burials overall had surpassed cremations. Persecuted Christians and Jews had already taken to the city's underground tunnels to escape Roman punishment and both groups preferred burials so as to preserve the body for the Resurrection.

All this brought about a significant move to burying people underground, in the catacombs. Rome had some 150 km of underground tunnels and branching of from there were countless storage rooms. When Warren and I went underground we encountered doorless rooms not with entire skeletons but independent rooms stacked almost to the ceiling with either thousands of leg bones or skulls or arm bones, on and on. Relentless rooms. Later in my travels I would see similar or greater devotion to this practice in Malta and Peru.

Back on the road we drove to Trieste, which is on a sliver of the Adriatic coast just before and below the border of Slovenia. From 52 BC it was being attacked by barbarians until in 46 BC Julius Caesar rode to the rescue, made it a Roman colony and gave it the then name of Tergeste. It was also interesting. We had a good look around and then crossed into Slovenia and its capital city, Ljubljana, which still incorporates significant olde-worlde charm. However we moved on to the other side of the city and into the Kamnick Alps where we set up our camp for the night in a lovely forest of beech, oak, fir, spruce and larch trees. In the early evening we had a fire going and a little home in the cool mountain air. After we had cooked and eaten dinner we had no sooner settled down for a relaxing chat than a noisy ruckus broke out from the nearest campsite some forty metres from us.

As the interference persisted Warren and I wandered over to see what the problem was. It took a while to understand but it transpired that the family whose campsite it was were in possession of an old but handsome full-length coat they had with them. The second family had come upon the scene and recognising the occupants of the campsite immediately tried to take possession of the coat, claiming they were the true and rightful owners of the venerable article. I asked a bystander why were they arguing if not now fighting over an old coat. My informant said, *my friend, is old coat but 300 years of old*. It turned out the two families, ancestors and descendants, had been fighting over ownership of the coat for the past 300 years. No wonder there are blood feuds and wars between neighbours and neighbouring states. I think I am right in saying that more wars have been fought in Europe than any other part of the world. Civilisation.

After a few days in the otherwise peaceful mountains we crossed the border into Croatia and its capital Zagreb. Another old-style city in appearance and I wouldn't know what lies beneath the surface but something gave me the impression it wasn't progressing as other cities do. I am certainly not a demographer but I looked up its population chart and today's number of 770,000 is within a few thousand of what it was in 1991. I found in 2024 that from age 0 to 23 there are slightly more males but from age 25 to 100 the females strongly outnumber the males. This might mean that the men are moving away to work or live elsewhere. Whatever it is they don't come back.

From Zagreb we drove down to the coast and followed the road south. At one point we saw a sign for the ferry to Krk, which is an island in the Adriatic Sea. Neither Warren nor I had heard of the island but thought we would give it a go. We drove to the ferry which was just big enough to take a few vehicles and set off to the unknown.

It was a short ferry ride and then we drove around until we came to newly constructed Haludovo Palace Hotel. It contained the Penthouse Adriatic Club Casino of Penthouse magazine owner Bob Guccione who invested US $45 million or $300 million today, into his venture. Although behind the Iron Curtain where gambling was otherwise illegal the casino attracted prime ministers, moguls, celebrities, billionaires, dignitaries and dictators including a young

Saddam Hussein. Mr. Guccione employed fifty scantily clad young women to keep the guests wined and dined, gambling and hopefully happily losing.

The casino overlooked the Adriatic but was otherwise surrounded by trees. Booking into the hotel was beyond our means so Warren and I parked the Kombi out of sight courtesy of the trees and with our sleeping bags slept under the protection of a large hedge. We were never discovered and during the day and into the night, pleased ourselves as guests. A plane load of wealthy gamblers flew from New York every eight days during which time the visitors did not pay for the air fares, accommodation, meals or drinks, so long as they maintained their addiction to gambling. We dressed to the best of our ability and mobile wardrobe and we did manage to fit in. On occasions American women would ask where are we staying, as in which room, and we always honestly replied, *We are in the starlight room*. At times we had to figure out ways not to show them the room.

With fifty girls to cater for some of our needs it was a rather mind-boggling experience. A special contact we made was with an Englishman of Greek extraction by the name of Nick, who was a croupier at the gambling tables. The tables catered to roulette where the ball will drop on a revolving circle, craps as in rolling the dice, keno which is a numbers game and my favourite blackjack where the emphasis is on attaining the number twenty-one using the value of cards. As we had to be seen at the tables lest we attract the wrong attention to ourselves by not gambling we did our best to comply with the expectations. Whilst I had lost at Monte Carlo luck was with me at the Penthouse Casino when playing blackjack.

We pushed our luck for five days and came out winners and in

American dollars which I thought was fabulous but would prove to be our undoing down the track. When he was off-duty we spent a good amount of time with Nick at the swimming pool. He was perhaps ten years older than us but we got along so easily and well that he insisted when we are back in London that we should look him up at his home. If he was there, day or night, didn't matter to Nick. Once again we found ourselves saying goodbye but hopefully more of a farewell.

I heard that once the celebrities, dictators, gamblers, politicians and others had been to the island casino once or possibly twice they did not return and as the locals who were all communists were not allowed to gamble the costly casino collapsed within a year.

CHAPTER FIVE

The KGB

The law locks up the man or woman, who steals the goose from off the common: but lets the greater villain loose, who steals the common from the goose.

Anon, *the Tatler Magazine*, 1821.

From Krk we headed inland to Sarajevo in Bosnia-Herzegovina and onto the border with Serbia and then its capital, Belgrade, camping out all the time and free camping at that. Belgrade has long had active history and from there we continued east where we followed the Danube River which flows between Serbia and Romania. This took us into the area known as the Iron Gates which are a series of rugged gorges that continue for about 130 km, passing through thick forests and high cliffs. We stayed on the road but where the waters narrow the result is challenging turbulence for those who navigate that far. In Roman times the Emperor Trajan had his soldiers build a remarkable 1,135 metre long bridge over the river, in the years 103-105 AD, in order to supply his men who were endeavouring to conquer the Dacians who occupied the Carpathian mountains and those who lived west of the Black Sea. Hadrian, who succeeded Trajan as Emperor dismantled the bridge in order to better defend the empire. However Trajan had and still has the honour of a Latin inscription carved into a rock face at the Djerdap Gorge. Because of rising water levels the ancient but clearly written dedication to Trajan can no longer be seen from the road but it can be if you venture down to the water.

We crossed over into Romania and heartily enjoyed our evening meals around the campfire as we continually passed by fields overflowing with sweetcorn and plums along with tomatoes, cucumbers, cabbages and apples. All fresh and delicious. Romania is Europe's largest producer of sunflowers and the national bird is the large white pelican, which is dominant in the Danube Delta. With a wingspan of up to 360 cm it is exceeded only by the great Albatross. I would like to add that the Ukraine produces thirty per cent of global sunflower crops and sixty per cent of global sunflower exports. Russia, with its massive area but harsh climate is in second place and with another reason to take Ukraine's riches by force let alone spill its blood.

Still trekking east we arrived in Bucharest, the Romanian capital and soaked up yet another sun-filled day in that relaxing city. It was quiet amongst the tree-lined streets dotted with café tables and chairs alternating in and out of the shade. In fact it was enjoyable to the point that as we had time up our sleeve before we had to be at the Romanian-Russian border, as planned, we decided not to go east but north, into those Carpathian mountains.

We set off the following day and the road took us to the town of Ploiesti, in Transylvania. It might surprise a lot of people to know that area has enormous oil deposits and the first large-scale petroleum refinery in the world opened in Ploiesti in 1857 and it is still ongoing with the city now having three oil refineries. That is more than we have in Australia but on the other hand, according to the analysts, while Australia imports 90 per cent of the oil it needs we only have enough home grown oil, the other ten per cent, for the next three and a half years. Our government talks of coal and gas as energy problems but I for one do not hear any discussion of our precarious oil situation. If that is correct it bodes ill for 26 January, 2029.

As we had only covered sixty-five km from Bucharest we continued on until we came to a fabulous town where seemingly all the buildings are constructed of magnificent local timbers. Not only that but the craftsmanship is of the highest order and I was so taken by the outcome that I did not note the name of the town, unfortunately, as you will soon read and then realise why we left that town in a hurry.

Romania has some of those tall and ancient giant Redwood trees. Other species include oak, both common and evergreen, spruce, beech and elm tree. We stopped in that town and walking around came to an irresistible timber building. Having climbed a few steps we entered what was a scintillating hotel and found ourselves in a bar. I cannot provide a worthy description of the building except to say it seemed as though everyone involved in its construction had contributed something of exceptional design. A great amount of expert wood-turning had gone into the all-timber building, bar the foundations and window glass.

Warren and I had a beer or two and it wasn't long before we were invited to join a group of men in their twenties. They drank

Chapter Five　*The KGB*

constantly and sang their hearts out. At that time the Jewish wedding song Hava Nagila was extremely popular in many countries and everyone in the bar was singing that song as loudly as they could and we were encouraged to join in. The song originated about 200 years ago, courtesy of Jewish families living in Sadagora, Ukraine, which is close to Romania.

As we did not speak a word of Romanian it was remarkable how enjoyable the night was. When the bar closed a man, Bogdan, who had been one of our group, invited Warren and I to stay at his place. As it was raining we wouldn't be able to sleep next to the Kombi in our sleeping bags and it was still loaded up with provisions inside, so we gratefully accepted.

We drove to his place, parked the Kombi in the open and took some of our gear inside. I had barely settled into my sleeping bag when Bogdan entered our room, came over to me and attempted to run his hands over me before trying to get in to the sleeping bag with me. That sobered me up and I gave him a touch of what-for Koolan Island style. He didn't fight back but went to Warren to try his luck but he walked into a bulldozer. We picked up our gear and went out into the pouring rain, leaving good old Bogdan sitting on the ground.

We were now cold and wet but inside the Kombi. Warren turned the engine on and pressed the accelerator. That was strange, we didn't go anywhere. I opened my passenger side door and stepped out to see what the problem was and that wasn't easy in the blackness of a night compounded by incessant rainfall. Then I saw or felt the problem. On the dirt road the wheels could not gain traction and were spinning. I don't know the composition of the soil but I knew we were moving into eastern Europe's and more so Ukraine's famous chornozem area which is renowned for its fertile black soil.

Whatever it was it had the better of us. Warren tried different pressure on the throttle and I went to the rear of the Kombi, between the wheels, and pushed as hard as I could but to no avail. When Warren revved the engine up in case that might work he had an unexpected result. From out of the nearby houses and through the gloom, like ghostly apparitions in their nightdresses, came at least eight if not ten women. Apart from footwear that was all they wore and now they hitched their nightdresses all but up to their thighs. I might have missed their spoken words in the heavy rain but I could not hear any instructions. As though this was nothing new to them the first of those ladies of varying ages took up positions behind the Kombi while their overflow held on to the side of the vehicle and they pushed with all their might. Warren eased off the throttle somewhat as he soon realised what I was seeing and that was that the women, especially at the rear, were being saturated by the mud from the spinning wheels. Thankfully the Kombi moved forward and on to firmer, safer ground. I tried to thank the ladies but they were already turning back to their homes to change out of those soaking, mud-caked nightdresses. Extraordinary.

The next day we headed north-east and came to the Romania-Moldova border, the border into the then Soviet Union where all the Soviet Republics were united under the control of Moscow. We could have continued to explore more of Romania, possibly seeking out Dracula's castle but it was essential we be at the border on time. We sacrificed that travel time. We looked at the border and nothing seemed untoward but we could not cross over for another three days.

We backtracked for five km to a likely but unofficial camp site we had earlier noticed, one with water from a well and available firewood and trees for shade and shelter. The only people there were a Polish family of two adults and their two children. Again we did not know a word of the Polish language and that was counterbalanced by them not speaking a word of English but we literally fed off each other. They also would be there for three days, not wanting to fall foul of the Russian border guards and visa schedules.

The husband's name was Mikolaj, which in Polish means victory for the people while his wife's name was Katarzyna which is the lovely Polish version of Catherine. Mikolaj was a doctor and also a major in the Polish army reserve. We had our evening meals with them around the shared campfire, exchanged food and somehow told them who we are and why we are here, as did they. I easily remember that good-natured and most likeable family.

They came from the city of Lodz which is in the middle of Poland and about one hundred and twenty km from Warsaw. I shall mention some historical items. At the beginning of the 14th century the ruler of Poland was Wladyslaw the Elbow-High and he was followed by his nephew Wladyslaw the Hunchback. At the beginning of the 15th century and up until the latter part of the 18th century Lodz was a private town owned by the Kuyavian bishops and clergy. Later Roman Polanski would live in Lodz and thus the city became known for its National Film School.

On the morning of the due day we were up early, eager to enter the Soviet Union. When we reached the border Mikolaj and his family were already there. As we pulled up alongside their car I was about to say good morning but one look at his face instantly discouraged me. I met his eyes ever so briefly before he turned his head away and looked down, ignoring me as if I carried the plague. Without a word said he was succinctly telling me not to acknowledge him and I didn't but I was shocked at his subservient way.

Mikolaj was a man of means, well educated, surely of good family and high standing with important career roles in his profession and military endeavours but he was kow-towing to men who, combined, would never rise to half the heights he had assiduously attained. I had yet to be shocked into understanding the Russian way of life.

I turned my back to him as a guard told me to open up the Kombi van. He was suspicious of our many cartons containing food. He was in a state of surprise when he opened up some of the boxes and found not one but half a dozen large packets of Weetbix. Not believing we could eat so much he opened them all, looking for things untoward. Vegemite of course totally confused him as it could not be food. This went on for more than an hour and took us nearly as much time to neatly repack the van.

Perhaps acknowledging Mikolaj and sharing the language to a degree the guards let the good Polish people pass well before us but sadly I could not say goodbye. When the Russians could not find a fault and had meticulously checked our passports, visas and just as importantly our detailed route, accommodation and itinerary they allowed us to proceed.

As we were no longer free to camp out we headed straight for Chisinau, the capital city of Moldova, which in centuries past was the country known as Bessarabia. A portion of western Ukraine was included in Bessarabia. Along the way we stopped in a village to top up our supply of fresh fruit. We were somewhat taken aback to find most of the grocer's shelves empty except for the dust. There was nothing more appetizing in the village and it was our first taste of what rural citizens of the Soviet Union put up with. They had small farms, hard work and little return in those Soviet days. Without Soviet suppression the country's low hills, sun-drenched plains, flowing rivers and moderate climate of the nearby Black Sea basin should have showered the people with abundant rural blessings.

We found that strange as agriculture has long been the mainstay of Moldova, which is landlocked between Romania and Ukraine. It is a small country but blessed with good soil and its arable land accounts for seventy-three per cent of the entire area of Moldova. I realise there are vast differences but the fact is that only six per cent of Australia is arable. Moldova's exports include oil seeds, cereals, apples, vegetable products, edible fruits and nuts and especially, wine. Over the past thirty years Moldova's agriculture sector as a percentage of GDP has declined from fifty-six per cent to twelve per cent as the country becomes more of a services-based economy.

The primary religion is Christianity with ninety per cent of people adhering to the Eastern Orthodox way. While suffering Russian interference the country is still a parliamentary democratic republic. That interference runs to the establishment of a sliver of eastern Moldova being carved out and occupied by Russian connections and so-called gangsters. Today there are 1,500 Russian soldiers in the illegally occupied area known as Transnistria, which translates as across the river. That is a Romanian word and not surprisingly so as trans is Latin for across and nistria refers to the Dnistria river but the hijacked territory is not recognized by any government or authority, bar Russia.

Warren and I stayed in Chisinau for three days and when we learned about Moldova being a significant wine producer it was too late for us to explore the underground tunnels of wine. Moldova has more than 150,000 hectares of vineyards and that means it has the highest density of vineyards of any country in the world, producing in excess of two million hectolitres of wine.

This is limestone country and up until 1960 a limestone mine existed. Limestone blocks were dug out and used in building the city of Chisinau and when the company ceased operating the empty underground tunnels were used for storing wine.

Sixteen km north of Chisinau is the Milestii Mici vineyard which has the largest wine collection in the world. It stores nearly two million bottles eighty metres below ground in tunnels that are two hundred km in length. The wines are seventy per cent red, twenty per cent white and about ten per cent dessert wines. The most valuable, priced at €480 or A$800 a bottle are exported only to Japan.

Twelve km to the south of Chisinau you will find the captivating Cricova winery and its cellars, which hold thirty million litres and are ninety metres underground in tunnels that extend for one hundred and twenty-five km, with streets and avenues running off to the sides. At that depth the wines are kept at twelve to fourteen degrees with ninety-seven to ninety-eight per cent humidity, which I gather is ideal for wine. Every two days each bottle has to be rotated forty-five degrees. That is done manually by women as each day they rotate up to thirty-five thousand bottles.

It is said that Yuri Gagarin, the first man to travel in outer space and who completed an orbit of the planet in one hundred and eight minutes, entered the cellars and emerged, two days later. Some of

Nazi Germany's head of the German Air Force, Reischsmarshall Herman Goering's fabulous but stolen wine collection was recovered at the end of World War Two and sent to the Cricova winery. Of some 3,000 bottles of Mosel white there are now only one hundred and twenty-nine bottles, each priced at US $15,000. Visitors are advised not to remove the dirt, even the dust is valuable. Goering's favourite wine was Chateau Lafite Rothschild and today even a late vintage will set you back US $1,000. His manor house cellar held 16,000 bottles of the best of wines.

Vladamir Putin celebrated his fiftieth birthday at the Cricova cellars and he holds far greater bottles of wine than Goering did. Putin has been to the Cricova cellars many times but he became infuriated when the Moldovan government decided to become friendly with the European Union. He then ordered a ban on the importation of Moldovan wine into Russia. That pettiness cost Moldova, and also Georgia for speaking its mind, thirty per cent of their wine exports and his friend China's Xi Jinping later performed his childish banning acts on the Australian wine industry. To show just how vindictive Putin is you should know that up until then every second bottle of wine consumed in the Soviet Union up to 2006 was produced in Moldova. Thus his nastiness affected Moldovans and his own people of Russia.

One customer who behaved herself and was a regular procurer of Moldovan wine was Queen Elizabeth 11 of England. She was fond of Negra de Purcari, an aged dry red from south-east Moldova, which consists of fifty-five per cent various French Cabernet Sauvignon, forty per cent Saperavi from Georgia and five per cent Rara Negra of Moldova. The grapes are hand-harvested and the wine held in oak barrels for eighteen months.

From Chisinau we drove still further east to Tiraspol, the l is pronounced as r, which when we were there was in Moldova proper but is now in the renegade breakaway/hijacked area known as Transnistria. Back then all the streets that we came to were dirt roads. That wasn't a problem, I am just letting you know the state of play in eastern Europe and the Soviet Union outside the major cities. We checked into our pre-arranged hotel and then set off to find Lara's family home. We managed that, met her parents and with their permission arranged to come back the next day and take her out, so that she could show us around.

For the next few days Lara took us here and there and I suppose I should say she took me in particular most of the time. Warren was not up to speed with the Russian language which was a drawback for him but he said he was ok with everything and sometimes went his own way, without getting into trouble, leastways not then. I won't dwell on my time in Tiraspol at the moment but you will know something of interest there soon enough.

I mentioned the Russian intervention into Moldova by carving out the area now known as Transnistra. Unfortunately these days Tiraspol is part of the area annexed by Putin and whilst it is a humble and relatively poor area there is something there of great interest to Russia; that being the 1411th Artillery Ammunition Depot, otherwise known as the Cobasna Depot. It was established by the Red Army general Staff in 1941 and is now regarded as one of if not the largest ammunition depot in Eastern Europe. It once held 40,000 tons of Soviet Union -era weapons and ammunition. Russia did remove half of that amount which still leaves 20,000 tons. Putin stopped that removal agreement in 2004 and it is probably no coincidence that

Chapter Five   The KGB

Map of Moldova but altered. Russian forces have illegally occupied the narrow and very lightly shaded, almost faded, blue strip of land on the eastern side of Moldova, adjoining Ukraine. It is now known as Transnistra and sadly incorporates Lara's family home town of Tiraspol.

Russia's 1411th Artillery Ammunition Depot in the illegally annexed part of Moldova known also as the Cobasna Depot

while the depot is in Moldova it is also only a few km from Ukraine. Presumably much of that would now be too old for practical use but who seriously knows. Putin has been using Soviet tanks from the late 1950s in Ukraine. Moldova has long wanted it removed as it is mostly stored in the open and dangerous as it deteriorates but Putin is not agreeable. The Academy of Sciences of Moldova determined that an explosion at the depot would be the equivalent of the atomic bombings of Hiroshima and Nagasaki.

Jumping ahead we left Tiraspol and still moving east crossed the border into Ukraine. When Lara's mother had recently wanted to visit her sister in Ukraine she first had to go to the police station and ask for their permission. That was a normal requirement. When we checked in to the attractive Krasnaya (Red) Hotel, Odessa, we were given a room on the second floor. As there were no lifts one walked up and down the stairs, not steps but broad staircases and that was fine, it was a little exercise after driving 3,500 km. When each level was reached and you left the stairs and walked down the corridor to your room there was always a watchful Russian lady, seated at a large table and chair at the beginning of the corridor. She saw every person who went along the corridor, which room they went into, at what time, when they came out and who was with them. She wrote down the details. I imagine today that Russian spy technology is sophisticated but that was the way of it then.

At midnight of our first day in Odessa the phone between my bed and Warren's rang. I certainly wasn't expecting a phone call from anyone but I picked up the phone and said Hello, in English. A female voice and definitely one that was young, polite and intriguing asked, *Is that Bill?* in impeccable English. I came awake and said it is and waited. The young woman told me her name, Katerina, and said she would like to meet me and my friend tomorrow. I asked where and how will I know you. She told me where to meet at 1 p.m., at a certain point on a particular street and that she would be wearing a red dress. I agreed.

At 12.30 the next afternoon Warren and I deliberately arrived early at the meeting point. I suggested he go across the road and stand behind a large tree. If I am in trouble he can either seek help or come and save me depending on the circumstances. He was good with that and crossed the road. The footpath in either direction at that hour of the day was chock-a-block with pedestrians, probably good if someone wanted to disappear into a crowd. I couldn't help but notice every person was wearing what I would call drab coloured clothing, such as grey, brown, off-brown, black or faded black.

A few minutes before the appointed time I looked along the footpath and there she was, in the distance but ever so clearly discernible. She was not wearing a bright red dress but a bold red dress of class and amongst everyone else she could not be ignored. Even at that unknown moment I thought how that colour must reflect her intrepid persona. She would be oblivious to the opinions of others and yet when I discovered her line of work I wondered all the more how does she expect to go unnoticed?

Katerina took Warren and I to a café for light refreshment and heavy discussion. After learning something about us she asked if we had American dollars in cash and I told her we do. She wanted to trade our dollars for far more Russian roubles than we could expect to receive from any bank or government office. We agreed to that illegal arrangement and resolved to meet two of her men that evening. She would not be there as she does the arranging and never the transacting. She would meet us tomorrow for lunch.

The deal went faultlessly and we met her the following day. Being in a generous mood and just possibly taken in by her delectable figure, shoulder length black hair, gorgeous face, her enticing voice, the feeling of sheer excitement she generated by her mere presence and our fistful of roubles we paid for a sumptuous luncheon. Katerina ran a gang of black marketeers and her appearance aside, being a low-profile leader she had not been picked up by the authorities. She was such a pretty girl that everyone would at least notice her. I began to suspect that she was a protected person. I was partly right. She later told me her family was in a position of power and influence in the communist party with her father commanding permanent accommodation in a leading hotel. He would not have approved of her being involved in these illegal activities, which was why she never appeared to or with her associates and she conducted business by phone and relays. I am certain she did not need the money but the thrill of the chase.

We agreed to another dollar exchange and the day after that she kindly devoted her time to showing us around Odessa and there are many places of culture and history to absorb. Odessa was established in 1794 by the Empress Catherine the Great. She made that possible by sending word to European tradesmen and those with other skills throughout Europe that she was offering such migrants their own land, tax exemptions and religious freedom. The historical centre of Odessa retains wonderful buildings of the nineteenth century which are World Heritage listed but that has not stopped Putin bombing them. On 31st January, 2025, Russia hit our hotel, the *Krasnya* with a

Chapter Five   *The KGB*

The Krasnaya (Red) Hotel Odessa, Ukraine

ballistic missile, damaging the building and injuring seven people. As you know we drove to Odessa but coming into the harbour is impressive as the city rests on a high steppe plateau looking out to the Black Sea. To connect to the harbour below the Potemkin Stairs were built. With twenty steps to each flight and ten flights the stairs can be challenging. The staircase extends for one hundred and forty-two metres with its lowest level being twenty-two metres wide. The stairs at the top are twelve and a half metres wide and join Prymorskyi Boulevard where houses are expensive to say the least.

The attractive city of Odessa is known as the *Pearl by the Sea* and is situated on the north-western shore of the Black Sea, with a population of one million people. The Potemkin Stairs were constructed in Odessa in memory of the Russian battleship

Potemkin whose sailors mutinied in protest at their treatment under the naval officers of Czar Nicholas 11.

I place Odessa in my list of favourite cities of the world along with New Orleans, Varanasi, Istanbul, Kolkata, Tokyo, Samarkand, Aleppo, Jerusalem, Yogyakarta, Cartagena and London.

Katerina asked if we would sell clothes, specifically anything with colour. We weren't travelling with many clothes but I let her men buy a yellow jumper and a pair of what I called my crocodile trousers as they were a combination of green and grey vertical lines. We would dine out every night as now we could easily afford to and one evening in a good restaurant a man walked in wearing the bright yellow jumper which I had only recently sold.

Usually those good restaurants were fully booked or there would be a queue out in the street. Even though we spread ourselves around it didn't seem to take long before the security men were letting Warren and I go straight inside. They would see us in the line and motion us to come forward. Someone must have told them we were good custom. Except for one thing. The one item the buyers wanted most of all were our blue jeans and jackets. I didn't but I nearly sold my jeans as the price was outstanding but there was no way I would sell my denim jacket. That was number one on every buyer's list and the money offered was outrageous. I knew I would not be able to replace my jacket for some time and I still had more than enough roubles. Every young Russian wanted that western clothing.

We did have something else that was in big, big demand and that was our Kombi van. Numerous taxi drivers, nearly every day, would offer us many times what we had paid for the Kombi, not for the vehicle itself but for the engine. It had a German engine and compared to the Russian Lada it was light years ahead. The Lada had many followers in Russia and by their standards it probably wasn't too bad but a major problem was the customer had to wait up to thirteen years after ordering one to receive it. Production was not the industry's strong point. A better Russian car was the Volga but sixty per cent of those were reserved for state and communist party officials. I often heard tales of woe in those days about the East German Trabant, a 500 cc or 1,000 cc runabout known as a spark plug with a roof. Years later in Germany I met a young woman from Czechoslovakia who in earlier days had a boyfriend from East Germany. They had a major dispute over something and in a tantrum the boyfriend destroyed her car, a Trabant, by burning it. She was still heart-broken, not by losing the boyfriend but her beloved Trabant.

Our Kombi had a tyre blow out and we needed to replace it. In Dubbo I can have that done in fifteen minutes, on a bad day. The tyre shop owner did not stock the VW type tyre and had to requisition a new tyre from his supplier, across town. Both he and I had to complete a two page form explaining who we are, why we wanted the tyre, where we live, what we do and on and on. All up it took a full half-day to be approved and to comply with the Russian system of everyday life that allows the authorities to know all about the individual.

One evening as we entered a more upmarket restaurant than usual we bumped into another diner and in apologizing to him realised he spoke excellent English and that he was impeccably dressed, right down to his shoes. He introduced himself as Arkadi and suggested we might like to share a table with him. His handsome appearance instantly reminded me of the Egyptian actor Omar

Sharif and remarkably they were the same age, forty. Omar Sharif had already starred in *Lawrence of Arabia* and would later make *Dr. Zhivago* and *Funny Girl*. The resemblance was uncanny.

Arkadi told us he owned two shoe shops and that he made a lot of money doing so. No wonder I had noticed his hand-crafted shoes. We enjoyed our dinner and then he ordered a bottle of X.O. cognac. I like beer and a full red wine but I do not have a leaning towards champagne, white wine or whisky. For a while I did acquire a taste for brandy but I could never afford to graduate to cognac, let alone the X.O. cognac which Arkadi ordered for us. The X. O. marking indicated the cognac is at least ten years of age and I have never enjoyed a drink of anything superior to that cognac except water on an outback day.

I think I am right in saying that when cognac in its early stages goes into oak barrels it is seventy per cent alcohol by volume. After staying in the barrel for ten years the alcohol by volume should be reduced to forty per cent and can be put on the market. X.O. cognac nowadays sells for $300 a bottle and upwards. The high price is justified by the fact that cognac makes up less than one per cent of the world's spirits by volume. As the night was still young Arkadi bestowed a second bottle of X.O. cognac upon our table. Unfortunately I have not seen Arkadi since for apart from having the drink of my life both Warren and I were delighted to be in the company of such an impressive and welcoming individual.

I did ask him how is it that a man of obvious commercial success and wealth such as he has attained can operate in a severe communist state? He told me that as long as he keeps his head down and does not attract attention to himself the authorities leave him alone. No doubt they also know where to shop.

At the other end of the ladder I could not help but notice there are many Russians with a low standard of living but one that they seem to accept and tolerate, probably because many have had no choice, know nothing else and have become accustomed to their lot. Being ignorant I had vaguely but always thought that all Russians are dyed-in-the-wool communists. The reality is far from that. It may be different now although I doubt it as this is how the Communist Party of Russia keeps control of the people. Only seven per cent of all Russians are members of the Communist Party. Those members have the best jobs, income, houses and pretty much everything that matters. They control everything. They can enjoy holidays on the coast, they are permitted to travel, have access to the best schools and hospitals. The list goes on. That's the way it is in Russia. You don't want to be one of the ninety-three per cent. English Prime Minister Winston Churchill once said, *Communism is alright if you have the mentality of a termite.*

Thinking of benefits to be had in Russia I wondered how would it be to go to a race-horse meeting. I had heard there was a club in Odessa so I asked the hotel manager could he please find out if Warren and I could attend a meeting. I told him, truthfully, that I am a

member of the Australian Jockey Club, as it was then. The manager came back to me and said there is a meeting today. He gave us a letter of introduction to hand to the club officials and off we went by ourselves. Somewhat surprisingly we found the track, which is known as the Odessa Hippodrome, entered, parked and showed the letter until we were taken upstairs in what turned out to be the main grandstand.

We followed a man in a modest uniform into a long room with

floor to ceiling windows that looked down on the racetrack and the crowd below us. Three men were in that large room and they turned as one to see Warren and I enter as our guide called to them. Then he left. A man about sixty years of age, large and heavy, read our letter of introduction and told one of the others to bring Daniil, an English speaker to the room. Daniil arrived, translated and introduced us to the big man, Maxim, who was the chairman of the Odessa Hippodrome.

Those people, whom I would call Ukrainians today as the Soviet Union no longer exists, endured terrific sufferings meted out to them over the centuries, by the Russians, such as in the 1930s when Stalin imposed the Holodomor, meaning *death by hunger* upon them. Stalin confiscated all their grain and caused five to seven million Ukrainians to slowly die by starvation. Countless millions more were sent to concentration camps in Siberia. On this day the Ukrainians were most welcoming to Warren and myself. I did learn however that the letter to Maxim might have mislead him when I later realised, as he introduced us to others, that he was referring to me as the Chairman of the Australian Jockey Club. I hoped that my visit in that unintended unauthorized capacity did not become known to the AJC.

Maxim ensured a steady stream of trays loaded with sausage rolls and jugs of beer never ended as he and Daniil explained the racing. The Hippodrome had been built by Czar Alexander 111 in 1890 and its two kilometre dirt track with whitewashed buildings and green grounds became a mecca for the entire Soviet Union. A successful jockey was a feted public figure who could name his riding fees. The Hippodrome was a summer playground for the Russian aristocracy and other wealthy citizens who gathered for the gambling, champagne, caviar and the best horseflesh in the Russian empire. The Black Sea climate of Odessa of course is far superior to that of St Petersburg and Moscow.

Competing horses came from Kyrgyzstan, Belarus, Altai, Kazakhstan and all over Russia. At the meeting on our day there would be a race for thoroughbreds followed by a race for trotting horses and then the thoroughbreds again followed once more by trotting, all afternoon. No bookmakers were in evidence and wagering was done on the totalizer but it had a reputation for not paying the best odds and not allowing the winners to keep all their gains. Russians. Many people were betting amongst themselves and Maxim suggested we do that. After a boozy lunch he told Daniil to take us downstairs and keep an eye on us.

Apart from physically assessing the horses we had no idea of a horse's form and how it might run over a distance with weight, let alone the quality of the jockey. About all we knew was the barrier draw. Anyway we would choose a horse to win and Daniil would find someone in the crowd who would happily bet against it. The locals had the better of us and fair enough, we were on their turf.

Later in the day Maxim went downstairs, made a couple of speeches, presented trophies and posed with the winning connections for photos. Before we left he gave me a photo of himself on the track, his track. His name comes from the Latin, Maximus, meaning strong and it suited the big feller.

Over the years there have been wealthy people who have one way or another purchased a two-seater Russian Mig-jet, a high-performance fighter plane and used it to take paying clients up and away for joy-rides. Another form of entertainment and income was to go to a shooting range and fire Russian machine guns and other former military weapons. I soon found that was possible in Odessa and thought long and hard about the Mig option. The passenger sits behind the pilot for up to forty-five minutes in the plane, a Mig-21 which is capable of doing twice the speed of sound. I didn't have enough money with me but even so I thought it was a fair price. I presumed I could have drawn funds from my bank account in London to cover the cost but on the other hand I had little doubt that would be a most protracted if not wasteful and futile Russian exercise. In the end I decided that even then it would restrict my further travelling and declined. I have since regretted that decision.

Someone had said to me that if I am going to Russia to avoid going to prisons and hospitals. The hospital came first. Warren had stomach pains and as a doctor could not relieve his agony I drove him to a hospital. My goodness what a morbid establishment. It was like being in an old black and white film. The grim-faced patients that were not bed-bound shuffled along tall faded of-white hallways in structures that were outdated to say the least. The narrow, metal beds were surely hangovers from the Russian Revolution of 1917 and there was a distinct lack of the tang of hygienic practices and surrounds, let alone a few flowers, anything to brighten the day. Ugh.

I handed Warren over to a nurse after explaining his problem as best I could and was told to wait. Just sit and wait. Do not go walking around. Warren was led away and I hoped he would return. He was not happy. Half an hour later the nurse brought him back, with something akin to a small smile on her face. It transpired that Warren had gas in his stomach and the hospital had done something to relieve him of it. He would be alright.

He was grateful to the hospital staff but somewhat dazed by the experience so I drove him to the harbour and its more cheerful surrounds. We left the Kombi and began to walk as his discomfort was now alleviated and the fresh sea air did him the world of good. Besides the naval ships, tankers, cargo ships, ferries and pleasure craft I noticed one boat which struck me as different from everything else. It looked modern and I discovered later that it was 232 metres in length. What was unusual to me were the many antennae, discs, aerials, odd panels and domes. I had not previously seen such a ship so I took several photos.

When I felt Warren was his old self I suggested we go out that night but with a difference, to experience the best of something Russian, no less than the pride and joy of the city, the Odessa Opera and Ballet Theatre. The first Opera House was built there in 1810 and after it burnt down in 1873 was rebuilt. Please take my word for it, the Odessa Opera House has to be seen to be believed. Before one enters you pass between two massive statues on either side of the main entrance, known as Tragedy and Comedy. The theatre was constructed in the Vienna Baroque style while the architecture of the luxurious audience hall is of the late French rococo era. The unique acoustics of the horseshoe shaped hall allows performers to deliver a whisper-low tone of voice from the stage to any part of the hall.

To keep patrons comfortable in the summer and before the advent of air-conditioning, workers would lower wagonloads of ice and straw down a nine-metre shaft before carrying them through a tunnel to a basement beneath the hall. From there, cool air rose up from vents beneath the seats.

I need to give a little background to the next item. From 1346 to 1353 the Black Death or the plague, killed some 75-200 million people around the world. During this time ships arriving in Venice were commanded to sit at anchor before unloading for *quaranta giarni*, which translates as forty days, and thus we have the English word, quarantine.

In 1831 it was decided to assign the old instituted quarantine fees to the Odessa Theatre. One of the medical inspectors involved in assessing visitors who might need to be quarantined was also the owner of the Odessa Theatre. When theatre ticket sales were low he would announce the outbreak of an infection among newly arrived passengers and order them to be quarantined in established quarters for that very purpose but at their own cost. He then took the fees and used them to engage superior performers in the Odessa Theatre to boost attendances and financial returns. Imagine that happening in Russia.

The interior of the theatre is overwhelming. The seating, the boxes, all are a flowing combination of red and gold. I would have been to more recently constructed theatres which because of the technology of the day could claim to be better serviced but I have never entered a more compelling theatre to be swallowed up by and joyfully immersed in. It is magnificent. The opera we were privileged to see was *Carmen*. The exciting dancing and the singing were alive with perfect movement and tone. It could not have been better.

I had been able to make contact with Lara back in Tiraspol and decided I would go back there and see her. Of course I had no permission to do that but what the heck. I dug out my oldest clothes and made my way to the train station. With my limited Russian language I told the ticket man he must excuse my poor speaking but I am from Estonia and asked for a return ticket to Tiraspol departing tomorrow. I held my breath as he remained silent for a time that seemed endless and then producing the precious ticket said something I could not understand but he nodded his head to me as if to say ok. I exhaled with relief.

After that I met up with Warren and we went to a Russian school. We had met a lady in the dining room of our hotel and the subject of Russian schools came up. After I realised how depressing and unsavoury the hospital had been for some reason I wondered about education. She said she had a cousin who is a teacher and it might be possible to meet her.

We drove to the school and met the lady, by the name of Varvara. It turned out to be a pre-school and that was a start. Pre-school is optional but over eighty per cent of children aged one to six attend for free or low cost, depending on the parents. Primary school is mandatory and begins at ages six or seven depending on the child's individual development. The pre-school children seemed full of life, happy and active. I thought the routine must be good but Varvara took the edge off my positive assessment when she told me that once they reach the age of five the system takes over and that *they belong to us from then on*. Her exact words. The communist party takes over and influences their onward life.

The next day my train left Odessa in the mid- afternoon for the 140 km journey to Tiraspol in Moldova. When Warren and I had driven the reverse route from Tiraspol we went past a forest which I noticed for its lovely oak trees. The train line was on the other side of the forest and afforded me an entirely different view of the trees.

Several dozen of the oak trees had been felled and trimmed and were being carried or dragged away to the open ground by at least thirty women. They had no machinery let alone men to assist them in their manual labour. The majority if not all the women wore headscarves, had heavy boots and wore long dresses. They looked to be aged in their thirties and forties and not one of them was taking it easy.

During that journey it was obvious we were now amongst the famed chernozem plains of Ukraine. Chernozem is the almost unique-to-Ukraine black soil made fertile by way of its organic matter, phosphorus and ammonia, which in turn are derived from a high percentage of humus or decomposed organic material. I shall include a photo of the soil which will make most farmers in any country highly envious. The texture of the soil is such that it provides moisture retention and is another additive to ensuring healthy plant growth.

An area of the remarkably productive Chernozem black soil of Ukraine

Chapter Five   *The KGB*

The sun was setting when we pulled into Tiraspol and I left the train. Thankfully Lara was there to meet me and we commenced the long walk to her home. I was greeted warmly by her mother and even-handedly by her father who invited me to be seated while he told Lara to bring beer for he and I. He settled into what was obviously his favourite chair and I suppose as fathers around the world do, he asked numerous questions of me, in Russian. My 200 word vocabulary could not cut the mustard and Lara had to relay the Q&A session until he sank deeper into his chair and eventually his beer supply.

Both her parents were a little on the short side and perhaps a tad heavy but it only made her friendly mother cuddly and her father carried it well. A nice couple. I liked them.

When it came time for dinner I was taken aback for her mother had prepared not one but two tables each the size card players use that were all but groaning with the weight of the dishes and plates of food that the good lady had prepared. I thought to myself I don't know what Lara has told her but I don't deserve all this and I wondered how on earth I could consume enough of it to do justice to the preparation her mother had invested in my visit.

Russian meals can contain sour cream or smetana and that is not my forte as it often includes soured dairy products and pickled vegetables. Anyway I determined to do my best. I was ok with the colourful borscht soup with its meat, cabbage, carrots, potatoes and onions as I often had that when dining out on our roubles. I also went for the other soup which mother had made, perhaps in case I did not fancy the borscht. This was shchi, chicken with either fresh or fermented cabbage. Fortunately it was fresh cabbage. I tucked into the pirozhki which are baked or fried pastries packed with meat, potatoes and cabbage or cheese, delicious. Pelmeni is perhaps the national dish and that is dumplings filled with minced meat and wrapped in a thin pasta-type dough. To myself they are good the way they are but people like to add butter or sour cream. I could not pass on the beef stroganoff, with its sauteed beef strips served in a cream sauce with mushrooms. Mouth-watering.

There was so much there and we lingered long over that meal so as to relish it all the more. I could say the above were the entrees and then we started on the main courses before the desserts, cakes, ice creams, chocolates, fruits and brandy. Well, it seemed like that.

After clearing the tables away and Lara and her mother having made inroads into the kitchen work the four of us settled down in the lounge room and relaxed in good chairs. I thanked my hosts with sincerity for a night that dementia will hopefully not obscure. The occasion had developed into a unique good feeling in my relatively young life.

It was nearly midnight and father had dropped off to sleep in his chair. I was thinking I should not keep Lara's mother up any longer when the euphoric evening was shattered by loud banging on the front door of the house. Its persistency woke father up but by then mother had opened the door to reveal two startling figures. Two men, both a good 183 cm in height and looking bigger by virtue of their uniforms filled the doorway. One wore a brown uniform with epaulets and badges of rank, the other wore a three-quarter length black leather coat over a black shirt and topped by a black peaked cap. Shades of a Gestapo officer for that was precisely what the second individual looked like to me.

Chapter Five *The KGB*

They saw me and without a by-your-leave stepped past mother as though she did not exist. I wasn't going to take this sitting down so as they advanced to me I stood up determined not to budge. In their language they demanded to know why I was there and why without permission? Knowing my language predicament Lara attempted to tell them I am a guest of the family. Their voices had woken Lara's father and he was surprised to see such men in his house. He proceeded not to ask them but to tell them to leave his house. Mother tried to calm him down for she was now concerned what might happen to him as when the two men tried to get their words through to me tempers flared between father and they.

Mother said I had been invited to their house and they should respect that. Through Lara I told them I would leave to keep the peace but it was now midnight, I did not have a vehicle and there was no public transport available, least of all to Ukraine. The two officers agreed I could stay for the rest of the night but I must leave the house and Moldova by sunrise.

Talk about a turnaround. It was disappointing but I had experienced a wonderful evening with Lara and her family. I apologized to her parents, thanked them as best I could, said goodnight and went to bed. I was up with the first light of dawn and this time Lara walked me to the bus station, before sunrise. The trains were not running at that hour. Lara said someone would have noticed us walking from yesterday's train, seen me as a stranger and dobbed me in to the authorities, just to be in their good books. The Russian way.

I did not have to wait long for a bus, bought a ticket and said goodbye to Lara. I took a seat up the back of the bus which in ten minutes was full, even at that hour of the day. We were probably half way to Odessa and out on the open steppe county when I noticed the bus was coming to a stop beside the only tree in sight.

I sat upright to see what was going to happen. A woman was sitting on the ground under the tree and as the bus pulled up she rose to her feet. I thought it an odd place to be waiting for a bus and when the driver opened the door she stepped inside. Instead of proceeding down the aisle to look for a seat she stood by the driver and looked down the length of the bus and at the passengers. I could feel a sudden tension in the air and the people around me somehow shrivelled up in their seats. No one uttered a sound. I took a good look at the woman and sunk down in my seat as instinct told me this is not good.

Did you ever see the 1963 James Bond film, *From Russia with Love*? Bond's female enemy was the KGB Colonel Rosa Klebb. I have always remembered that name, Rosa Klebb, it stuck to me for over sixty years. She was a small, feisty rather unattractive woman in her sixties. When Bond tried to take hold of her a knife-like weapon protruded from the front of her heavy shoe and she tried to stab him with it. The woman now running her eye over the passengers could have been her older sister. Scary.

Whoever she was the passengers were in dread of her. Rosa, my name for her, talked or perhaps lectured the passengers for a good six minutes and received not one word in return. Then without further ado she turned, stepped down and left the bus to go to her tree. The bus driver continued on as though nothing had happened but the still silent passengers were not so at ease. I dared not ask anyone what had occurred for fear of giving myself, Estonian or Australian, away. It remains a mystery to this day to me but it showed me the power and control selected people in Russia have over their brethren.

We rolled on to Odessa and I met up with Warren and told him how I had been kicked out of Moldova. He had gone to the Botanical Gardens of Odessa which are now 150 years in existence. He took in the scenery which included two friendly young ladies with whom he spent some time as they showed him around the gardens despite the language situation. Katerina probably knew I had been away but she certainly knew I had returned as she phoned that evening and arranged a currency exchange for the following night. This time two of her men would come to our hotel room. That duly happened and after we admitted them we proceeded to place our currencies on the flat and open carpet on the floor, just so that everything could be easily seen and assessed. I had come to trust Katerina but she always sent different men for some security reason I suppose and I simply wanted to be certain of everything. However I deluded myself in that regard.

The counting was underway when the door to our room was opened with haste and fourteen people burst in upon us. I say upon because the two women in the party were photographers while the twelve men were there to strongarm the two Russians, Warren and I into immediate submission. Despite that Warren had the presence of mind to act quickly if not correctly and he scooped up all the American dollars that he could in an instant, raced to the open window and threw the dollars to the wind, if not down to the street to the possible benefit of passers-by. Yes, we had the window open which is not always possible in hotels and apartments these days, so that was old-school. I was just as quick off the mark but on the other side of the carpet and I took my dollars to the nearest disposal facility, that being the bathroom. I beat my pursuers there and jammed the money down the toilet but by the time it flushed many hands were already plunging into the rather ordinary water. I could do no more but I was aware that my actions and the swirling dollars were being photographed by one of the women. I was on film in Russia. That left twelve secret police officers to frog-march the four of us downstairs. At odds of three to one against there was not much we could do. Photographers aside there were four crows waiting for us downstairs and outside the hotel entrance.

Since 1820 the police in England used a horse-drawn black carriage for moving prisoners from place to place. It was made of timber, held six prisoners who were each in a narrow cell without windows and only a small ventilator in the roof for air. The carriage was known as the Black Maria. In Russia, when we were there, the secret police used one modern day vehicle for one prisoner. It was a black van and known as the Black Crow. Warren and I plus our two colleagues were each assigned to an individual Black Crow. In Australian English we talk of a crow per se but in Russia because of their language they can speak of a male crow or a female crow, the ending of the one word signifying the difference, as in Latin.

When our convoy of Black Crows stopped we were taken out and I had time to see that we were being marched into an unmarked and bland three story high concrete building. As we were escorted along the ground floor corridor they directed each of us into separate rooms. I could say we were interviewed but as it was dramatically one-sided it was more of an interrogation. It started alright with questions about who I was, from where, what am I doing here in

Russia, how am I travelling, who do I know in Russia, where have I been and what do or did I intend to be doing. Then I had to tell the man what I knew of Warren and especially of the two Russian men I was with. What transactions had occurred with them prior to tonight? Where did I get the American dollars and how many more did I have? Who else have I met or do I know of in Russia and what transpired with those people? How did I make contact with these two Russians, what are their names and where do they live? what did I intend to gain by dealing in the illegal black market, not complying with Russian law?

Often I could not answer the questions because I did not know the men, they had contacted me out of the blue and I didn't think bargaining for extra roubles was a big deal. I did have my doubts about that though because since arriving in Odessa I heard of an Englishman who had traded the currency, been caught and only two weeks ago was sentenced to two years in prison. I was concerned about that. A man came into the room, said something to the interrogator and left. I was then taken out of the room and escorted along the corridor. At one point the wall jutted out into the corridor and I saw one of our Russian colleagues curled up on the floor against the section that protruded. I was shocked. His teeth were bared, his lips drawn back over them, like a dog that has been thrashed and knows it is going to happen again. Fear glowed from his eyes. He cringed as we approached along the corridor but he was by himself. There were no guards near him, no need for them now.

I never saw him or his companion again. I entered another room with two KGB officers present and was told to sit on one side of a table. The senior man, tall and well-built with fair but thinning hair spoke slowly in English and he held something in his hands that was half covered but seemed familiar. He told me that I would be charged with black marketeering and something else, as he opened his hands and laid my camera on the desk. Spying. Now I was truly worried even if the charge was absurd. Like many countries who engage in spying Russia itself does not like to be spied on.

In 1934 The People's Commissariat for Internal Affairs, otherwise known as the NKVD was founded under Josef Stalin as the Interior Ministry for the secret police of the Soviet Union. After Stalin died the KGB was created and that did not make life for Russian citizens, or foreigners, any better. In 1937 the NKVD instruction regarding *On Foreigners* stated that *almost all the foreign nationals are spies*. The punishment for spies was severe or fatal.

I heard his colleague call the senior man, the tall one, Borislav. In my mind I called him Boris but not to his face, an overseer of course. Boris said they had found certain photos on my camera that indicated I am a spy. I asked what would they be and he told me they had the proof that I had been to the Odessa harbour and taken photos of the Russian ship *Kosmonavt Yuriy Gagarin*, which at the time was the world's largest communications ship and was the flagship of a fleet of communications ships, that belonged to the Soviet Academy of Sciences. The *Kosmonavt Yuriy Gagarin* was a Soviet space control-monitoring ship devoted to detecting and receiving satellite communications and could track the orbits of cosmonauts and unmanned missions when not over the Soviet Union. I though this is a long way from Koolan Island and not what I expected. How do I convince this Boris I know nothing about the ship, no one asked me to photograph it and I only did so because I

Chapter Five   *The KGB*

The Russian science ship named after Yuri Gagarin and for which Bill was accused of spying

had never seen anything like it. I suppose that sounded like a weak excuse and they certainly were not going to return my camera. That was evidence. They did not physically ill-treat me but mentally it was becoming a worry. I was taken to a basement in a lonely place and confined there. Warren eventually joined me.

I thought they can't be serious about me being a spy but Warren said that they knew he had been to the Botanical Gardens when and where he met the two young women. They accused him of soliciting prostitution. That ridiculous assertion made me feel better. These people must jump at shadows. Capital punishment is still legal in Russia but President Boris Yeltsin enacted a moratorium in 1996 that ensured no executions have since been carried out. In earlier times convicted people died by drowning, being buried alive or having hot liquid metal forced down their throat. Today's Black Crows are large Avtozak vehicles that resemble a metal fortress with grid windows for transporting up to thirty-six prisoners with little to no air ventilation, exhaust fumes that often find their way into the prisoners' cabin, are extremely hot in summer and freeing cold in winter. I am told they are deliberately seen so as to intimidate the people and regarded as the ultimate symbol of Russian authority.

Each day Warren and I were questioned more and more about our activities and while I confessed to the black market trading and travelling to Moldova without a visa I never mentioned Katerina. After two days Boris eased off, he was no longer so cold, officious and inquiring. After five days Boris said we were free to go. He almost smiled. Thank goodness. However a problem arose when the Immigration Department or Border Security or Internal Affairs, the ones with the control over who comes and goes, said during our extra five days in Russia our visas had expired and it was illegal for us to leave the country. We could not attain another visa to leave Russia within Russia and we could not go to another country to obtain a visa. We were stuck. Immigration would not budge.

It is interesting to see how the tide ebbs and flows. The KGB now wanted us to leave and Immigration would not let us leave. Apparently the two authorities were arguing and debating the situation for hours on end, until the KGB came up with an agreeable solution. We had driven into Russia and our original visa said we must leave Russia by driving out, on a certain date. We could not get the date back but the KGB proposed getting around the lack of an approved road exit by allowing us to leave by sea. If we did that Immigration said they would overlook the visa exit by road arrangement.

Warren and I were let out after five days and driven to the harbour.

Chapter Five   *The KGB*

The Black Crow stopped by a cargo ship and as we stepped out of the vehicle I looked up to see our Kombi van high above our heads. It was gently swinging in the air as a crane loaded it onto the ship. It might sound odd but I had forgotten about the Kombi and now I was stunned to see it anywhere let alone high in the sky. I turned to Boris as he told me, *This ship will take you to Bulgaria and then on to Turkey. Be careful.* As he turned away I had to know and I said, *Thank you but what happened to the two men who were with us?* He answered, *They were shot.*

CHAPTER SIX

Opposite the Blind

The wisdom of the one who travels to many countries and serves the learned there, increases as an oil drop spreads on water.

I looked back as we sailed out of Odessa harbour, having enjoyed the city and then being disappointed our visit ended as it did but overall I had a soft spot for Odessa and still do. By the way Yuri Gagarin, who I referred to earlier at the Cricova winery, met a sad death and I might mention that.

He was fortunate to be alive as in 1941 German soldiers occupied his town and took over the family home. The Gagarins were allowed to build a mud hut, three metres by three metres, behind their house. The family of six lived in the hut for ten months until his older brother and older sister were deported to Poland for slave labour.

Alexei Leonov, the first man to walk in space, was in a helicopter in the area on the fatal day and he heard two booms. The first emanated from an Su-15 fighter jet breaking the sound barrier and the second two seconds later from Gagarin's plane crashing into the ground. The Su-15 was meant to be flying at 33,000 feet but somehow was at 1,500 feet. While afterburning the Su-15 passed close by Gagarin, turning his plane over and sending it into a tail spin, a deep spiral at 750 kilometres per hour. A jet plane can sink into a deep spiral if a larger, heavier aircraft passes close by and flips the jet over with its backwash. Yuri Gagarin's ashes were placed in a wall of the Kremlin, on Red Square. On the anniversary of his space flight people in seventy-five countries celebrate his achievements on Yuri's Night, 12th April. Yuri's single pilot spacecraft, Vostok-1 was 4.5 metres in length while his spherical module was 2.45 metres diameter, a coffin. Immediately prior to blast-off his heart-rate was 64.

The cargo ship was making for Varna in Bulgaria, a journey of 700 km by road or 380 nautical miles by sea which meant we were crossing the Black Sea by day and all through the night. Warren and I were allotted a basic cabin and we were happy with that, after being held for five days in isolation. There were ten other passengers, three of whom were of interest to us. The first was Viktor, a man of about thirty years of age. He had been born in 1942 or perhaps 1943, he wasn't sure, in a distant village in Ukraine. Not long after his birth his parents were killed by German bombing and he was raised by survivors in the village. When he was about eleven years of age, an international aid organisation moved him, ironically, to West Germany. From there he was one of many orphaned boys who were sent to other countries where they might have a better chance in life and he was assigned to Australia. For his teenage years he lived in Sydney and when old enough to work he began as a truck driver. Lately Viktor had been driving fuel trucks in the eastern suburbs of Sydney and being well paid for what can be a hazardous vocation.

Viktor spoke fifteen languages. They came to him like seagulls to fish and chips. For a boy with no early education he was

Yuri Gagarin

extraordinary for he only had to hear a foreign tongue for the first time and it resonated with him. The second and third passengers of interest were two beautiful and intriguing young women in their early twenties from Japan. After two days of listening and learning from those girls Viktor was deep in conversation with them.

He said he had just made his first trip to Ukraine to see where he was born. When he drove into the isolated village there was no one to be greet him. He told us that the villagers, like others in the Soviet Union, knew from harsh experience that when a black car came their way it was always occupied by a German or Russian hardheaded official who was only there for his benefit not for the villagers. When they saw his black car approaching everyone ran into the nearby low hills and hid. Viktor simply called out and hung around until the boldest ventured forth.

Before the slow-moving cargo ship reached Varna a crew member took us to see the captain. A large photograph of Leonid Brezhnev who was the leader of the Soviet Union for eighteen years after succeeding Nikita Khruschev occupied pride of place in his cabin. He wanted to let us know that when we dock in Varna he will not mind if we go ashore even without a visa. We will have one full day in Varna and depart at 9.45 the following morning. If we do not return to his ship he will not be looking or waiting for us. If that means we have to stay in Bulgaria that is our concern, not his. Do we understand?

Warren and I readily accepted all that he said and thanked him for having us on board his ship. We assured him we would not do anything to embarrass him. We did not mention that so far nobody had asked us to pay for anything such as our transport and meals on his ship. Someone had authorized the crane be used to load the Kombi on board and nothing had been said to us. It was strange but we decided we would not prod the Russian bear.

The following morning we descended the gangplank and were in Varna. Bulgaria was not a country I had anticipated visiting and we would not have much time to make the most of the opportunity but we did our limited best. Varna is the third biggest city in Bulgaria and its port is the biggest and most important for its good position on the Black Sea coast but even so it is not a major world port. Today eight million tonnes of cargo are processed per year in Varna. Sydney ports handle some 180 million tonnes of cargo annually.

Not being able to communicate with anyone of note in Varna I do not have much to say except that I know in the Crimean War against Russia the French and British forces used Varna as a headquarters. Unfortunately an outbreak of cholera killed many soldiers. Later the Orient Express train from Constantinople to Europe passed through Varna.

Then, even while we were in Varna something extraordinary happened. A workman doing excavation work prior to construction had dug into what turned out to be an ancient necropolis or cemetery. It was only four km from the centre of the city and initially some 290 graves were uncovered. There were several differences from other burial grounds.

The Varna cemetery was not the first in the world to place decorations about the graves but it was definitely the first to place gold and gold artifacts therein. The oldest gold treasure and jewellery in the world dating from 4600 BC to 4200 BC was discovered there. This pre-dates the ancient Egyptians doing that

Chapter Six *Opposite the Blind*

and it is considered to be one of the main archaeological sites of world history. Unfortunately we could not access the site and it would be some months before the gold was moved to the Varna Archaeological Museum. Three thousand gold artifacts have been found and grave number forty-three held more gold than has been found in the rest of the world during that time frame, some researchers claiming for the millenium, i.e. 5000 to 4000 BC. I have a photo of a skeleton with ever so much gold of varying sizes over his bones, his arms still clasping some of the larger items.

Exposition of the skeleton and the objects found in grave No. 43, which can be seen at the Varna Archaeological Museum

Skeleton of ancient man buried with much gold in Varna, Bulgaria

Back on the cargo ship that night we continued talking with Viktor, admired the culture of the Japanese girls and looked with interest at a chart of the Black Sea. The following morning we stayed on board, not taking the opportunity or the risk of going ashore for just a couple of hours and by misadventure missing the boat. I didn't ask to go to Bulgaria and I mean no offence but I did not want to stay there at this time in the current circumstances.

We sailed into Istanbul. What a wonderful way to arrive in one of the great cities of the world. In my early years of travel London was far and away my favourite city but as the years went by that changed as did London. The city became so crowded, I saw the makeup of the residents change significantly and I felt the character difference caused a loss of the natural and national British way of life. A generation later when my son was living in north London's Finchley he claimed everyone else in Finchley was Russian and he did not come across a native Englishman speaking English. A slight exaggeration perhaps but seemingly so and definitely not the London I had lived in. I love its heritage and history but the more I visited Istanbul it became my number one city. I regard Istanbul as a living museum.

Cruise ships with thousands of tourists arriving from European ports come from the Mediterranean, from the south-west into the narrow channel of The Dardanelles, where the ancient city of Troy once stood, 300 km to the west of Istanbul, then through the Sea of Marmara, which is the smallest sea in the world, and on to Galataport, to disembark in Istanbul. Our cargo ship crossed the Black Sea from the north and sailed through the Bosphorus to Istanbul. The Bosphorus is that strip of water from the Dardanelles to the entry into the Black Sea.

There is a strong belief that up to 7,500 years ago the Black Sea was a freshwater lake, separated from the Mediterranean and the Sea of Marmara by a cliff at the end of a valley known then as Bosphorus. Earthquakes typical of the area caused the cliff to collapse with the result that the Mediterranean waters poured into the Black Sea at the rate of fifty cubic kilometres of water every day or 200 times the flow of Niagara Falls. A cubic km is measured as one km x one km x one km and its volume is 1,000,000,000,000 or one trillion litres.

Frightened Stone Age people would have witnessed this flood and as it was no doubt a terrifying sight they would have told their children and their children's children. Along with the flooding of the Persian Gulf at the same time this event has been proposed as one source for the biblical story of Noah's flood.

The Bosphorus is now a deep strait of thirty km in length and no wider than seven hundred and fifty metres at its narrowest point. It separates Asia and Europe and connects the Black Sea and the Sea of Marmara. The area is of strategic transport, trade and military importance, certainly for Turkey, Ukraine and Russia. It is interesting that two currents flow through the Bosphorous. The surface current flowing from nor-nor-east to sou-sou-west carries the excess water from the Black Sea through the Sea of Marmara and on to the Aegean Sea. Below the surface the counter current brings saline water from the Sea of Marmara to the Black Sea and that is lukewarm in winter and cold in the summer.

In 667 B.C. a Greek from the coastal city of Megara, south of Athens, by the name of Byzas sought new lands and asked the oracle of Delphi where should he find them. He was advised to seek them opposite the city of the blind. While sailing through the Bosphorus where it meets the Sea of Marmara, Byzas saw the Greek settlement of Chalcedon on the Asia Minor side. It was unremarkable compared to the body of water that he saw flowing inland on the opposite or European side of the Bosphorus.

Byzas followed its course and discovered it went well inland, was protected from the fast-flowing waters of the narrow Bosphorus and as Captain Arthur Philip would also say 2,445 years later when he initially sailed into Sydney Harbour, *it will hold 1,000 ships*. This natural deep-water harbour would become known as the Golden Horn. The land on one side formed part of a wedge-shaped peninsular, adding further to its attraction on which to build a fortified city. Being a modest man he named the site Byzantium which would later become Constantinopolous after the Emperor Constantine, then Constantinople and today Istanbul.

Byzas and his people were amazed to realise that the founders of Chalcedon seventeen years earlier had missed seeing this extraordinary site that was available to them. As the oracle had said to Byzas, *you will find the land you seek opposite the city of the blind*.

The Turks kindly unloaded the Kombi, a Russian sailor said, *Do suidaniya i udachi* or *Goodbye and good luck* and we farewelled Viktor and the Japanese ladies. We might be out of the frying pan but heading into the fire. We set off to find Shona and Michelle.

At first I had thought it was a stroke of luck that the KGB had sent us to Bulgaria and Turkey, especially to Istanbul which was where we had agreed to meet the girls. I have had luck now and again but this release and deliverance at times seemed unreal. I began to wonder how can this be? Then a possibility struck me. During the five days the KGB held us the daily questioning slowly changed to discussions and the atmosphere was somewhat relaxed. I could not be sure but perhaps I had told Boris that we were headed to Istanbul, although he had to send us somewhere by sea if we were to exit the Soviet Union and there is only one way out by boat from within the Black Sea. Heaven knows we had discussed some things for hours on end. If that was so and Boris knew our immediate plans it might be possible that he had a change of heart about us. He could get us off his hands, keep the peace with Immigration and simply do something for the good.

In the glovebox of the Kombi I had the name of the campsite where we were to meet the girls and somehow without any knowledge of the Turkic language we eventually arrived there and found them in a cabin in the camping ground. I thought we might be in the doghouse but it turned out they had only been there for a couple of days as the time we were delayed we would otherwise have spent driving to Turkey. Thank goodness for that.

Istanbul has so much to offer that I will mention a few happenings now and more when I later return, once on my honeymoon and again on another journey to soak up more of the historical city.

I am biased regarding the Hagia Sophia as it has become my favourite building, anywhere. As a result of civil wars let alone defending its borders and fighting off barbarians the large Roman empire was becoming unmanageable and it was decided to transform the empire into two realms. Rome would be the capital of the western Roman empire consisting of western Europe and western North Africa and the capital of the eastern Roman empire that included Greece, Turkey, Syria, Israel/Judea and Egypt would be Constantinople.

In 532 after riots in Constantinople in which 30,000 citizens were killed and the fourth century Hagia Eirene church was burned down the Emperor Justinian began immediate construction, on the same site, of the Hagia Sophia cathedral. 10,000 workmen completed the magnificent Christian structure in 537 with pillars and marble from countries far and wide. The building is remarkable, even today after some 1,500 years for its architecture method of using pendentives to support, unseen, the huge dome which resides fifty-five metres above the ground. I will not delve into the architecture more than that but the entire building is to be admired both from the exterior and the wonder of the interior.

One of the exquisite and colourful mosaics of the Hagia Sophia presents from left to right the Emperor Justinian holding a model of the Hagia Sophia, the Virgin Mary holding baby Jesus and the Emperor Constantine holding a model of the city of Constantinople. That mosaic was added in the ninth century and it is an amazing grace that this unique building with its contents from the past can still be witnessed and treasured today.

Shona, Michelle, Warren and I usually walked as that is the type of city Istanbul is. It surrounds you with its life over the ages. Those surrounds brought us to the remains of the several walls which over the centuries kept all but a few invaders at bay. The walls ran along the Bosphorus, turned into the Golden Horn and then on for six km over land to the Sea of Marmara. There was a ring of three walls, the low, outer and inner walls, one after the other and each taller than the last. The final and tallest wall was almost five metres thick and twelve metres high with ninety-six towers at a height of twenty metres. In front of those walls was a moat which could be flooded on demand via a series of pipes that ran the length of the first wall and provided instant defence should the city be threatened. To prevent attacking ships from entering the Golden Horn a chain with the thickness of a man's arm was winched across the water at the entrance of and to the far side of the Golden Horn, according to the research of Paul Cooper. In addition the Cambridge Ancient History says the walls were *perhaps the most successful* and *influential city walls ever built—and to survive for more than a millenium.* Istanbul has a reconstruction program that is restoring sections of the walls to their past glory and they look fabulous.

The Topkapi Palace was home to many of the Ottoman rulers of Constantinople which the Turkish government renamed Istanbul in 1930 and converted the building to be a museum. One of its many treasures is the Arms Collection which incorporates one of the richest gatherings of Islamic weapons, from the 7th to the 20th century. The Conqueror's Pavilion houses the Imperial Treasury with its vast array of accumulated treasures from the Ottoman dynasty which includes items such as an iron mail coat decorated with gold and encrusted with jewels. Gilded swords, thrones of ebony and ivory, jewel encrusted looking-glasses and a gold elephant from 19th century India are also to be seen. The hilt of the Topkapi Dagger has three large emeralds topped by a golden watch with an emerald lid while the head plumes of white herons enriched with diamonds, rubies and emeralds adorn the turbans of sultans, their horses and women of fashion. The Czar of Russia, Nicholas 11, made a present of a jade bowl. The famous Spoonmaker's Diamond is set in silver and is surrounded by two rows of forty-nine diamonds. Two fabulous solid gold candleholders, each weighing forty-eight kilograms and set with 6,666 cut diamonds were a gift from the Ottoman Sultan Abdulmecid 1 to the Kaaba in the holy city of Mecca. Under Abdulmecid the Ottomans fought alongside Britain and France against Russia in the Crimean War.

Elsewhere in the Museum we came across what is purported to be the forearm and hand of John the Baptist in a golden covering, gifts from the Emperor of Germany and clocks given by Queen Victoria. We were allowed into the Harem which was for women but eunuchs and young boys were able to enter on occasions. Next was the Privy Chamber which contains what are regarded as the most sacred relics of the Muslim world. These include the cloak of Muhammad the Prophet, his battle swords, an autographed letter, a bow, a tooth and what I found quite remarkable, a single hair from his beard. I realise teeth can last for centuries and in the British Museum I saw the body of a man who had been preserved for 5,000 years by way of being buried under desert sand. His body had all its skin and there were tufts of hair on his head. The hair was attached to the body but in the case of Muhammad to claim an unattached single hair from a beard draws a long bow and surely an even longer faith. I saw the sole hair and to a degree I understand what faith is to the believer. It is everything.

There is far more to Istanbul but I do not want to overload the system for now so I will relate more when I later return to the fascinating city.

Shona and Michelle told us they had received an offer to go back to do contract work at their former hospital in London and whilst there was no rush they would accept the offer. It was decided we would all go on to Athens and split up then so we made the 600 km

Chapter Six   Opposite the Blind

drive to Thessalonika, bush camping as we went. We stopped for a while in Thessalonika as it is rated the second city of Greece. It was founded in 315 BC by Cassander of Macedon who named it after his wife Thessalonike, the daughter of Philip 11 of Macedon. This is interesting as Thessalonike was the half-sister of Alexander the Great. In addition Philip 11 led one of the more than twenty armies that attacked Constantinople but failed to breach its powerful limestone walls. Limestone again, similar to the structure of the underground winery tunnels as seen in Moldova.

In earlier times Thessalonika attracted Christian followers and Paul the Apostle numbered several visits to the city's synagogue while on his second missionary journey. Another point of interest is that from the 16th to the 20th century Thessalonika was the only city in Europe in which the majority of the population were Jewish, mainly Sephardic Jews. In the early years of the Byzantine Empire it was considered to be the second city of importance after Constantinople. In 1881 Mustafa Kemal Ataturk, the founder of the modern republic of Turkey was born in Thessalonika and I imagine it fair to say that his influence on and leadership of Turkey has at least matched that of any other world leader. In 2014 the Financial Times magazine, Foreign Direct Investment, paid the city a compliment stating that it is the best mid-sized European city of the future for human capital and lifestyle.

While in Thessalonika Warren and I were having a quiet early evening drink at a bar when we were welcomed by four United States Air Force officers who suggested we join their table. I don't believe there is an American base there but the men were certainly present and we all talked and enjoyed the company. They asked what we were doing and we said we were travelling around as it comes. One of the Americans said that if we were ever looking for work to sustain our journey and found ourselves in Heidelberg, Germany, we could go to the American Army base, Patrick Henry Village and enquire. He thought they would likely find suitable work for two fit young men. I made a note of that and thanked him.

We set off for Athens and followed the coastal road as much as possible. In doing that we came to an old-style village and stopped to look around and meet a few of the locals. As it happened there were only a few. A man came out of an older restaurant and explained that the tourist season was over and most of the village businesses had closed, the owners or managers going back to other interests. We chatted and he asked where were we heading? Athens, we told him but looking around along the way. He asked if we were in a hurry and the girls said no to that. He then told us he has two villas behind his restaurant and we could stay in one of them for a week at no cost. We looked at the beach across the road and didn't hesitate to accept his generosity. He added that he would be staying on for another month and he could supply us with evening meals in his restaurant, if we would like that?

The temperature might have dropped but the water was not cold. I know because the first thing I did every morning was to go for a swim and more importantly try to catch a wave. Once or twice I latched on to a rare half-metre swell and made a little progress but that was the best of it. Still and all we enjoyed splashing around in the Aegean Sea, going for long coastal walks and dining out each night to a different marine menu. A week was enough.

We moved on to Athens, a popular city soaked in history and

still oozing with life. We covered all the tourist areas and you have probably seen and done similar so I won't overdo it now, except for one small item. In a flea market I came across an old, old knife, an ancient knife in a heavily engraved scabbard. It was one of those few moments when I saw something for the first time and instantly desired it, irrespective of not knowing anything about it. The blade was twenty-three cm in length and narrow while the handle I thought short. Perhaps that makes it a dagger and certainly a stabbing implement. You wouldn't use it in the kitchen, for throwing or for skinning sheep and kangaroos as I have often done.

The handle is special if not spectacular for the top and sides of it are in the shape of a triangle with the bottom descending into a slight taper until it reaches the hilt whose arms spread to the two sides like an albatross on the wing. When you pass your hand over it the markings are raised above the flat of the surface in relief style. Also the engraved area is the colour of worn gold with a background of faded black. The triangular top section carries the design of the double-headed eagle and below that are three circular lines within which spreading arm-like tentacles or languid vines appear to create movement.

I do not say that this knife is as old as what I am going to allude to but it is of ancient age. I have had it now for fifty-three years and there may be a century or more that it has been around. I would like to know for certain. Consider the following if you will. The double-headed eagle originated in the Hittite empire which I think was more or less southern Turkey, from the 18th to the 12th centuries, BC. The Byzantine empire of the Greeks at Constantinople was conspicuous when the Palaiologan emperors notably wore the double-headed eagle on their clothes to show they were members of the imperial family. They also used the double-headed eagle on a red shield to indicate they were of Constantinople. When Emperor John Palaiologos sailed to the Council of Florence his ship's flag was adorned with the double-headed eagle.

The official symbol of the city of Christian Constantinople was the crescent moon and that first occurred long before Islam came on the horizon in the seventh century. When the Muslims finally conquered a heavily outnumbered Constantinople in 1453 they took the crescent moon and made it the symbol of Islam and of Turkey that we see today. Which reminds me that when Aboriginal people in Australia talk of the Dream Time it is unfortunate that they do not point out that the Dream Time was a concept and words named by a white man. That gentleman was Francis Gillen, an anthropologist and ethnologist while being the Telegraph Station manager first at Charlotte Waters and then at Alice Springs for twenty -five years where he was in regular contact with Aboriginal people.

Back to the dagger. The intrigue extends to the well-worn scabbard with the top segment again being of that raised and engraved style which goes down from the top of the scabbard for seven cm. In the centre of that section is a small circle that is raised higher again and the circle is empty. The jagged edges of the circle clearly show that a precious stone was once held therein but it has been long gone. That which I have described on one side of the blade and the scabbard is repeated on the other side, so both jewels are missing. The top and lower ends of that seven cm section are connected by a chain so I presume the knife could have been attached to a belt or similar.

Chapter Six *Opposite the Blind*

There is one more item of interest, in fact I believe of great interest. Similar to the double-headed eagle being engraved on a raised surface so does the lower half of the scabbard have something engraved in gold and black on a raised platform. This is a ship, definitely of the type that existed long ago. I thought it might have been Persian or Greek and I have found drawings of a Greek ship identical to this one on the dagger. You will know of triremes, which were ships of those ancient empires including the Romans that had three decks for 170 rowers. A bireme had two decks but this ship has one deck for fifty rowers, being twenty-five men on either side of the ship. Such a vessel was known as a penteconter, meaning fifty-oared. The clincher is that the Greeks built that size ship with one mast placed precisely in the middle of the boat, the same as this dagger has. The engraving is so fine I can count the number of oars on the side of the boat and the single large sail is also typical of the size and shape used on a Greek penteconter. I am confident I know what I have but I would like to know when this dagger might have been crafted. At times the word penteconter also referred to a military commander of fifty men in ancient Greece.

The four of us explored Athens for five happy days and Warren reminded me he had previously arranged to meet two Sydney friends of his, Geoff and Ian, in Barcelona. So we suggested to Shona and Michelle they might like to stay with us until then. The girls felt that as they had accepted the new hospital contracts they should honour them and so we parted. We offered them a refund on their investment in the Kombi but they said they had been happy with the arrangement and to let it be. Make it a deposit on the future.

We drove them out to the airport, farewelled them and had an early night. I now had plans for the morrow and wanted an early start for the road ahead.

You will soon see where we were going but before that I will relate how we arrived there. There are two roads to travel to what I will call O. The best road and quickest way is to drive west from Athens to Patras and then turn south to O. As we intended to leave Greece from Patras we did not want to be back-tracking and so we took the slower south-west route to Corinth, Tripoli and Magalopolis before turning north to Zacharo and then arriving at O.

Before reaching O we stopped in Zacharo which is on the Peleponnese, by the Ionian Sea and has a beach, Mediterranean climate, hot springs, a lake and nearby mountains. St Spyridon is the Patron saint of the town and the central church bears his name for the 8,000 residents. He is the Patron saint of Piraeus and also the island of Corfu as he created the miracle of removing the plague from Corfu. He later died and was buried in Cyprus but when the Muslims occupied that island his body was removed to Constantinople. There his remains were found to contain a sprig of basil, which besides being popular around the world is regarded by the Hindus of India as the royal plant and the queen of herbs. That internal basil was seen as divine confirmation of the sanctity of St Spyridon.

When the Muslims took Constantinople in 1453 St Spyridon's remains were moved once again, this time to Rome. When the relic of his right arm was later found it was given to Pope Clement Vlll, who *handed* it on. Basil had a lot to do with that and my dear basil-growing wife, Janice, otherwise known as Mrs. Google, tells me that after Herod Antipas had John the Baptist beheaded, his head was preserved in a pot of basil. Perhaps.

From Zacharo we had no more than twenty km to cover to see our destination, Olympia. We had arrived at the site of the first Olympic Games in 776 BC. There are buildings but the area is not so much a town with its 3,000 citizens but what it always was, the home of the sporting events of the Ancient Olympic Games and the Temple of Zeus, which is dedicated to the father of the gods. Inside the temple doorway there was once a statue, crafted of ivory and gold of Zeus, to whom the games themselves were dedicated as originally they were a religious festival. The low-lying temple remains are close to the original stadium. You can see several marble lions' heads which were used as waterspouts at the Temple of Zeus. Alongside the temple is the Heraeum, the temple of Hera, wife of Zeus. Her temple was of the Doric order and within that were stored the garlands of flowers to be awarded to the Games winners. Another building of note is the Philippeum, a circular building of the Ionic order which consisted of using slender columns, with scroll-like swirls at their top and bottom. It is said that the Philippeum was dedicated to Phillip 11 of Macedon, by himself. As we have seen he was the father of Alexander the Great. The Ionic order of architecture was popular in the Archaic Period which extended from 776 BC to 480 BC. Archaic in this context meaning old, not decrepit.

To the east of these temples were the stadium for the athletes and the hippodrome for horse and chariot racing. The western side of the temple saw the wrestling and gymnastics. The Olympic Games continued for 1,169 years, until the Emperor Theodosius 1 cancelled them in 393 AD. Worse destruction came in 420 A D when Theodosius 11 destroyed the site. He did this in order to wipe out paganism while promoting Christianity. In 551 A D the area was hit by an earthquake and later repeated tsunamis flooded the site with metres of deep silt and sand that included marine matter.

We made our way to the running track where the main foot races were conducted. It still exists from that ancient era due to its being covered over and left undisturbed for centuries before being eventually uncovered, restored and maintained.

Only a handful of people were about at the time but unlike the ancient competitors I did not make an animal sacrifice or run naked. The original clay and sand covered running track measured 192 metres but the stone slabs with parallel grooves for the runners' feet were not introduced until about 350 BC. They are still there today. I glanced around and no one looked twice

The running track of the original Olympic Games in 776 BC. Bill ran the full 192 metres

Chapter Six Opposite the Blind

as I readied myself on the starting line. In my mind's eye I saw a white-robed youthful priestess drop the white flag and I was off. I ran as though Hades, the brother of Zeus and Poseidon, and who ruled the land of the dead, was after me. I gave it my all and ran to the old finishing line to ensure I ran the one hundred metres at the Olympic Games.

I suppose there are always people who will do anything to gain an advantage. There were cheats then as there are now. At the original Olympic Games if an athlete was discovered in serious cheating he, women were not allowed to compete, was fined, named and shamed. It is known that certain boxers and wrestlers bribed their opponents to lose. A zane, which is a bronze statue of Zeus, paid for by the monetary fines, was erected at Olympia for one and all to see. Sometimes the cheaters were also subjected to physical punishment or excluded from the Games. At the base of each zane or statue was a pedestal on which the cheater's name and home city was clearly written so that all would know his shame. The sixteen zanes of Zeus have long gone but there are at least seven pedestals still standing in a line. The word zane is the plural of Zeus.

From Olympia we drove on to Patras and camped nearby as the city was too big for us. The following morning we boarded the ferry from Patras to the southern Italian port of Reggio di Calabria. I believe the di has been dropped from the city's name since we were there and sometimes the Calabria is not used. Long ago and for centuries Reggio was a Greek colony. The city seemed a mixed bag of life with a reputation for blatant corruption, periodic earthquakes and population overcrowding offset by an attractive waterfront, a favoured pedestrian street known as the Corso, similar to the Corso in magnificent Manly as well as Australian Moreton Bay fig trees and above all, the rather incredible Riace Bronzes.

According to a study of 386 European cities Reggio has the least amount of green space per person. Another assessment says Reggio has three to four square metres of green space per person while cities such as Liege in Belgium and Valenciennes in France provide more than 300 square metres of green space per person.

Just months before Warren and I arrived in Reggio there were exciting headlines reporting that a local man had been snorkelling 200 metres from the coast at nearby Riace.

At a modest depth of seven metres the snorkeller saw what he first thought was a man's arm protruding from the sand below. It turned out to be one of two extraordinary bronze statues of naked, bearded warriors, in excellent condition despite being created about 460-450 BC. The statues are remarkable as they are incredibly impressive and are known for their anatomical details, powerful musculature and nudity which symbolizes their divine or heroic status. One man is 1.98 metres tall and the other 1.99 metres. The statues were crafted by using the lost-wax casting method which I know a little of but I would take too long to describe it adequately.

When people talk about their old or ancient cultures they should be aware that this art was being practiced in Bulgaria in 4,450 BC, Pakistan 4,000 BC, what is now southern Israel 3,500 BC and Iraq in the third millennium BC to name but a few.

We drove north to Naples and while staying there took a ferry to the Isle of Capri, as you do. There is no doubt it is lovely and well worth the little effort to arrive there. Apart from the beauty bestowed by nature the Roman Emperor Augustus assisted the island's development by creating his own private seclusion entwined in man-made attractions. Augustus directed aqueducts for the gardens, temples and numerous villas be erected for his pleasure.

There is interesting history here which I would like to mention. Julius Caesar was not an emperor of Rome as it was still a republic and not yet an empire. His title was *dictator perpetuus* or *dictator forever*. Shades of Putin. Caesar's great-nephew, Augustus, was the first Roman emperor, his full name being Gaius Julius Caesar Augustus aka Octavian. After the death of Julius Caesar, he was granted the title by Augustus.

Tiberius also was in love with the Isle of Capri and built no less than twelve villas there to varying degrees of opulence although only three remain today. The most extravagant by far is the *Villa Jovis* or *Villa of Jupiter* but it is difficult to access on its headland positioning.

Maria Carey owns a villa on the island but I am more interested in the Russian writer Maxim Gorky who owned a house, the villa Behring, near the gardens of Augustus, and his writings regarding the hardships of everyday people. Vladamir Lenin came to visit Maxim Gorky.

Like others Warren and I took a rowing-boat into the island's Blue Grotto, which is a sea cave. The entrance is only a metre high and the boatman had us lie down. There are times when the swell is too high or the numbers of other tourists with the same intent also too high and you might have to wait for an hour to enter but we were in luck and incurred no delay. The cave measures sixty metres by twenty five metres and the bright blue effect of the water is caused by there being an underwater opening precisely under the mouth of the cave.

When bright sunlight takes advantage of that the water appears to light up. During the reign of the lecherous Emperor Tiberius the Blue Grotto was used as a marine temple.

After looking around Naples we drove north for twenty-five km to the ancient city of Capua. The city had long supported ancient Rome with thousands of infantry and cavalry but after a political dispute it sided with Hannibal and the Carthaginians. Hannibal is one of my heroes, so to speak so I will mention this. He and his men, and elephants, who had crossed the Alps, stayed in Capua with that city's blessing for a winter before resuming the war with Rome.

Capua is also known for another Roman war incident. In those times slaves were numerous, they were everywhere and the Romans were austere masters in war and peace. Eventually there was a revolution and it was led by a slave from Capua, by the name of Spartacus. The slaves were initially successful as Spartacus led by example and he was a true leader in addition to being a fighter. Eventually two Roman armies brought the slaves undone and 6,000 of them were who were taken alive were then crucified along the road from Capua to Rome, the Appian Way.

We followed that road from Capua to Rome as much as was possible, for about 200 km. I gather that today some sections of that road are reserved for local residents only but fifty years ago that was not an issue. As we drove the road of history it was not hard to imagine cross after cross on both sides of the road bearing the dead and dying slaves. Some say Spartacus was one of them but my limited knowledge says his body was never found.

We settled into a camping ground in Rome and used it as a base to explore the Eternal City as many poets have nominated it. We

Chapter Six Opposite the Blind

did not see everything Rome has to offer but we had the pleasure of visiting the Spanish Steps, the remains of Circus Maximus, the Colosseum, the Vatican and its museum, the Sistine Chapel, Baths of Caracalla, the Trevi Fountain and the Forum. I would later return to experience more.

One morning in the camp Warren was halfway along a line of men waiting to have a shower. The current occupant finished his shower, came out and looked along the waiting line. He recognized someone and called out to him, *Warren, Warren*. The caller was Geoff from Sydney, one of the two blokes we were to meet in Barcelona. Shortly afterwards the four of us were together and I met Geoff and Ian for the first time. They were going off to visit Hadrian's Villa and Villa d'Este at Tivoli so we went together in their better Kombi.

When I came to write this segment I could not recall the name of the place we went to no matter how hard I tried. So I changed tactics. I told my so-called brain to remind me of the place name and no more. Then I deliberately forgot about it. The next day, twenty-seven hours later and after more than fifty years ago the name, Tivoli, came into my old head. Bingo, it worked. I planted the seed and let it be.

Tivoli is twenty-nine km east of Rome and many say it is Ancient Rome's greatest theme-park. It is renowned for the breathtaking undulating landscapes and elegant villas, such as Villa Gregoriana which was established by Pope Greory XVI in the 1830s and Villa d'Este which was created for Cardinal Ippolito d'Este in the 16th century.

The Villa d'Este has to be seen. You have not lived until you have seen for yourself the villas and other structures about which I am lost for words and yet they are matched if not exceeded in their wonder by the gardens and their accompanying fountains and waterfalls. They include fifty sculpted fountains, at least 450 spouts and jets and sixty-four cascading waterfalls all watered by a kilometre of canals flowing across the terraces in a brilliant display of engineering. The Hundred Fountains incorporates a walkway where strange and hideous masks, various animals, plants and eagles spout water in absolute co-ordination. I have visited and explored the best gardens in Canada and America and they are equal in beauty and design but here are added extraordinary buildings. Beneath Hadrian's perfection for maintaining the smooth operations above ground for his elite visitors, let alone himself, was an underground system of tunnels that connected all the buildings to ensure that the thousands of working slaves who were necessary were not seen.

Included in Tivoli is Hadrian's Villa and all that accompanies it and I shall say something of that for the Emperor Hadrian was different to most of his peers. Hadrian appears not to have been interested in expanding Rome's empire. He was content to consolidate and hold it as the world knows by his building Hadrian's wall as the northern extent of Roman rule in Britain and as Warren and I saw at the Iron Gates on the border of Serbia and Romania.

Hadrian is said to have travelled to every corner of the Roman empire and with his penchant for architecture and engineering he doubtless drew on the works of many master craftsmen in building his villa and surrounding gardens. He attained a wide collection of antiquities and art from Greece and Egypt in particular. He was inspired by a water feature at Alexandia and so constructed a canal, one hundred metres in length and edged with statues and curved colonnades of overwhelming brilliance.

Chapter Six *Opposite the Blind*

Many thousands of people were required to build and maintain the works of Hadrian's innovative mind which included Latin and Greek libraries, bathhouses, numerous pavilions, temples, underfloor heating, banquet halls, private suites and alfresco dining halls. Hadrian's villa is regarded as the epitome in architecture of the elegance and opulence of the Roman Empire and significant proof of that can be seen today. His villa is designated a UNESCO World heritage site

Having a fear of assassination Hadrian was at all times protected by the Praetorian Guard which was the personal bodyguard for emperors. Their quarters can still be seen today. Those select soldiers were paid three times that of other ranks, had superior swords and oval shields and grew in numbers, prestige and power.

The next day I told the boys that when we were in Bocca di Magra, my brother-in-law, Mario had told me a friend of his, Harry, lives in Rome and might possibly be able to give us advice or even work as Harry writes scripts for films. I had Harry's address and the boys agreed we might as well talk with him.

We found Harry's apartment in the centre of Rome and were made welcome. We had a good meeting but it so happened that at the time Harry was writing a script but not working on a film so unfortunately he could not offer or help us into the Italian film industry. However if we are interested he has a Welsh friend who owns a vineyard in Chianti and he has been looking for willing workers, if we wanted to go and speak to the man. Phones in those days were not as readily available as they are today and being positive about the outcome we decided to drive.

CHAPTER SEVEN

Men of Iron

Twenty years from now you will be more disappointed by the things that you didn't do than by the ones you did do. So throw off the bowlines. Sail away from the safe harbour. Catch the trade winds in your sails. Explore, Dream. Discover.

Mark Twain.

Our destination was *Venosa* vineyard at the nearby medieval hilltop town of Radda-in-Chianti, 255 km north of Rome. Not only is Radda-in-Chianti in Tuscany situated between two of Italy's most famous attractions of Florence and Siena but it is in the heart of the Chianti wine industry. Wine has been grown there since the 13th century and in the Middle Ages three villages including Radda-in Chianti formed the League of Chianti. Today that area is itself within the official Chianti Classico Denominazione di Origine Controllata e Garantita.

Arriving at *Venosa* we met the owners Annaliese and Dafydd. Annaliese's mother was German and her father Italian while Harry's friend Dafydd was Welsh through and through. Fortunately we could understand his English but when he spoke Welsh we were stranded.

Dafyyd, or David in English, had lived on the Isle of Anglesey which is an island connected to the Wales mainland by a bridge. In that environment he had several jobs before settling into later life as an author. Annaliese had inherited the vineyard from her parents.

They had been attempting to improve the production of their vineyard and a contractor had recently used heavy machinery to carve out a deep and long trench which angled down and across a field that Dafyyd wished to convert to more grapevine country. The intention of the trench was to fill it with large rocks and then overlay it with earth so that when heavy rains came the trench would carry the excess water away and the grape vines would not be adversely affected. There were ample rocks in that field so the two jobs could complement each other as in clearing the land for the vines to be planted and ensuring the water run-off. The problem was that Dafyyd did not have machinery to carry rocks to the trench and workers to throw in as many rocks as might be required. Perhaps being an author he was not conditioned to such physical activity but he must have been confident because the trench was there, although empty.

Having explained his intentions he asked if we would be interested in doing the required work for him? He said we would have two large bedrooms, with two beds per room, in the lovely old two story house built entirely of stone, three full meals a day, certain times off and we could drink all the Chianti we wanted as he had two partial vintages on hand. The clincher was that we would each be paid 10,000 Italian lira a week, in cash.

It did not take us long to realise that in those days 10,000 Italian lira converted to A $14 a week or A $2 a day. Now to you today that will sound ridiculous but up until then close to 200,000 copies of

Frommers book, *Europe on $5 a day*, had been selling each year. By our time the cost was probably up to $8 a day. The fact is that the $2 a day didn't matter in the slightest. Those long, fun-filled months were amongst the happiest of my life and I think the other boys would agree. Besides which we only left when one day Dafyyd said he was out of wine, we had drunk him out. An exaggeration perhaps but no matter how much Chianti we consumed every night we never had a hangover from that subtle and smooth as silk red wine.

Talking of earning $2 a day I might point out that at the same time, in the early 70s, you could rent a two bedroom, all electric cottage with all conveniences and close to transport at no less than Bondi over the Christmas holidays for $40 a week. Otherwise you might like to spend Christmas at a holiday cottage at Brunswick Heads, eleven km north of Byron Bay, with accommodation for two people for the princely sum of $16 per week. That makes our weekly $14 salary, plus wonderful accommodation, look good by comparison.

The four of us began work the next morning by cleaning out the pigpens. After cleaning ourselves we set off to the trench and for most of the day, every day, we picked up not just rocks but the biggest rocks we could and dropped them into the trench. The first days were hard, I won't deny that but it was pleasing that each of us settled into the routine and as our fitness improved so did our work. Dafyyd was pleased and I don't know if Annaliese took it upon herself to provide a magnificent lunch every day or if Dafyyd asked her to do so but I can say that Annaliese spoiled us.

They were an odd couple in some ways. Both of them were obviously intelligent, as befits an author and writer similar to Dafyyd's friend Harry in Rome but perhaps Dafyyd also belonged in the big city. He was tall and lean, easy to talk to and to be credited for having a go at the rural life but with all due respect he did seem uncomfortable about it at times. He was about forty years of age and I sensed he probably thought he had to have a crack at working with nature now rather than later in life and if that is accurate then good on him.

Annaliese was perhaps two years younger and also good to talk to, with us. It was none of our business but she and Dafyyd did not seem to talk to each other, except in passing so to speak. Like Dafyyd she was a willing worker but more relaxed about matters. You would have to say she was quite attractive even though she was always in farm work clothes. I think the only time she dressed up was when we went to the circus. With her intellect, dark shoulder length hair casually falling about her shoulders, lovely complexion and good nature it was felt she could be doing better for herself in many facets of life. She and Dafyyd probably found us to be different in many ways and if we had not performed the work to their satisfaction they would not have tolerated our differences and we would have been back on the road quick smart. You meet many people in your travels but you don't always stay or live with strangers under their roof where they abide by your little peccadillos.

It was uncanny how good the weather was for it never seemed to rain during the day, only at night. Each day we would come in from the field for lunch and find a substantial timber table set up in the shade of long-established grape vines, laden with freshly baked bread, tumblers of cool water, bowls of pasta, a variety of salads and carafes of mild red wine.

Then we would happily and although well fed, not sluggishly, return to our duties. There were days when men armed with shotguns would walk by us or pass in the distance. We had to ask why this was so and learned that in some countries and especially Italy, the hunting and shooting of quail is a long-time and popular part of life. There is a three-month season in the year when some 600,000 Italians go walkabout with their guns and each can kill forty quail, let alone other species of birds. The hunters have free access to public lands but I could never work out if private land is off-limits as they seemingly help themselves.

The hunter must hold the *porto d'arama* which is the right to own a gun in addition to holding a hunting licence and the latter is valid for six years. This type of hunting is concentrated in Tuscany, Umbria and Sardinia. It is the rich protein in the quail that makes them desirable and those people who cannot bear to kill the little creatures often keep them as pets. They are tiny as the male quail weigh little more than 100-140 grams and the heavier female up to 160 grams.

Shotguns are used as the quail are ground feeders and only fly short distances but they are quick on the move. The lightest shotgun is the 28-gauge variety, the most popular seemed to be the 20 gauge and the 12 gauge was used for heavier shot or pellets. The meat is dark with the taste of mostly chicken and a touch of duck. Their popularity has seen the price of the little bird recently reach $6 each. In Australia quail are now the most popular of the game bird industry with 6.5 million farmed and slaughtered for an annual return of A $35 million. China of course is the biggest producer and consumer of quail.

I later went on a circular road-trip around Oklahoma, Kansas,

Chapter Seven   *Men of Iron*

New Mexico and West Texas with my wife and John, a friend from Oklahoma. We three had sailed together as voyage-crew on the three-masted, square-rigged barquentine 'Europa' around Cape Horn from east to west, to celebrate the 400th anniversary of the first rounding of the Horn. Apparently we were the first three-masted, square rigger to make it around the Horn from east to west since 1939. John was so thrilled by the venture that he suggested we do something else together. Along the way we crossed from New Mexico into the West Texas city of Lubbock where there are two museums of note. One is devoted to the hometown rock 'n roll singer Buddy Holly which is well presented while the other is the outstanding American Windmill Museum. Set on eleven hectares of hill there are 161 fascinating windmills of many types. A good number of them are inside a massive building where the base of some are set deep in the concrete floor that enables the exceptional guides to explain up close and in intriguing detail the workings and the differences of these historical behemoths. America developed along many lines but it was the windmills that supplied water to the trains and then to the homes and towns that followed that helped dreams come true.

I mention this because a little north of Lubbock is the land that was home to Boone Pickens. This self-made man established what might be the most imposing property in the world. You might like to google it lest you do not believe me as there is so much to what he has created. The relevant point here is that when he put the 64,809 acres of Mesa Vista Ranch up for sale at US $220,000,000 he was adamant it contained the world's best quail hunting.

There is another animal praised but not raised in Italy and that is the Italian wolf believe it or not. The wolf is considered the national animal of Italy on account of Rome being founded by the legendary brothers Romulus and Remus who were raised by a she-wolf.

One night we all went in to Radda-in-Chianti to see a performance by a visiting circus. After all these years I cannot recall individual acts but I can say with absolute certainty that it was the best time any of us ever had at a circus. Many animals and a variety of performers did their thing and while the animals were faultless it was the men and women of the circus who exemplified their profession at the highest level of competence performed to a backdrop of sublime comedy. Similar to the others I laughed and I laughed, not at the circus folk but sincerely with them. They were wonderful with their multi-skilled acts and defied logic that they were not touring Milan, Venice and Rome. You have to realise that Radda-in-Chianti back then had a population of 710 so the supposed top circus performers in Italy let alone Europe were unlikely to come calling. So all the more accolades went to the minority league which performed with such rare panache. Today Radda has only 1,500 residents but there has been a local explosion in the numbers of up-market villas for visitors. All the while Radda has retained its magical fairy-tale appearance of a genuine medieval town.

A few days later the four of us were doing our convict act of moving rocks to advantage when the morning air was shattered by the most tremendous roar, as though a large plane was flying low over our heads but as the plane moved on the sound stayed with us. It was deafening and then mysterious for the noise only ceased gradually and we could not see anything out of the ordinary.

The field containing the trench sloped down for quite some

distance, for three hundred metres or more, until it reached a creek, the boundary of *Venosa*. The land then rose up in similar fashion on the far side of the water for some two and hundred and fifty metres where it was interrupted by the presence of a small village. As Dafyyd and Annaliese would soon tell us an earthquake had struck on the far side of the creek and it was strong enough to bring down several of the ancient stone houses in that village. We did not hear the quake but we heard those two-story stone houses come crashing down, with that frightening roar. I won't be sorry if I never hear that sound again for it carried itself into our very beings. I did not find out the extent of suffering to the people but I know their homes were gone.

Dafyyd later took us on a tour of the wider area of Tuscany and what a treat that was. We visited several larger and long-established Chianti vineyards. The entire countryside was picture perfect from the point of view of soft light and gentle colours of the landscape, the quality and reverence of the buildings which were evidence of the work of master craftsmen and the geometrical precision of the vines themselves in God's garden. To see the result of centuries of endless devotion to those vineyards was humbling.

The nights had become cooler and we were taking it in turn to go out and collect firewood. No doubt that activity had been going on for centuries but there was still timber about.

The next time I went out I was looking for better firewood so I took the wheelbarrow and the chainsaw further than I had gone on previous expeditions. As there were no fences I kept going until I saw timber that looked similar to grey and yellow box trees back home that make for good firewood. I stopped there and cut enough to fill the wheelbarrow so I had exercise going home. I carried the wood in relays up the exterior stone stairs and unloaded it by the open fireplace as Dafyyd came along. He looked at the wood and asked where did I collect that? I described the area and he responded by saying, *I would rather you don't go back there for more firewood*. I replied it is good wood and could he tell me why he said that? He told me, *That land and the timber on it, belongs to the Pope*.

Situated between Siena and Florence has meant that Radda-in-Chianti often had to choose sides between those two cities when they were at loggerheads with each other. After numerous battles between the two over the centuries Radda-in -Chianti eventually became part of the province of Siena which is much smaller than Florence.

Siena is a UNESCO World Heritage site and as with Radda but larger, its historic centre is the embodiment of a medieval city with an emphasis on the Gothic style. Both are a delight to see and walk amongst. They take one back to the years 1,300 to 1,550, unique and lovely. This beautification came about in no small measure as Siena was so often in competition with Florence and Pisa and Siena's Gothic appearance was implanted over the 12th to 15th centuries. It is said that the entire city of Siena was produced as a work of art that is absorbed by the surrounding countryside. Worth travelling much further than we did.

The most important event in Siena is the annual Palio when two horse races take place on 2nd July and the 16th August. When each resident is born he or she becomes a member of one of the seventeen *contrade* or groups such as the Porcupine, Unicorn, Owl, She-wolf and others, along with their contrade's colours, emblems and flags.

Chapter Seven   *Men of Iron*

The horses race for three laps around the Piazza del Campo which is Siena's main square and covered for the racing with tuff clay, which is a prepared surface designed to assist a galloping horse by producing a surface that lessens the jarring of its hooves and feet. On the other side of the coin each jockey receives a whip made from ox sinew. A lot of horse racing occurs over four days and the venue is packed with supporters and tourists. We were not so fortunate as to be there for the race days but we did walk the circuit and revelled in the architectural wonder of one of the world's most intriguing and eye-catching cities.

After labouring at the trench where by now we had made good progress and were nearing completion we went into Radda on a Sunday and sat outside a café in the main square. It was a pleasant experience to be seated in surroundings that had barely changed for generations and yet had not deteriorated. You could almost feel history oozing out of the cobblestones while we bathed in the morning sunshine. A few of the men of Radda sat at tables around us and after greeting us in general terms then said of us, *The Men of Iron*.

They were referring to the work we had undertaken on *Venosa* which they said in various ways, had impressed them. Not many of them had seen the result of our labours but from what they said the word had circulated far and wide. We were humbled.

Not long after that the trench was finished and we told Dafyyd and Annaliese we would be leaving in two days, if that was alright with them. We phrased it like that because they had been good to us and if ever we enjoyed work it was on *Venosa*, which I think means Venus.

The next morning I was up early, about dawn and made my way to the kitchen. I remember I wasn't my usual hungry self but something different stirred me to go that way. I had hardly been there for a minute and was idly standing when Annaliese entered the room. She silently walked to me and took my hands in hers. You might say she looked into my eyes and I know she then put her arms around me and drew me to her. Crikey, I hadn't expected this for breakfast. Annaliese kissed me and again and I could not insult the lady by declining her approach. In a low voice she said that after we leave *Venosa* I must meet her in Rome where her girlfriend has an apartment. We would stay there.

At thirty-eight she was eleven years older than myself and the way she looked that was not a problem at all. In fact her actions were now making her even more desirable but she put me on the spot. I could hardly expect Warren, let alone my new found friends, Geoff and Ian, to hang around while I enjoyed myself. Not only that but we were about to set off for more of Italy, a dash of France, a look at

Bill, Geoff, Warren and Ian plus Kombi in Rome camp site

Chapter Seven   *Men of Iron*

Andorra, a fair bit of Spain and a hell of a lot of Morocco and that was before we even turned around for Portugal and whatever else came our way. Our discussion ended abruptly when Geoff appeared looking for an early breakfast.

I did give the matter serious consideration. I imagined Dafyyd would not be pleased and that was only if he were to find out which might not eventuate anyway but then again he had shown no sign of being close to Annaliese as one might expect and I did not believe any of my three companions would have hesitated if they were in my position. I decided to go to Rome, swim with Annaliese and see where the current of life takes me.

As the day wore on I had second thoughts. As enthralling as it might be initially the Roman adventure could be short-lived and I would miss the boat to Morocco along with my three amigos, whom I could reasonably expect to be in my life as the years rolled by. I found time to be with Annaliese and told her how I felt, in full, as did she. It was touching but no.

We farewelled *Venosa*, Annaliese and Dafyyd and travelled via Florence to Bocca di Magra. Warren and I left our Kombi with Wendy and Mario, transferred our gear to Ian and Geoff's Kombi and set off on our way to Morocco, resuming our camping mode of travel. We went via Marseille as the ancient city has a reputation that links the past to the present. Believed to have been founded in 600 BC the city nowadays has the largest Jewish population in Europe after London. It is still famous for its large and vigorous port, trade, industry and transport but overall has swung from manufacturing to hi-tech, large services sectors and to having ninety per cent of its business stemming from small and medium enterprises with less than five hundred employees each. Although there is high youth unemployment some 7,200 companies have been created in Marseille since 2000, suggesting it is now the most dynamic city in France. It was in Marseille we bought cassette tapes of Cat Stephens and others of the day to play as we went along. Cat Stephens' style of music was out on its own at that time.

From Marseille we took the road to Nimes which is a remarkable city in southern France. It is widely known as the best Roman city outside Italy for its well-preserved Roman buildings. Highly regarded is the Roman amphitheatre known as the Arena of Nimes.

This Arena was built about or just after the Colosseum in Rome, around 80 AD, and could hold 24,000 spectators on its thirty-four terraces and is still in good condition. In fact it is probably fair to say it is in excellent condition. The Arena holds Spanish-style bull-fighting and concerts, on separate days. Nimes also is the home of *Maison carree*, the square house. That is one of the best-preserved Roman temples and of impressive design. So much so that Thomas Jefferson, third president of the United States of America, had a stucco model of the temple made while he was the Minister to France in 1785. From that came the Virginia State Capitol, completed in 1788, as the First Fleet arrived in Australia. It houses the oldest elected legislative body in North America, the Virginia General Assembly.

There are many other items of interest in Nimes but of particular interest to myself are the Roman baths courtesy of the Emperor, Constantine the Great, whom we mentioned when we were in Constantinople, for his many great achievements. To defeat inflation Constantine introduced a new gold coin, known as the solidus. This coin became the standard for Byzantine and European currencies for more than one thousand years. I sometimes think it may have been a pity that our world order dropped the gold standard but I gather the economic world outgrew the supply of gold. Then inflation took off. If the gold standard had been maintained it would have been beneficial for Australia today as the country is the world's third largest producer of gold and the price has reached A $6,000 an ounce.

There is a more modern item about Serge de Nimes to give it the full name. Denim, the fabric of the blue jeans you might be wearing derives its name from Serge de Nimes as it imported the blue dye for the worsted fabric. Just to add to the mix, in case you don't know, the word worsted stems from the town of Worstead in Norfolk, England, where that high quality wool yarn was spun.

It was a pleasant fifty-five km drive to Montpellier, which is ten km inland from the coast. For the past twenty-five years Montpellier has been the fastest-growing city in France with a population now in excess of 300,000 people. The city's nickname is *gifted* so I presume it is favoured on many fronts. The University of Montpellier was established in 1220 with a strong emphasis of teaching and learning being on medicine. One student was the French astrologer, apothecary, physician and reputed seer, Nostradamus, 1503-1566. His forecasts for 2025 are not enticing so I won't drop them on you and spoil the day. Nostradamus was expelled from Montpellier University because he had already worked as an apothecary or chemist, and the trades were frowned upon by universities in those times. He became famous for creating a *rose pill* allegedly for giving protection against the plague. In Montpellier today all public transport is free for residents.

In France it seems that towns and cities are well spaced out, allowing room for each to develop and grow. So it was that after another 90 km we arrived in Beziers. Unfortunately the long-established city is known for the Massacre of Beziers in 1209. The Crusaders were in the area and the Catholic faith was perturbed by the presence of the people known as Cathars, whom the Catholic Church deemed to be heretics and also living in Beziers. The Catholics requested the Crusaders to take out the Cathars for them. After they had taken the city the Crusaders asked how would they identify Cathars from Catholics? The Abbot then supposedly replied, *Kill them all, for the Lord knoweth them that are His*. I only repeat this dastardly remark because it has been quoted so many times in history since. It is claimed that if not everyone was killed, then only a handful of the almost 20,000 survived.

Away from that Beziers is better known for its annual Feria de Beziers. This is a five-day bull-fighting event attended by a million visitors. That magic number.

Moving on we came to Perpignan which being in the south of France is a strong Rugby Union area but there is an intruder in the town, an Australian Rules football club known as the Perpignan Tigers.

Now we headed into the eastern Pyrenees mountain range until we entered Andorra, a landlocked country of 467 sq km, with France on its northern border and Spain the southern border. For the 80,000 residents Catalan is the official language but French and Spanish are regularly spoken. Two matters draw up to nine million tourists and/or investors each year. The first is tourism with an emphasis on ski-ing and other snow activities. The second is financial advantage.

For decades there were duty-free goods and overall taxation was minimal but eventually it was acknowledged that taxes would have to be applied. Nowadays finance and international banking are coming to the fore in Andorra.

Andorra was not engaged in World War One but three volunteers fought against Germany. There is zero-tolerance regarding the possession and use of illegal drugs accompanied by various forms of punishment. I am not alone.

Dual-citizenships are not permitted in Andorra and what I find interesting and rather like is that non-citizens are not allowed to own more than thirty-three per cent of a company and until they have lived in Andorra for twenty years they cannot own one hundred per cent.

All very thoughtful but we were there to see the snowfields and the capital, Andorra la Vella. We were not set up for ski-ing on this trip but the 300 km of ski runs have enough variety for one and all. We could hardly roll out our sleeping bags in the plentiful snow so we found rooms in the centre of town and after dining out walked the streets of the good city taking in the well-lit night sights. The following morning saw us continue our exploration and we found the adjacent ski slopes covered with a deep layer of welcoming snow. Andorra seemed well priced against the regular and more favoured European runs. It would be a good place to return to without having to be a gun skier or have deep pockets.

The road to Barcelona is naturally down-hill and an easy 200 km drive but some people take two, and I know of even three, days to take in the sights along the way. I will mention a few, starting with what is regarded as one of the top ten castles in Europe, that being the castle at Cardona and the nearby Salt Mountain. One of the many religious sites is the Cave of St. Ignatius at the ancient, as in pre-Jesus days, town of Manresa. The stand-out Montserrat Abbey is home to the famed Black Madonna.

We found a camping ground in Barcelona but then unlike today there was ample space. Barcelona is a great place to visit even though the average person stays only three nights, according to the trade figures. I couldn't place it in my top ten cities but it is has an air of excitement about it and places to see and explore. Like everyone we walked the Las Rambles boulevard that runs through the city centre with its restricted vehicular access. There are live performances, human art, bars, flamenco shows, all manner of things to see and do. The statue of Christopher Columbus is placed where he landed on his return from the New World, the Americas. I had to go to the Segrada Familia, who wouldn't, to see that astonishing building. It is the largest unfinished Catholic church on the planet and I suppose the largest of any religion. I know of mosques that might cover more ground but that is only so more people can be catered for in the otherwise empty interior. The Segrada is a unique building and once again I must ask you to do a little research and discover it for yourself. That process will draw you in and you will feel you know it better than my humble knowledge. Better still, if you have not been there, you might consider doing so.

Briefly, the work was begun in March, 1882 and the man whose dedication has brought the building to somewhere nearing completion, Antoni Gaudi, took over as Architect Director and assumed that post in 1884. For a long time the costs were paid for by public donation. I don't recall having to pay an entry fee, like everyone else we were free to walk around at our pleasure. Today there is a entry fee of thirty-three euros for adults, eighteen euros for children over ten and free if under ten but if you also wish to access the towers the cost is twenty-nine to forty-nine euros for adults and twenty to twenty-nine euros for children. Except for the interruption caused by the Spanish Civil War the building has been ongoing ever since. Antoni Gaudi died in 1926 when twenty per cent of the work was completed. To those who suggested the construction was slow, Gaudi replied, *My client is not in a hurry*.

We walked through what I thought then, more than fifty years ago, was a massive, massive building. Nearly all the construction material is stone but it is interesting to know that modern technology has been introduced such as computer-aided design and computerized numerical controls which have seen faster progress.

Talking of progress I have to wonder about that at times. In the early 1970s Barcelona had about two million visitors a year. According to The Local Spain information outlet for English speakers in Spain there are now an annual fifteen million serious visitors to Barcelona and another seventeen million visitors who are regarded as day trippers, such as the three and three quarter million people who arrived in Barcelona by cruise ships in 2024. That is accounted for by Barcelona having the largest port in the Mediterranean. I don't know how the rest arrive but they are there. Apparently Las Rambles now has high noise levels until 3 a.m. and a major section that has become a seedy red light district.

My point is that there are now ten times the number of tourists in Barcelona than we encountered and whilst we may have missed some of what is to be seen nowadays we did it without having frustrated locals telling us to go home or authorities placing restrictions on our intentions. Other cities are doing likewise, Amsterdam with a population of one million people was inundated by some twenty-five million visitors in 2024. UNESCO has suggested that Peru only allow 2,500 tickets per day for visitors to Machu Picchu, which in its time had 750 people living there while Paris and Rome are considering banning large coaches from the city centre, in Mallorca which some days sees 17,000 passengers come ashore from cruise ships, and Venice, visitors are now charged a tax per person per day, governments are cracking down on Airbnb listings, Iceland is imposing tourist taxes and fees while restricting rentals to control its housing shortage. Japan has banned tourists from certain streets in the popular Tokyo geisha district and has limited the number of trekkers who can climb Mt. Fuji. I don't recall tourist numbers ever being an issue. During our stay on the Trobriand Islands, to the east of Papua New Guinea and otherwise known as the Islands of Love, after an Israeli couple departed Janice and I were the only foreigners amongst the 12,000 islanders.

Next stop was Valencia but before we came to the city we parked by the side of the road. All that we could see were orange groves, full of those delicious Valencia oranges. Valencias are claimed to be the only orange with a peak summer season.

There were literally millions of them so we thought someone might not miss a few, as there were no fences or guard dogs to hinder us. We opened the sliding side door of the Kombi next to a grove of orange trees. Two of us walked to the nearby shed to slowly buy a few oranges while distracting the vendor as our third man harvested plenty of oranges and threw them to the fourth man who caught and stored the oranges in the Kombi and we had fresh oranges for the next two weeks. Naughty but ever so tasty.

William Wolfskill came from Kentucky and moved to Santa Fe, New Mexico, where he became a fur trapper. He later migrated to California which was then part of Mexico so he became a Mexican citizen. As a citizen the Mexican Government gave him a land grant. There he grew excellent wine grapes and oranges. He then created a hybridized orange and named it after Valencia in Spain on account of its sweet oranges. Today that hybrid Valencia is the most popular juice orange in the U.S.

We also came to Alicante which I particularly mention because the city was fortified about 235 BC by the legendary Hamilcar Barca, father of the great Carthaginian commander Hannibal. The Carthaginians were originally Pheonicians and that extraordinary race of sailors, traders and long-time enemy of Rome are one of my favoured peoples of all eras.

Granada in Spanish translates as pomegranate and the city of that name sits at the foot of the Sierra Nevada mountains, no doubt because that is where four rivers converge, at an elevation of 738 metres and only an hour's drive from the coast that we had been following for some time. From 711 to 1492 Muslims from Africa controlled much of Portugal and Spain and Europeans often referred to them as Moors. From 1232 until 1492 the Emirate of Granada was the last capital of the Nasrid rule, which was an Arab dynasty and the last Muslim-ruled state in Spain. In that period twenty-three sultans ruled Granada.

From Granada we drove eight km to explore the magnificent Alhambra, which was a self-contained complex of forts and palaces.

In addition to the regular Friday mosque, public baths, artisans' workshops and tannery, a good water supply and roads and houses for the public at large, the Alhambra supported six major palaces with their various attractions, one of which was the Palace of the Lions. This is a palace where the central courtyard has a circular fountain surrounded by carved lions. It was built as a victory palace and said to represent the strength of the ruler.

The Alhambra Museum has excellent artworks from the Nasrid era and I loved walking the passageways that depict Arabic writing and are open on one side, perhaps to take advantage of the nearby gardens that are placed throughout the Alhambra. I gather that in the Muslim world gardens provide the possibility for a touch of paradise on Earth.

The Hall of the Abencerrajes is a high vaulted room with a honeycombed ceiling that must have been a nightmare to create but the end result is stunning in its shape with heavenly shades of light. One of the best of rooms. The Queen's Dressing room has a coffered ceiling, which means it has recessed panels. Many of the surfaces of the countless walls are completely carved with exquisite patterns, tiles or covered with written poems or texts from the Koran. A water stairway is a four-story staircase with descending water features.

At the Hall of Beds the ruler would survey his naked wives and throw an apple to the one he wished to favour that night. The Court of Myrtles is a large pool of water with its myrtle bushes. The sultan's wives and concubines all had chambers which connected with the pool's surrounds. One Muslim ruler, Muhammad V was on terms with the Christian King of Castile, Pedro 1, the Cruel. For his evil ways Pedro was ex-communicated by Pope Urban V.

The Palace of the Comares stands as the most complete of all Alhambra's offerings. It served as the Sultan's residence and contained the throne room. Comares baths had steam rooms and marble floors. There is much to see in the Alhambra including more than 900 tiles which each say in Arabic script, *Wa-la galiba illa Allah* or, There is no conqueror but Allah. This was the personal motto of the Nasrid dynasty and a decoration not to be missed.

Another 130 km and we arrived at magical Malaga. Leastways that is how I felt about one of the prime towns on The Costa del Sol. I didn't know what to expect, in fact I hadn't heard of the place. So the fact that I fell in love with it straight away did mean something. I can't describe any one thing as bowling me over I simply felt right at home in Malaga. Of course, the beaches, warm weather and colourful surrounds helped but overall it just hit the spot.

In the past fifty years the population has slowly grown from 400,000 to 600,000 but the number of tourists in 2024 is 14,400,000, a ratio of twenty-four visitors to one local and as with most popular centres it is now dominated by apartment towers, human rabbit warrens. I would rather live with my memory than return to that lifestyle. I never envisaged the degree by which tourism would develop and I appreciate being there earlier.

Pablo Picasso was born in Malaga and lived there for the first ten years of his life. The 18th century family home, Casa Natal Picasso still exists as does a museum in his honour, not surprisingly. I don't know the finer points of Picasso's life but I believe he was the best painter of his type and probably of any era. Picasso was influenced by African art. It is said he produced 13,500 paintings and possibly many thousands more as well as 100,000 prints and engravings,

300 sculptures and 34,000 illustrations. Picasso painted 400 portraits of his second wife, Jacqueline Roque, but I can top that. I have more than 600 portraits of my wife, Janice, although I confess taken with my camera on our trips.

Another similar drive, this time of 135 km saw us pass through Fuengirola and on track to Gibraltar. I recently saw a beachfront photograph of Fuengirola from the air and that makes Malaga look alright for Fuengirola appears to now have a beachfront that is reinforced by an unbreakable linked line of shoulder-to-shoulder apartment towers, the same height and dimensions providing a bland barrier to the otherwise God-given salt air.

Back in Mudgee the publican of the Sydney Hotel, now the Waratah Hotel, was a good man by the name of Alan Hoad, who was assisted in running the main street pub by one of his sons, Larry. Alan's other son was living and working in Spain and as Alan knew I was going to Europe he said if I did make it to Spain I might drop by and say hello to his other son, Lew. A little past Fuengirola and half way between Malaga and Marbella, thirty km from each, we turned of the main road and arrived at Lew Hoad's Tennis Club.

We had not met before but Lew was there and when I explained why we had called in he welcomed us warmly, like old friends, at least of his father and brother. I have never met a man with such a powerful hand. When we shook hands, and he did not so much grip me but held my hand it was as though his was of iron. I have met shearers with powerful hands but after hitting out with a tennis racquet for decades Lew was No 1.

Lew Hoad won fifty-two career titles including the singles titles for the French Open, the Australian Open and Wimbledon twice.

He played right-handed but I also admired him as he had a superb one-handed backhand. Unlike his long-term opponent and doubles partner, Ken Rosewall, who liked to play from the baseline, Lew Hoad was always an attacking player.

Lew introduced us to current players and guests including the quite handsome American film star, Ty Hardin. In our day Ty Hardin was big-time but I wouldn't expect the younger generations to know of him. He had served in the American army, became a pilot and then played football. Trying to break into the film world he missed out on a supporting role in the film, *Rio Bravo* to that cool singer, Ricky Nelson, of *Garden Party* and other hit songs.

However John Wayne then saw him while visiting Paramount studios and recommended him to Warner Bros. They paid out Ty's Paramount contract and gave him one for seven years. When Clint Walker walked out on his *Cheyenne* contract, Jack Warner gave Ty the lead role and from that he gained his own western series, *Bronco* for four years. Ty made a number of films such as *The Chapman Report, Palm Springs Weekend, Battle of the Bulge, Beserk, Custer of the West, One Step to Hell, Death on the Run* and a lot more while he guest-starred often on TV top-rating shows such as *Maverick* and *77 Sunset Strip*.

He came to Australia and made the two-year series *Riptide* about an American running a charter boat company on the east coast of Australia. During that time he told a journalist, *I'm really a very humble man. Not a day goes by that I don't thank God for my looks, my stature and my talent.* Well Ty would be humble otherwise he would use his real name, *Orison Whipple Hungerford*. His philosophy would fit in well with some others these days but I am pleased to say Ty Hardin was inquisitive and friendly towards the four Australians.

Lew Hoad was gracious, modest and a joy to talk with. He was also generous as he kept the four of us in food and drink for a good half day as I later told Alan and Larry in Mudgee. We thought his tennis camp was brilliant, well laid out, easy on the eye and lacking for nothing. These days it is bigger with seven top class courts. Whilst it still draws the tennis players and those who want to be it is also a major wedding and hospitality venue of significant renown.

Gibraltar, now I had heard of that but probably only because of the Pheonicians going that way after they founded Malaga in 770 BC and also of events in World War Two. Late in the day we came to the town with a population of 34,000 at the foot of the Rock of Gibraltar. With an area of 6.8 sq. km and a mountain occupying most of that there isn't spare space. To reach Gibraltar proper we drove along a narrow isthmus just above the level of the water.

Gibraltar has long been important due to its unique location, situated as it is at the narrow Straits of Gibraltar where the Mediterranean Sea joins the Atlantic Ocean. In days past the Greeks named the Straits, *The Pillars of Hercules*. After a combined Anglo-Dutch force captured Gibraltar during the War of Spanish Succession Gibraltar was ceded to Great Britain in 1713, in perpetuity. The British Navy has maintained a strong and influential presence and not surprisingly there are numerous tunnels in the protective Rock. Members of the public are not allowed that far. At one point the road crosses the airport runway and when a plane is about to land or take-off the barriers go up and obviously no one can continue driving or walking.

The people living in Gibraltar have good incomes and a high and comfortable standard of living. Most of that derives from shipping, on-line gaming, the millions of tourists and favourable and flexible taxation, financial and banking systems. On an average day 300 ships pass through the Straits and that is one every five minutes or about 110,000 ships per year.

There are several hotels but The Rock is the most sought after. Opened in 1932 and set in 3.6 hectares of its own gardens opposite the Botanic Gardens, The Rock Hotel is dug into the western slope of the Rock of Gibraltar. A ten minute walk takes one to the cable car for a lift of 400 metres up the mountain. With terraced restaurants, lounge bars, the biggest swimming pool in Gibraltar and class all through The Rock has long been favoured by such notable visitors as Royalty, world leaders and celebrities including Winston Churchill, Errol Flynn, Sean Connery and my wife, Janice.

There is some background to my last comment which I would like to mention. Janice's father worked his way up in the business of salvaging ships that were in difficult circumstances around the world. In 1956 the Suez Canal was owned by the Egyptian Government but operated by a concessionary company of French and British shareholders. The Egyptian President Gamel Abdel Nasser nationalized the Canal and the French and British thought military response was required. Thus President Nasser blockaded the Canal by sinking ships in it. Janice's father, Philip B, was later called in to clear some of the ships which he did. On account of his good work at Suez the Chinese Government asked him to go to China and salvage ships for them. He did that and the Chinese Government paid his fees and all his expenses. That included putting him up in their hotels. In those years China was nowhere near as developed as it is these days. In one major hotel he was kept awake most of the nights by rats running around his room. So he was forced to turn the lights on, get out his revolver and stay up shooting rats in the hotel room. This continued for so long that he left the hotel and slept on the ships he was salvaging. Yes, why didn't the hotel staff do something about it? I thought they would still have had rat-catchers then.

I don't doubt for a moment the story that Janice's father had to shoot rats in his hotel on account of the man he was but I would like to add more rats to it. More than forty years later Janice and I were travelling around China and found ourselves in Chengdu, out in western China. We took a bus down to Chongqing and I mention that because of the number of car and truck smashes we saw on the way. The bodies seemed to have all been removed but the vehicles were left on the road precisely where the accidents happened. From the burn damage it appeared some of those wrecks had been there for weeks at least. Not one vehicle had police security or keep away tape around them and the worst one was a truck spread across the centre line of the road, so every motorist had to drive around it.

We arrived in Chongqing which I call the blast furnace city of China. It is hot climate and heavy industrial. Two things of note hit us immediately. Roads were being constructed and that is nothing new except that in Chongqing as one highway road was being built another was being constructed over that one from a different direction. A third was then overlaid above those two. As if that wasn't enough a fourth road was being built almost alongside those three and a fifth road over the fourth. I took photos for proof. Only in China.

Our bus dropped us at its depot which was about 80 metres above the river and at the top of a steep incline. Janice and I were

Chapter Seven   *Men of Iron*

about to board a boat going downriver to Wuhan, later to be covid town. For such travel there are two options for the three-day, 890 km journey. You can pay top dollar and travel in comfort on an American style boat or take a Chinese boat for one sixth the price and whilst you go first class it is rather rough. We opted for the experience of the cost-saving Chinese boat. Three other couples did like-wise, a Polish duo, a Dutch doctor and his wife and an interesting husband and wife from Vienna, Austria. All great people as it turned out so we were lucky in that regard. The other 380 passengers were Chinese and they travelled second class at best. They received three meals a day but we were advised their food would not be at all suitable for us and we should bring three day's food with us, which the eight of us did. There was to be no inter-mixing on board. First-class passengers had the sole use of the top deck of the boat to have their meals and to relax and enjoy the sight-seeing as we went down the Yangtze River.

There was a problem and I do not exaggerate. Looking down on the Yangtze on such a clear day one might have expected the river to sparkle in the sunshine but that would never happen. The colour of the famed Yangtze river was brown, rust-brown. It was a sickening sight, like sludge, from bank to bank and as far as one could see up and down the river.

People might say what on earth has been dumped into that huge waterway but the better question would be what has not been dumped into that mighty river. Australia is not perfect but Chongqing and China, you should hang your collective heads in shame.

The eight of us bought our supplies of dry foods, fresh fruit and water at local shops before we boarded the boat. The journey itself was good with several shore excursions but there was another problem. For each of the three nights we all ate our prepared meals up on the top deck and after long and informative talks into the night we retired to our individual cabins for two. Before long we were awakened by repetitive rustling sounds in the cabin.

Turning on the dim lights it didn't take long to discover the problem. The cabin was infested with rats, eating out at our expense. We had not left food out per se but on the other hand there were no refrigerators or cupboards to safely store the goods. Each night we bundled our food up as best we could but the rats kept coming, as they did in all the other cabins. I couldn't imagine this happening on the American boats but who knows. Chinese rats are many and determined. My point is that the passing of four decades since Philip B was shooting rats means he didn't get them all and the problem persists.

When Philip B finished his salvage work in mainland China he flew to Hong Kong where he was literally mobbed by journalists wanting to know what life is like in China as no one else of note had been there. This was about ten years before President Nixon made his historic trip to China in an attempt to have the Chinese government open up the country for trade.

Later he had completed other salvage work and then flown to Gibraltar where his wife and his daughter, Janice, had arrived from London to meet him. To avoid paying tax he always spent at least six months of the year outside England, which wasn't hard to arrange on account of his line of work. Janice has shown me several of his passports and some he filled in eighteen months. He listed his occupation as shipowner. One stamped but with a handwritten

Chapter Seven   *Men of Iron*

Warren, Geoff and Ian cutting each other's hair so as to enter Morocco

entry states *approval to visit a sheikhdom in the Persian Gulf* while another has the Foreign Office stamp and then above that is a handwritten note saying *also valid for Iraq and Syria*. Yet another Foreign Office stamp has the added handwritten notation, *Also valid for China*. From Iceland to Brazil, Burma to wherever he went, he was always on the go.

Their accommodation was booked at The Rock Hotel and Janice recalls that one day a car called for them and they went out for lunch. They were driven along the 135 km road trip from Gibraltar to Malaga in the opposite direction we had just come from. That car journey of Janice and her parents is what I have been leading up to. Today that 135 km comprises the major towns of The Costa del Sol but believe it or not back then there was not one hotel along the entire journey for the family to have lunch until they arrived in Malaga. Now you might say as I thought that Janice might be in error but for the fact that back in London whenever someone said to her mother they were going to The Costa del Sol, she told them there is no hotel along that road where you can stop for lunch. Perhaps there were hotels of a sort but if they served lunch it was no more than a counter lunch, not a formal lunch. Now if ever there was an example of how tourism has changed I think that is a great example.

You might remember the actor Richard Green who played the lead role of Robin Hood in the film, *Sword of Sherwood Forest* and then as Robin Hood in 143 episodes for TV. When Janice and her parents were staying at The Rock so was Richard Green. He was having an affair and it wasn't with Maid Marian.

As usual we camped out but not in The Rock's gardens or even the Botanical Gardens. It was no matter as we had to be up at 4 a.m. the next morning to board the early ferry at nearby Algeciras to take us to Morocco.

I have only just remembered this incident and for the life of me I could not pinpoint exactly where. However I have now found the photo to substantiate the moment and it was in Spain coming down from Andorra towards Barcelona. We were driving along the main road with a three-metre high embankment on the right-hand side, the sight of which brought us to a halt. People had used picks and shovels to dig out doorways and windows in the bank that lead into rooms which they had also excavated. Part of the outer wall looked like a layer of plaster had been applied to it and then white-washed to tart it up. People were living in the dug-out bank on the side of the road.

Homes built into the side of the road, Spain

CHAPTER EIGHT

Morocco on twenty cents a day

These words were not stated in Morocco but by Kenya's first President, Jomo Kenyatta.

When missionaries came to Africa, they had the Bible and we had the land. They said, Let us pray. We closed our eyes. When we opened them, we had the Bible and they had the land.

We boarded the first ferry of the day at 5 a.m., one that would take us across the Straits of Gibraltar to Ceuta, which is an autonomous city administered by Spain. It is a Spanish enclave, military post and free port on the African coastline, carved out from Morocco. Ceuta is on a narrow isthmus that connects Mt. Hacho, also held by Spain, to the mainland. Mt. Hacho is believed to be one of the two Pillars of Hercules, the other being the Rock of Gibraltar with both guarding the Straits of Gibraltar.

The Pheonicians realised the narrow isthmus made Ceuta a strong defensive outpost and they created a base there to add to their nearby settlements and silver mines at what would be Cadiz

Chapter Eight   *Morocco on twenty cents a day*

to the north and their trading centres to the south along the coast of Morocco.

It was peaceful in our time but things have changed. Twenty years ago, 2005, a groundswell of anti-immigration sentiment towards African migrants arose. In 2018 this resulted in the erection around Ceuta of two parallel six metre-high fences topped with razor wire and augmented by underground cables that connect spotlights, video cameras, movement sensors and the military to keep illegal migrants and smugglers at bay.

There have been many attempts to break through these impediments with the defenders of Ceuta being subjected to having urine, excrement, acid and other burning substances thrown at and all too often landing on them.

We passed through Spanish Customs and immigration at Ceuta and came to the Moroccan equivalent, which prevented us from being accepted and entering Morocco. Men with long hair were not allowed into the country. We were not the only transgressors. There was a veritable line-up along the road with men cutting each other's hair off and not being too fussy about their handiwork. Fortunately we had suitable scissors and Warren showed he must have done something similar in another life.

Feeling light-headed we drove into Morocco and on to Tangier. The Pheonicians and later their offshoot the Carthaginians established the town about the 9th century BC as again it is beautifully situated, for many reasons on the very north-west tip of the African continent. The climate is good, the beaches are better and today I hear the jet-set is invading the city, whereas it used to be the Romans, the Vandals, Byzantines, Arabs and Portuguese who came to conquer.

We parked the good old Kombi and walked to Tangier's medina and bazaar. The city was and I hope still is one of colour and vibrance. The medina is the historic part of town which is always my favourite with its narrow and winding streets and alley ways. The bazaar was not on the scale of Istanbul but just as absorbing. Now and again we were the only foreigners to be seen but that was never an issue as we were comfortable with the surrounds. So we had to discretely laugh when we came across six young Japanese men walking towards us, linked arm-in-arm apparently for the sake of security. I would definitely go back to Tangier.

The city is a melting pot of people perhaps unlike any other. Tangier may be equal for its position to my beloved Istanbul for it sits at the crossroads of Africa and Europe as against Istanbul's Asia and Europe. There is nothing dull about Tangier and yet the world's greatest traveller of the 14th century was a man who was born and raised there but who left to see the world for himself. His name was Muhammad Ibn Battutah and he travelled from Tangier to Timbuktu in Mali, to what is Saudi Arabia including Mecca, the Maldives, much of India, China, Afghanistan, Constantinople, Egypt, Russia, Sri Lanka, South-East Asia, Turkestan, the Steppe of Ukraine, to Persia, Syria and Iraq. In total he travelled three times as far as Marco Polo and those who should know say that our world today knows much of what occurred in the 14th century thanks to the written words of Muhammad Ibn Buttutah. I feel privileged to have a book detailing many accounts of his remarkable life. He can be excused for bias in saying, *Morocco is the best of countries, for in it fruits are plentiful and running water and nourishing food are never exhausted.*

We stayed awhile in Tangier and then left for the 280 km drive

Chapter Eight   *Morocco on twenty cents a day*

south to Rabat, the capital of Morocco. All good but we moved on to something a little more exciting, such as Casablanca. It is Morocco's biggest city by far with a lot of up-market life to it yet Fez and Marrakech are said to be more attuned to tourism and good times. Perhaps. We did not set out to test that theory but probably for the first time we did go out heavily, explored a few bars and clubs and indulged in more drinks than usual. When we finally left the last club we were quite happy but we forgot to go to the bathroom. As we started to walk that oversight kicked in but it was too late to go back to the club. A passing wall appeared or maybe we were passing the wall, it was something like that. The four of us lined up against the wall and were much relieved.

Geoff was the first to be hit, as he was the nearest to our attacker. The man then continued, going along the line as quickly as he could while we had our backs to him in order to teach all of us a lesson. His blows landed thick and furious as you might expect from an angry man even if he is on crutches. He stood and then hopped on one crutch and one leg while hitting each of us in turn with his second wooden crutch. We did not retaliate as it was his country and we were in the wrong. However we could not stay to apologise as he did not relent. Everyone by now has seen the film *Casablanca* with Humphrey Bogart and Ingrid Bergman. A great film so it was disappointing to learn that the film was made entirely in Los Angeles and not one Arab or north African character has a speaking role.

It was a 245 km drive from Casablanca to Marrakech along an inland road but most of the time we had to drive slowly if not carefully as the majority of the traffic was people riding bicycles or walking and the last thing you want to be involved in is a road accident. In the early hours and again in the evening some people were hard to see on account of colour. The morning and evening light was not bright and the roadside was usually sand colour, much the same as their clothing. Outside the towns there were barely any cars on the road.

Marrakech is another matter. It has its weak spots as most places and people do but it is a big and progressive place to live and work. Similar to Sydney and Melbourne in that it has long competed with Fez as the country's top dog and as with Canberra so the Moroccan powerbrokers anointed smaller Rabat as the nation's capital city, favouring neither of the two combatants. France has long tinkered with controlling Morocco at best or its attributes at least. The groundwork for that seems to have occurred over a century ago.

In 1907 Pierre Benoit Emile Mauchamp was a French doctor working out of a Marrakech pharmacy. By all accounts an innocent man he was brutally killed in an unprovoked attack by a cruel mob near the pharmacy, having been accused of pernicious Christian objectives. France was outraged across the land and awarded Emile Mauchamp the Legion of Honour. This period marked the beginning of the French conquest of Morocco.

Antagonism flowed from both sides but today the majority of Marrakech's citizens appear to do well. The city now has more than a million people, 400 hotels, five-star resorts, golf clubs, increasing numbers of Europeans, especially the French buying Marrakech property to live in and the International Film Festival of Marrakech, the Moroccan answer to the Cannes Film Festival. Marrakech has been well attended by Francis Ford Coppola, Jeremy Irons, Roman Polanski and Martin Scorsese along with European, Arab and Indian film stars.

Chapter Eight *Morocco on twenty cents a day*

This has all happened since our visit more than fifty years ago but the souks or market places we trawled were just as colourful if not more so for the characters of the day were less restricted by the laws of the land, the square was used for public executions to deter the plebs from opposing their rulers and is now used for more mundane matters, the city's magnificent six-metre high red walls with their twenty gates and two hundred towers were far more prominent without today's all-encompassing tall buildings to hold as many people and pollutants as possible while the famous private and public gardens of the city had their beginnings even before we ventured there. The 340 hectare Agdal Gardens were begun in the 1160s and the Menara Gardens in 1157 and are still thriving, thank goodness.

If they take your fancy you can see many palaces, mansions and historic residences with the oldest dating back to the 16th and 17th centuries. Quite fascinating especially if you have an eye for Islamic architecture. In the backstreets you will come across metal workers still turning out their iron lanterns, brass lamps and engraved tea trays along with cedar wood crafts and Arabic and Berber shawls and carpets made from cactus silk. Then there are the superb paintings to be uncovered besides figurines and sculptures. A craftsman's paradise.

Just meandering around the markets, drifting along and drawn to the sounds emanating from their activities you will come upon snake charmers, mystics, sellers of herbs and potions, story-tellers to be heard, acrobats fast coming your way, magicians appearing, musicians of note, the ever-popular monkeys and their tricky trainers, entertainers clothed from medieval days, water-sellers and

A camel sale in a remote part of Morocco

other professions as varied as pickpockets and dentists. We didn't miss much and never tired of it.

After leaving the enticing, upmarket city of Marrakech we covered 177 km to Essaouira. Until 1960 Essaouira was known as Mogador which derived once again from the Pheonicians who in the 5th century BC made the coastal town their main trading centre on the Moroccan coast. The Pheonicians' homeland was what is today northern Israel and the cities of Tyre, Sidon and Byblos in Lebanon. Byblos comes from the Greek language and means book and from that is derived the word Bible. The alphabet most of the western world uses even in differing counties today is directly descended from the twenty- four letter alphabet created by the Pheonicians. The Greeks added but two letters to the Pheonician creation. Similar

Chapter Eight   *Morocco on twenty cents a day*

to their original home at Tyre, Lebanon, the Pheonicians found rock snails or murex at Essaouira and from them made the rare purple dye much favoured by Roman emperors and royalty down the centuries. They made huge fortunes from selling that dye but it took fifty kilograms of rock snails to produce one gram of product. When it is non-season time it is possible to take a boat out to the Iles Purpuraires and you can see where the Pheonicians worked. Essaouira has a crescent-shaped beach much protected by Mogador Island which wards off the strong marine winds and ensures a placid harbour and beach.

The writer of *Lord of the Rings, J.R.R. Tolkien* was so taken by the name of Essaouira's Mogador that he created the dark land Mordor, to the east of Gondor. Mogador was also known to the Arab trade caravans bringing their craft goods and black African slaves from Timbuktu to Essaouira which they referred to as the port of Timbuktu. Depending on where the caravans reached the coast and then went north it is a journey of about 2,400 km.

The next day saw us continue south for 190 km along the coast. Nineteen km before we arrived at our destination of Agadir we came upon a village which we all instantly fell in love with. We parked that in the memory bank and continued on to stunning Agadir. What a beach that is, long, wide and handsome with good sand and surfing waves. Great. There was a good sized town with adequate facilities and provisions and it is no surprise to learn that one million people now reside in Agadir and tourists flood in from Europe in winter. Not surprisingly the name Agadir comes from the Pheonician word *gadir* meaning fort or wall.

Ancient Agadir is at the foothills of the Atlas mountains, on the edge of the Sahara Desert, blessed by beautiful beaches and with today's splendid golf courses. A recent photo showed me a breakwater leading into a marina which on three sides is hidebound by apartment towers and hotels shimmering in their white array. If you are going to Spain or Portugal may I suggest you travel further south.

Most Moroccans thereabouts are Berbers, similar to the people of Algeria. Polygamy is legal if the first wive gives her approval in writing and the man can afford the second wife, or more. Kissing in public in Morocco is not allowed and unmarried Moroccan couples cannot share a room. Be respectful and adventurous and you should have the time of your life.

Something from the past may interest you and it was certainly news to me. The Agadir Crisis occurred in 1911 when French troops upset the balance of power and Germany sent a gunboat to Agadir to deal with the problem. It has been firmly stated that incident was instrumental in World War One beginning three years later between France and Germany.

We camped on the edge of Agadir for a few nights which was good but there were many people around us, mostly set up in tents. One of those tents, close by, was occupied by the so-called Prince of Morocco, some bloke who fancied himself and as I was told was a dealer in drugs. I suppose we had to run into that sometime, somewhere. As I earlier mentioned when I was in Panama City, I don't like the drug world so when asked if I wanted to go to that tent I declined. I mention this not to grandstand my opinion but to tell you that a man who went there told me the going price for a kilo of marijuana or hash was US $1.

Chapter Eight   *Morocco on twenty cents a day*

We spent enjoyable days at the beach and exploring Agadir and not making a Casablanca mistake but decided to move back to that village we had seen nineteen km north of Agadir. The village goes by the name of Taghazout but before that we stopped at nearby Aourir village. The villagers of Aourir grow bananas as rarely seen elsewhere. It is hard to see anything but bananas wherever your sight takes you. A few years before we arrived the musician Jimi Hendrix called in and apparently was blown away by seeing so many bananas. He coined the nickname Banana Village and it stuck for that is how it is still known. We later came back and bought hands of bananas, that is a bunch of up to twenty bananas still on a single stalk and probably paid no more than one cent per several bananas.

At Taghazout village we put our swags on a grass section above the beach, collected wood for a fire to cook on and to provide some warmth into the now shortening nights. We had thought it looked good but there were hardly any other campers and yet as we later found out, Taghazout is nowadays reputed to be the gun surfing beach on the Moroccan coast. How good was that, for lucky us. There were minimal but adequate facilities and once we learned where to buy fresh vegetables such as onions, beans , carrots, potatoes and other items locally such as seafood from the fishermen we hardly lacked anything. One day we bought a slab of camel meat but as an experiment it failed. We put the meat in the big pot, gave it a long head-start and then added vegetables as required but while they cooked well the meat didn't. We added a stone to the pot to see if it would boil before the meat, so frustrated were we. I think the butcher conned us. The best meat is not from the hump but from the section below the hump, probably because it has been pounded by the rider for so long that it tends to soften. Most likely we had the sinews from a camel hoof or two.

Otherwise we dined like kings and at our leisure. It is remarkable but true that we ran a cost program over the nine days we stayed at Taghazout, surfing and playing beach cricket. The cost for the food we consumed per person per day came to a total of twenty cents per day. When we bought a bottle of Moroccan red wine at eighty cents a bottle that would blow the budget out to one dollar per day, if each of us had a bottle of wine. Five years earlier people had been travelling around Europe on $5 a day according to the guide book.

The surfing at Taghazout was so good and I believe ever since its reputation has been rising to the heights. I read an article on the internet by a lady who lives there and she advises potential visitors on what is now available. For example the bananas haven't changed but the surfing has. There are now numerous surf schools, some of which offer accommodation as well as individual or group surfing lessons at up to $1,000 a week, resort type rooms at up to 200 Euros a night, work-stations for freelancers and others, garbage cans, yoga, kite surfing and horse-riding while policemen patrol the beach on horseback, cafes and restaurants, motorbikes and camels, workout stations with bars and poles for exercise, fishermen supplying fish and crabs--- as they did for us and southern Morocco goats that climb eight to ten metres to the top of the argan trees in order to eat the delicious pulpy fruit and we saw that transpire many times.

Taghazout was wonderful not just for what we experienced but for the freedom of those unspoiled days, however we needed to move on. Most people come to Agadir for the warm all year-round weather but unlike us they sleep indoors. As it was becoming cooler

Chapter Eight   *Morocco on twenty cents a day*

and we were continuing south to the Sahara Desert we stopped in Agadir to buy some djellabas.

A djellaba is a long, loose-fitting outer robe or dress with full sleeves worn by men and women. It is a traditional Moroccan garment made of sheep's wool although in more recent times cotton has been used. It has a pointed hood for protection against the sun, the sand and for us, the coming cold. Moroccans have worn the djellaba for centuries and to them it represents a way of life. While used for daily activities it partakes of religious, weddings and festive occasions, incorporating meaningful designs, culture and social status. Colours carry meaning such as a young man wearing a brown djellaba to indicate he is not married. Of course I did not know that at the time and selected what I thought was impartial, being of brown, white and black stripes from top to bottom. I wore it in Morocco and later on our honeymoon when traveling on an ex London single-decker bus overland from London to Kathmandu and it was a God-send for its warmth and durability. Also in Australia at times.

Next day four strange-looking Arabs were seen driving further south for another 200 km to Guelmim. Now there are many ways to spell the name but I use that because I saw it on a road sign next to the Arabic spelling as we went on our way. However the beads of that name are spelt Guelimine beads and that was what we were after. We had met enough westerners in Morocco by now to learn about their valued existence.

Guelmim is known as the *Gateway to the Desert* as it sits on the edge of the Western Sahara in southern Morocco, bounded by Mali, Algeria and Mauritania. During the 19th century it was an important crossroads between Africa and Europe and in that time large quantities of glass beads were traded there. These came to be known as Guelimine beads and whilst the Millefiori or thousand flower glass beads are of dazzling and colourful patterns they were actually made in Venice, as far back as the 16th century. They were the type we were after. Traders across the African continent, as previously stated those trading with Timbuktu, used them prolifically as much value was attached to their relatively small size. They came to be known as trade or slave beads, depending on which business the trader indulged in.

They were used on other continents and such was the demand that on suitable occasions they were used as ballast on slave ships for the outward voyage. Not only were Guelimine beads traded for slaves but for ivory, gold and whatever was the current rage in Europe. The beads were created by Venetian artisans creating flowers or stripes from glass canes that were then cut and moulded onto a core of solid colour. A thin hole was drilled from one end to the other so the beads could be used as a necklace and an easy way to carry them.

On arriving in Guelmim we discovered the weekly camel sale was to be held the following day and we agreed that was a must to attend as it is the biggest camel sale in Morocco. That shouldn't surprise considering the geographical area where camels are the mainstay of travel in particular and life in general.

The sale is so big it has to start at daybreak. I couldn't say how many camels were there but I did attend a similar sale in Rajasthan, India, where there were 50,000 camels and horses for sale but that was an annual sale not a weekly one. I confidently estimated there were at least 4,000 men at the Guelmim sale and every man had a

Chapter Eight   *Morocco on twenty cents a day*

rifle slung over his shoulder. Some of those hardy types were tall and with a turban on their heads I thought if they stick a knife in me no one who cares will notice. At times the mass of men was so intense I was separated from my companions. Many of these men are the Tuareg, an ethnic group of the Berbers. They are nomadic pastoralists utilising much of the Sahara Desert.

In Tuareg society women do not wear the veil but the men do so when they attain maturity. They believe that the veil wards off evil spirits. Tuareg clothing is dyed with indigo, a deep rich colour of blue and violet, a natural pigment derived from certain plants and that colouring is transferred from the clothes they wear to the skin of the wearer. This comes about because to save precious water the clothes are pounded and not washed in hot water. The darker the blue of his clothes is taken as an indication of a man's wealth. This gives rise to the name and appearance of the Blue Men of the Desert.

In the afternoon we were in the town of Guelmim when we met two Americans, Danny and Steve, blokes in their late twenties. We had a cooling drink or two with them and I suppose they felt comfortable and compatible with us. I say that because Danny asked if we could help him? He had arranged to sell his car to a local man, no less than the mayor. I took that with a grain of salt as even then Guelmim was a big town if not a city but it wasn't my business so I let that remark go through to the keeper. The buyer was indeed the mayor.

Danny was selling his car for a certain amount of cash and I don't remember how much, a large amount of Guelimine beads and a private showing by young women of belly-dancing. I remember that. Danny intended to join a camel caravan heading further into

Donkey and camel ploughing in tandem in Morocco

the southern Sahara and said he had no need for his car and Steve did not want to buy it. Danny was concerned about being robbed or ripped off in some way and asked would we come with Steve and himself to ensure the deal went as planned. Why not?

The following morning we went to the buyer's house, introductions were made and we were all seated in a large room. He did have a large house. The mayor gentleman and his off-siders produced the money, Danny the beads and both the mayor and Danny did the counting, twice. To us everything looked and sounded good. Glasses of black tea and plates of date cakes were handed to each of us and we relaxed. Then hands were clapped and the first of the belly-dancers stepped out from behind curtains suspended from an archway leading off the large room. All up the dancers performed to live music for perhaps twenty-five minutes and we took that as

Chapter Eight   *Morocco on twenty cents a day*

our fee. Danny had offered to pay us something but the transaction seemed above board and all was well. To us it had been interesting.

In fact Ian took advantage of the situation to ask the mayor would he be interested in another trade? Before meeting up with us Ian and Geoff had flown to America, worked in Chicago, bought a Pontiac and driven from Canada to Mexico. Being business types Ian had travelled with his dinner suit which he now offered to the Arab mayor and for a bagful of Guelimine beads the exchange was made. When Ian returned to Sydney he rented a flat in Cremorne. He sold the Guelimine beads for enough money to buy all the furniture he needed, second-hand but as he needed sufficient to start over again, a significant amount. Warren, Geoff and I paid cash for our Guelimine trade beads. I later offered my beads to my future mother-in-law for her daughter's hand in marriage. She was not taken by the idea.

Ian had somehow come up with the directions to an oasis further into the Sahara where palm trees surrounded a natural pool of hot water that came up from the depths and maintained the not-too-deep water level at all times. We agreed with him it should be a worthwhile exercise to find and enjoy it. The next morning we set off, quite excited.

The track took us though absolute desert country so I was surprised we could travel on it but I imagine it had been beaten into a solid base courtesy of centuries of wear and tear. After about twenty km we came up and parallel to a camel caravan going in much the same direction but on pure sand, no track. As we looked across we noticed one of the camel riders seemed like he was waving to us. He was. It was car-less Danny, late of America.

Ian's directions were spot-on and we soon came to the oasis. We didn't need the djellabas there and we soon stripped off and were basking in the hot water in the hot desert but sheltered by the cool palm trees. Heavenly. We fooled around, had a casual but healthy lunch and enjoyed the surroundings which for us were magical and no one else was there.

That night we camped outside Guelmim and the next day returned to Agadir where we stocked up with supplies for the road ahead, which would take us into and over the Atlas Mountains. They separate the Sahara Desert and the Atlantic Ocean and by traveling north we hoped to reach Fez and then return to Tangier.

After a drive of eighty km due east we came to Taroudant, which has the most complete ancient walls of any town in Morocco, not only that but with its surrounding ramparts it is likened to Marrakech. It is known as the grandmother of Marrakech and that says a lot.

Straightening up to the north we had to stop at Ouarzazate. Due to its striking scenery and fortress style buildings, historical architecture, suitable climate, availability of good technicians, low production costs and other technical efficiencies Ouarzazate is an excellent setting for film-making. These are just a few of the many films that have been produced in this area: Lawrence of Arabia, The Man who would be King, The Last Temptation of Christ, Gladiator, Legionnaire, Kundun, The Mummy, Kingdom of Heaven, The Wages of Fear.

Most houses in the Atlas Mountains are built of either baked mud brick, rammed earth, red mud clay bricks, even rough cut pieces of red rock. In the High Atlas the houses are built of stone while wood is often used for the ceilings. All of these techniques are required

Chapter Eight   *Morocco on twenty cents a day*

in an attempt to beat the heat of summer. At the town of Boumaln Dades regional nomads head up the mountain where they spend the summer in their traditional cave houses. Those people rarely accept visitors so we could not see their caves and underground homes.

We stopped at another of those small towns high in the mountains to stretch our legs and to explore. I don't know the name of the town as it seemed rather sleepy and uninteresting on account of the near empty main street. Anyway we pulled over, parked and began to walk that street and it was noticeable for its long length. As we walked like four gunfighters abreast, well, why not, down the middle of the wide stretch of street we were surprised to see two young women some way off but walking towards us.

As they came closer we could see they were not Arabic but western women. They stopped when they were a metre or two away and looked at us. The first thing one of them said, looking at me, was, *You're Bill Stanford, aren't you*. Not a question but a statement. I said, *Why do you say that?* because I had never seen this girl beforehand. She replied, *I am a friend of your sister, Wendy, and she often talks about you. I recognise you from her.*

Well I was gob-smacked and I think the other boys were also. Anyway I confessed to being he and after that we made introductions all round, found a place for morning tea and talked a while before moving on in opposite directions over the High Atlas Mountains of Morocco.

Continuing on we noticed some farmers were using a camel alongside a donkey to pull the plough. We had seen this method being used in Morocco on quite a few occasions and tried to find out why the farmer would use two such diverse animals as the camel and the donkey. Due to our lack of Arabic and those farmers being at the lower end of the socio-economic scale we were unable to converse with them. One day Geoff was talking with a Moroccan in English and he put the question to the man. He seemed a knowledgeable type and easy to speak to but his answer surprised us to say the least. He said the camel is strong in that it can carry much weight and go long distances but if left alone it tends to walk in circles whereas the donkey is remarkably strong and resilient and a counter-balance to the wandering camel. Due to the Russians having taken my camera and my not yet replacing it I do not have such a photo but I have seen Moroccan photos and postcards of that tandem method of farming. If you don't have the horse-power you use the next best. They say there are one million donkeys in the land and most of them are in the Atlas Mountains.

We did eventually find out how two animals of varying sizes, weights and strengths can work together and it goes like this. The two beasts of burden are harnessed with an unusual belly-yoke system characteristic of the region. The belly-yoke is a wooden bar suspended from straps around the withers, which is the point between the animal's shoulder blades, and it hangs under the chest of each of the two animals but without touching them.

The tillage implement is then attached to the yoke and since the individual yoke is suspended a set height above the ground, it can be used to harness animals of different sizes and types. The same system is used to plough with two mules, two donkeys, a horse and a donkey or as we saw quite often, a camel and a donkey. A few last words on the tough little donkey. If a male donkey mates with a female horse it will produce a mule. A horse has 64 chromosomes

Chapter Eight   *Morocco on twenty cents a day*

and a donkey has 62 chromosomes and as the resultant mule has 63 chromosomes it is sterile and rarely, if ever, able to reproduce off-spring.

All credit to the donkey as it is claimed that Cleopatra, Queen of Egypt, the vivacious Pauline, sister of Napolean Bonaparte and Poppaea Sabina, wife of Roman Emperor Nero all bathed in donkey milk to maintain the beauty and skin of their youth.

At length we came down from the hot, dry Atlas Mountains to one of the great cities of Morocco, that being Fez. At an elevation of 400 metres it is 200 km from the coastal capital Rabat and 300 km from both ocean-side cities Casablanca and Tangier. I like to see inland cities come good and prosper and I class Fez as one of those. I recall the city being large then and nowadays the population numbers about one and a quarter million people.

Fez is known as the Mecca of the West and the Athens of Africa along with being the spiritual and cultural capital of Morocco which should indicate the high regard in which it is held. It is a rare visitor who would be bored in Fez. There is surely something for everyone and we explored and enjoyed the city for a multitude of activities and reasons but I am only going to relate one aspect otherwise I will be here until the next Australian Federal election.

It is said more people visit this centre than any other in Fez and considering it has been operating non-stop for 800 years, since the 13th century, in the same traditional manner it commands respect even if it might not interest you. I refer to the Chouwara tannery.

The Chouwara tannery takes in goat and sheep skins along with camel and cattle hides and cures, stretches and dyes them. The curing is done by placing the skins outdoors in large, ancient, rounded-stone, open-topped containers and soaking them in a mixture of cattle urine, pigeon guano, quicklime, salt and water. Over three days this softens the coarse skins and induces them to be able to absorb the dyes. To obtain the required natural colours poppies are used to provide the red dye, indigo for blue, henna for orange. After the dye treatment the skins are laid out to dry in the sun which means many go on flat rooftops whereas on the Indonesian island of Sulawesi I have seen countless similar hides laid out on bare ground, which might be practical but possibly not so effective.

This long-determined treatment results in high demand from craftsmen who turn the famed Moroccan leather into coats, shoes, handbags etc. Apart from a mechanical rinser the process does not involve machinery and continues on as it has done since medieval days.

After Fez we returned to Tangier from where we took the ferry back to Algeciras, Spain.

CHAPTER NINE

El Cid

God, give me the serenity to accept the things I cannot change, the courage to change the things I can, and the wisdom to know the difference.
— Reinhold Niebuhr (preeminent American theologian of the twentieth century, who influenced Martin Luther King Jr, Hubert Humphrey, Jimmy Carter and Barak Obama)

We intended to visit Seville and good intentions are often interrupted, are they not? It is about 200 km from Algeciras on a decent road and should have been a quick trip but about the halfway mark there is a short turn-off to the city of Cadiz. I have tried to limit my comments about the Pheonicians as I find them of great interest but you may not, so this may be my second-last reference to them.

The Pheonicians carved out a settlement in southern Spain as they liked to do on a slice of coastal land about the 10th to 9th century BC. They established a port there in the 7th century. They called it Gadir or Agadir as they also did with Agadir, Morocco. Much later Julius Caesar arrived in the city when he was a junior Senator. He saw a statue there of Alexander the Great and morosely reflected that at the same age he had not achieved such success. The Pheonicians soon found the locals had substantial deposits of silver and preferred them to work the mines after which they bought the silver at low prices and then sailed off to various parts of the known world to sell the silver at high prices.

Men of other countries only had the skills to sail flat-bottomed river boats, not venturing out into open waters for another two thousand years because they did not know how to build their boats with hulls, as did the Pheonicians. They made Gadir, later Cadiz, possibly the oldest continuously lived-in city in Europe and cemented their power as one of the world's great trading and sailing nations. They sailed to Britain where they were amused to find men in small boats constructed not of timber but of animal skins. In the Cornwall area they came across tin mines, which are still active today and which they traded in great amounts and derived enormous wealth to the extent they paid mercenaries to protect their homeland while they continued to trade. They called that country Baratanac, which in their language meant land of tin and from that was derived the name of Britain. They named their new land Spain which means land of rabbits although they may have seen rock hyrax, a small creature from Africa that does look like a rabbit. I have seen them in inland Kenya.

On to Seville, another wonderful Spanish city and the name Seville comes from the Pheonician word *Sefala*, meaning valley or plain, when they colonised the area. It is eighty km from the Atlantic Ocean and sits on the Quadalquivir river which enables it to have the only river port in the country. Many of the buildings are large and quite remarkable for their imposing presence as is the Plaza de

Chapter Nine *El Cid*

Espana and the city is the third largest after Madrid and Barcelona. Our friend Julius Caesar turned up again, this time when he ordered the walls of Seville to be built. There is a bit of Australia in Seville, if I can put it that way. As I write this the temperature in my home town of Dubbo is 42 Celsius but that is not unique. All of eastern Australia, the day after Australia Day, 2025, is being tested by a heat wave. Today it is 43 in Penrith, western Sydney and also 43 in Tibooburra, north-western NSW.

Seville is also hot with the average temperature in July and August above 36 degrees. The 40s are regular and the city is known as the frying pan of Spain. I instantly had a good feeling for Seville and I rank it along with Malaga as my favourite Spanish watering holes.

We soon heard there was to be bullfighting at Seville's Real Maestranza bullring. I had never been to a bullfight, have not been to one since and I doubt I will ever see another but I make no excuses for saying I am glad we went to the one in Seville for it was colourful, exciting, full of drama and courage on both sides, i.e. the bull and the bullfighter.

The bullfighting which consisted of six individual bullfights each took twenty minutes during the afternoon and the sun shone at such a moderate temperature the event could not have been better presented.

In bullfights everything is combined : colour, gaiety, tragedy, bravery, talent, butchery, energy and strength, grace, emotion. It is the most complete of all spectacles. From now on I cannot do without bullfights. *Charlie Chaplin, actor, film producer.*

Official Summary:The bullfight is the oldest mass spectacle in Spain. In the bullfight several matadors take part on foot, usually three, assisted by their respective teams consisting of three banderilleros or peons and two picadors on horseback. In total are twelve bullfighters on foot and six on horseback who have to fight six bulls. The animals that are fought must be between four and six years old and have passed a veterinary examination certifying their suitability and must be killed by swordsmen who have received the *alternativa* as matadors of bulls, that is to say, who are maestros.

At the beginning of the modern *tercio de varas*, the bull gallops out of the bullpen and the matador normally stops it with the bullfighter's capote, then moves towards the picador in order to reduce the pass. There follows the distraction of the peons to separate the bull from the horse, which is protected by the pad, and the distraction test, which is normally performed by the matador in the order of the bullfight, to please the spectators or motivated by rivalry, immobile, waits for the bull to charge and uses the moment

Bull fighting

of crossing to plunge the sword in, *al volapié*, in which the matador, taking advantage of the stillness of the vanquished bull, falls upon the bull's cross and sinks the sword in, and the encounter, in which matador and bull attack each other simultaneously. The death of the bull is assured once it has fallen to the ground, by a dagger blow in the nape. The dead bull is dragged out of the arena by galloping mules while the arena workers of the bullring remove the remains of blood and certain assistants remove all blood from the capote, muletas and swords. In each sacrificial ceremony the evidence of violence is hidden.

In the few seconds during which the mules remove the bull dispossessed of his life, the spectators collectively express their opinion of the bull: they boo and whistle if it did not please them and they cheer and applaud if it behaved favourably and nobly. Presidents recently received the power to spare the life of a bull that

Part of the bullfight at Seville Spain, mules take away the dead bull

is considered exceptional in what is termed an *indulto*. The President, in recognition of a particular bull's great bravery can grant its return to the arena while the spectators standing, emotionally applaud the animal, whose name will be remembered by aficionados. *Real Maestranza de Caballeria de Sevilla.*

That night we free-camped in our sleeping bags outside Seville and went to sleep around a fire. When we woke up in the early morning we were covered in frost. To warm us up we used Ian and Geoff's cooker/stove to make pancakes for breakfast but it was time to move indoors and from then on we complied with Mother Nature's overpowering point of view.

Our next stop was to be Lisbon, the capital city of Portugal but before we arrived there we came across a Spanish farmer using a camel and a donkey to pull his plough, just as we had regularly seen in the Atlas Mountains of Morocco. Shortly afterwards we were stopped at the traffic lights in a rather large Spanish town or city. Geoff was driving and as he tells the story I was sitting in the back seat behind him. Along our side of the Kombi a group of Spanish schoolgirls were waiting for the lights to change before crossing the road. I could not see the girls as the windowless sliding door was between myself and them but for some unknown reason I pulled the sliding door back to open it. Geoff says I must have pulled it with some strength as the door hit the end of the runner quite hard and made a solid noise. He turned around to see what I was up to and I still cannot answer that.

He said I was sitting in my seat as the door opened up and he commented later on my blond hair which had grown back since our enforced haircuts. I had let it run wild since for most days we had no hot water to shave with. So there I was in my djellaba with the hood down showing my blond hair and beard. Geoff said in that moment the schoolgirls heard the door fly open and they looked to see where the noise had come from. What they saw was merely myself but my appearance caused some them to call out, *It is Jesus, Jesus Christ*, in alarm and wonder. Now I know you will think that is preposterous but Geoff is so adamant and he is an accountant so you have to believe him, that he tells me on certain occasions he has related that incident to more than a few people. Embarrassing.

Apart from that our trip to Lisbon was uneventful as was the city itself. It is modern, clean, beautifully presented and the second oldest capital city in Europe, after Athens. The nearest beaches were twenty-two km away but before we went there we made a donation.

One thing that caught our eye in Lisbon was that blood donors were being sought and the Blood Bank was paying donors A $20 plus a meal. $80 between us was handy money, in fact more than fifty years ago it was an astonishing amount and so we accepted the offer. It went well. For many years in Australia I have since donated blood, for a milkshake and a muffin but never for money so Lisbon was surprising. Then I went to Papua New Guinea for a while and when I returned home I was banned from donating blood for three years, like everyone else when they return. I was not told the precise potential threat but something nasty was in PNG but not in Australia, yet. When the three years expired Covid-19 struck and I haven't given blood since. The way it goes.

The water at the surf beaches was on the cold side and not necessarily because of the winter season but in comparison to the waters along the inland Mediterranean Sea which are warmer.

Driving twenty-five km along the coast to the north brought us to the upmarket resort mecca of Estoril which seems to lack for nothing if one has the money to enjoy the no expense spared luxurious playgrounds. They were interesting but out of our league at the time. If we had known then of Portugal's beautiful and historic Douro Valley I am certain we would have travelled that way but being ignorant of that at the time we set off to Madrid.

It was a long drive and sometimes we would stop at a pub for a counter lunch with the locals. They usually seemed surprised when we walked in wearing our cold weather djellabas but after a little joke or two they accepted us and we all had a drink and a laugh.

Personally I liked Madrid immediately. Due to the cold weather at night we took a room in the heart of the city and that made it ever so easy to have a central base from where we could explore. I came to think of Madrid as my blue city because at night the cobblestone streetlights around us had a soft blue glow about them which I found warm and attractive.

My favourite excursion was to the Museo del Prado where some of the world's greatest painters of the past have their works on display. Like so many people I felt privileged to visit the Louvre in Paris and admire its artwork but as soon as I saw and entered the Prado in Madrid I knew it was the one for me. I am not knowledgeable about art, absolutely not but as with a car, a cricket bat, a girl, a racehorse I simply know what I like. I wasn't disappointed and for one thing the Prado holds the work of my favourite painter, the Flemish, or Dutch born, Pieter Bruegel the Elder. There is no precise record of when he was born but he died in 1569, his early forties. I gather he grew up when religious subjects ceased to be the natural subject matter of painting. His strength was his ability to create worthy landscapes and most of all, at least to myself, scenes of the people, often the poorer types. He painted them in great numbers, in multitudes and to look at them I find is similar to reading a book for despite so many figures he coated them with extraordinary detail. Some of his paintings include The Triumph of the Dead, The Blind leading the Blind, The Peasant Wedding, Winter Landscape, Children's Games and The Hunter in the Snow.

The Prado also has the work of Titian, Goya, Jusepe de Ribera, El Greco, Hieronymous Bosch, Diego Velazquez, Pablo Picasso and Salvador Dali. Other Spanish painters include Joaquin Sorolla, Juan Gris, Francisco de Zurbaran and Antoni Gaudi of the Segrada Familie.

The next day we drove fifty km out of town to the *Valle de los Caidos*, otherwise known as the Valley of the Fallen. It is in a mountainous area with what is described as an underground valley that holds a basilica, an abbey and on top of the mountain the world's largest cross, that being 152.4 metres in height. A basilica is a church that has been deemed important by the Pope. All this is a gigantic monument to forty thousand soldiers of both sides, the Nationalists and the Republicans who died in the Spanish Civil War and who are buried in the Valley of the Fallen. In total 200,000 soldiers died and many of them came from other countries during the years of fighting from 1936 to 1939. The Republicans were supported by fighters from Russia and various countries of Europe while volunteers from Germany, Italy and Portugal fought for the Nationalists, many eventually under the command of army strongman General Franco, who became Spain's dictator overseer.

When we left Madrid we took the road north for 250 km on our way to Burgos. The countryside leading to and round Burgos was covered with good crops of barley and wheat. At an elevation of 865 metres Burgos is said to be on the cold side and for cities with a population in excess of 100,000 people it is the coldest city in Spain so once again our hardy and ever so practical djellabas came to the fore. At that height I thought the crops looked healthy and was interested to discover the land that they thrive on had supported forests long ago but they are now cleared and the soil consists of a lime and clay combination along with gypsum. Over time the peaks of the surrounding moors of the Douro Basin have released protective layers of limestone that settled within the soil.

We came to a stop in Burgos which is known for two of Spain's warriors in particular. One was General Franco whom I recently mentioned and he made Burgos the headquarters of the Nationalist forces to fight the Republicans.

The other was *Rodrigo Diaz de Vivar* who was a Christian knight known for his military prowess in the eleventh century that saw him proclaimed as the general who was never defeated. He fought for and commanded both Christian and Muslim armies and was known by one and all as *El Cid*, meaning the Lord or The Master. He was born in Vivar, a village near Burgos, the capital of Castille. His life story is long, memorable and worthy of a major film, which in due course is what took place, known as *El Cid*. He was a hero of Spain and today is still seen in that light. I found it to be an absorbing film and therefore I made a point of going to visit his tomb which is in the Cathedral of Burgos.

I walked along the nave of the Cathedral and where the transept is, under the dome of the nave, lies the top of his tomb. It is shielded

Chapter Nine *El Cid*

The tomb of El Cid, Burgos Cathedral, Spain

Tizano, the sword of El Cid, Burgos, Spain

from the public by no more than a rope cordon. I stood alongside it, being as close as anyone could be, mindful of the fact that he died in 1099. He is buried in a sarcophagus below, one that was made a few years later and said to have been sculpted by a one-time Christian colleague, King Alfonso X the Wise. In 2007 the sword of El Cid, Tizona, was sold for 1.6 million euros and is now at the Museum of Burgos.

The 1961 film *El Cid* starred Charlton Heston and Sophia Loren, who, by many accounts could not stand the man. If you see the film you might pay attention to her in the death scene.

Santander rests easily at the northern or top end of Spain, looking out over the Atlantic Ocean. The airport is named in honour of one of the true gentlemen of any sport anywhere. I write of Spain's golfing legend Seve Ballesteros, winner of ninety-three tournaments, fifty of which were on the European Tour, more than anyone else. His outstanding record lists five of the world's majors before his unfortunate death from brain cancer at age fifty-one.

Our immediate interest lay in the Cantabria Caves, about thirty km away and that was where we soon found ourselves. The Cantabria are a collection of thirty caves in which evidence exists that people lived in them at varying times in history. Most of the evidence shows they were there, 14,000, 18,000 and one example of 20,000 years ago. The El Castillo cave shows evidence of being in use at various times over the past 150,000 years.

In addition to scientific and archaeological evidence plus the remains of bears the regular visitors can see for themselves the rather extraordinary rock paintings which have survived. These artworks are wonders to behold for the bold colours of some and the artistic merit of others. Animals are the objects of many artists and they include horses, goats and cattle while the Altamira cave alone has sixteen bison plus red deer that are 2.25 metres tall. The coloured artwork is exceptional.

Back to Santander and from there we followed the coastline to San Sebastian, which put us about twenty km from the Spain/France border. With its warm summers and cool winters San Sebastian is a ready-made tourist town with the added attraction of a large bay that has good sand on its three beaches, which do yield some reasonable waves. When you stand at the head of Concha Bay and look out to sea there is a good-sized island almost equidistant between the two headlands which in their turn are as large as each other with the island between them being two-thirds their size. All-up the three outcrops of land appear well balanced so as to make

Chapter Nine *El Cid*

the bay an attractive setting as seen from the beach. One thing that I am not used to is its annual rainfall of 1,650 mm of rain. I am not speaking against it but pointing out that Dubbo has annual rainfall of one third that, of 550 mm.

San Sebastian is the capital of the Basque country and the people speak the Basque language, that being Euskara. Perhaps because they wish to popularize their preferred way of life the Basque people are strong on their cultural aspects. They have many events and festivals for music, their cuisine, theatre, film and of course, Basque week. One of their four universities has established the world's first degree in Gastronomy.

We stayed a while and I distinctly recall walking with Ian, Warren and Geoff along a wide promenade above the beach and looking out to sea. It was a lovely morning and we noticed a group of six people walking towards us. Amongst them was a woman of perhaps thirty years and I know she was 183 cm tall, the same height as myself because I looked straight into her disarming eyes which seemed to lock on to mine. Her long hair was tied at the nape, so as to reveal the character-forming and feminine aspects of her face. I mention all that because she had a distinct presence about her that, to my mind at least, stood her apart from mere mortals.

The other boys must have felt it too because as we closed the gap between ourselves and that group we stopped in our tracks. When they reached us they also halted and we greeted each other. I can't tell you about her five companions because I was mesmerised.

Fortunately she was friendly and from Brazil and nowadays that is all I remember, apart from the fact that I sensed, no, I knew, she was or would be someone special.

Taking positive memories with us we left San Sebastian and crossed the border into France where we soon stopped to fill up with petrol. While Geoff was seeing to that I left the Kombi to stretch my legs and bumped into a girl coming out of the service shop. I apologized and for some reason she stopped and we talked, not in my fragile French but her elegant English. Her name was Claudette and as I was about to go back to the Kombi she said if I am ever in Paris perhaps I would like to see her? Well that seemed like a possibility so she gave me her address, saying the apartment is on the seventh floor but there is no lift.

We drove over the Pyrenees and came to Toulouse, home to aviation manufacturer, Airbus. France and then Germany are the biggest shareholders in Airbus and in France there are 56,000 Airbus employees of which 28,000 work in Toulouse. The business language at Airbus is English but when a job is advertised so is the required language, French, German and Spanish being helpful. In November, 2024, Airbus had an order book for 19,075 of its best-selling A320 planes of which 11,865 had been delivered. Good business. Not so Boeing.

The most important part of Toulouse is that it is the absolute French headquarters of what really counts in the world today and that is Rugby Union. Toulouse has been the champions of Europe six times and of France on twenty-three occasions. Unfortunately there were no scheduled matches at the time and just as disappointing was the fact that we four were now splitting up. Ian and Geoff wanted to go back to England and Warren and I needed to return to Bocca di Magra to continue the travels in our Kombi van. Warren and I didn't expect Ian and Geoff to drive us back to Italy and Toulouse looked like an even split for us going in different directions. They took us to

Chapter Nine *El Cid*

the railway station and as we were early we checked our luggage in and then Ian dropped us downtown to have a look around Toulouse for a couple of hours. We said our farewells and went our own ways.

When it was time to return to the railway station we were unable to find the right streets so I used my knowledge of the French language and asked people for directions. When I did that each of them looked at me strangely and a few hurried away. I wondered what was going on, perhaps something untoward had happened at the station. I tried again, saying, *Excusez-moi s'il vous plais mais ou est la gare?* Which translates as Excuse me please but where is the railway station? It wasn't until an English-speaking French lady told me that with my inadequate pronunciation I was actually saying, *Excusez-moi s'il vous plais ou est la guerre?* Which happens to mean, Excuse me please but where is the war?

We took the train to Genoa, Italy, and from there a bus to the nearest stop to Bocca di Magra where Mario met and drove us back to Bocca. After a couple of days hospitality from Wendy and Mario we departed to make our way back to England but by a different route. We drove up to Munich and stopped to see where the 1972 Olympic Games had been held and the eleven Israeli athletes murdered, which hardened us up to go to Dachau.

We drove the sixteen km from Munich to the first concentration camp to be constructed in Germany in World War Two and the longest-running concentration camp in Germany. We parked at the nearest building and on stepping out of the Kombi encountered a large open-topped barrel. Rifles standing on their butt filled the sombre container and the barrel of each rifle was fitted with a deadly bayonet rising up as if to check one's movement. Welcome to

Adolf Hitler lived on the second floor of the Prinzregentplatz 16 in Munich from 1929 to 1939

Dachau, where the overhead greeting sign says *Work Makes You Free*. I would later see the same sign at the even more infamous Auschwitz concentration camp in Poland.

It is depressing to list the horrors carried out by men against their fellow men, let alone women and children. So I shall conduct a quick summary. The majority of the inmates were Poles, Russians, French, Yugoslavs, Jews and Czechs. They died of some of the following causes: medical experiments including lethal injections, deliberate malaria, typhus, pleurisy, tuberculosis, pneumonia, dysentery, shootings, hangings, the gas chambers, beaten to death, run to exhaustion and suicides. 4,000 Soviet prisoners of war were killed

Chapter Nine *El Cid*

The crematoria, Dachau concentration camp, Munich, Germany

at Dachau's SS shooting range and the crematoria used to seemingly make it all go away for Germany.

To make life easier for the wretched inhumane guards the prisoners were identified, to a degree, by different colours attached to their clothing. Political prisoners wore a red badge, professional criminals green, those who were considered work-shy black, idiots white with the word STUPID, Jehovah's Witnesses violet, emigrants blue, Jews yellow, gypsies brown.

Dachau has endless atrocities to its name. Here I will only mention one, the standing cell. Those cells were so narrow that the elbows of a standing prisoner would touch the sides of his cell and configured so that he could do nothing but stand, for days at a time. Think about that. If you have been to Tasmania's former penal colony of Port Arthur you might have entered one of the tiny and contorted isolation cells. I had trouble doing exactly that, entering it. Those cells are shaped to prevent the prisoner from standing, the opposite of Dachau. In Port Arthur's isolation cells you cannot obtain a comfortable position.

We left Dachau and breathed out, settling down for the run north to Heidelberg. It was one of the few German cities that for the most part avoided WW 2 Allied bombing, perhaps because it did not contain military or war manufacturing facilities but also because it was and is one of the most beautiful cities in Germany. This good fortune of war was notably made possible by the thoughtful American Brigadier General William Beiderlinden whose soldiers had the city at their mercy in 1945. He contacted the city burgomaster or mayor and told him that if the Nazi troops withdrew he would not shell Heidelberg. Crucial to the decision to comply was the local wish to save Heidelberg University and other civic treasures. Typically mayors under Nazi rule were not allowed to enter into such negotiations but the brave mayor stood his ground, the Germans withdrew and the city was saved and preserved thanks to the American general.

The University, which opened in 1386 is the oldest in the country and has produced fifty-seven Nobel Prize winners. This may account for the city of 150,000 people today, having twenty-five per cent of them as students. Heidelberg Castle, constructed by 1214 is a major attraction although damaged over the centuries by two substantial lightning strikes. A popular area is the Philosophers' Walk where university professors and philosophers have and still do, discussed worldly matters during their perambulations. The older sections of the city are highly regarded for their baroque style of architecture, drawing as they do on exciting detail, contrast, grandeur and deep colours.

Chapter Nine *El Cid*

Being happy with what we saw of Heidelberg Waren and I then proceeded to the American Army base known as Patrick Henry Village. This deceptive title then hosted 18,000 American soldiers and was the headquarters of the American Army in Europe. At that time it was commanded by four-star General Michael S. Davison.

I cannot exactly recall the way it went but we rolled up to the entry gates, gave our names, said that we are looking for work and that we have been recommended to apply here by officers of the American Air Force in Greece. From there we were passed along to more senior personnel who interviewed us with the outcome that we were offered work that day.

We were not allowed to live on the base but we soon found cosy accommodation nearby and I say cosy because by now there was snow everywhere. The next morning we joined a squad of fifteen civilians of mixed nationalities and began our work, most of which consisted of putting in place whatever was required for General Davison. Being such a senior officer he was always holding meetings, talks, appointments not only with his own immediate officers but also those from the German military, other American units from throughout Europe, politicians, NATO members, occasionally the media and who knows who else.

We often saw General Davison but of course never to talk to. He had graduated from the United States Military Academy in 1939 and was posted to a cavalry unit at Fort Brown, Texas. During WW2 he served in North Africa and Italy, participated in the Anzio invasion, served in France, was wounded twice and rose through the ranks to that of Colonel.

Our job was to ensure the presentation, the setting and the

seating for General Davison's meetings were always faultless. At times he only required a single room but his needs ran the gamut from there up to catering for hundreds of attendees in a large auditorium. It was not just the meetings but often the guests needed to be supplied with morning tea and or lunch and the dismantling and tidying up probably took longer to deal with than putting it all in place. Our duties were separate from the chefs and waiters but we needed to work in with them so that no one could find fault. The numbers of people who came to the auditorium naturally varied so moving furniture was a major task.

After little more than a week Warren and I were put in charge of the civilian team, which came as a pleasant surprise. Now I was a joint overseer working with the American Army. That probably made us even keener to do a good job and after another two weeks we were invited to an after work evening party for the officers and their families. It was an informal gathering whereby they did not wear their uniforms. Warren and I were the only ones from the civilian group invited so we thought we must be doing something right.

Drinks were on the house which was tasty and a colonel started talking with me. When he asked what were we doing in Germany I told him a little of our travels and he was so interested we must have talked for forty minutes. I met a major and his attractive wife and their daughter was in the same category. She was a nice girl and I was lucky that over the next few weeks we went out whenever it was possible.

Other people were good to us in different ways. The kitchen was massive and staffed by American soldiers and they were all African-American. To feed so many soldiers one of them told me he had to stand there for hours just cracking eggs for their breakfast. We first

Chapter Nine *El Cid*

met some of those blokes shortly after we arrived and they kindly said that if we came in early, before the officers were about, they would give us breakfast. We always had lunch care of the army but officially not breakfast or dinner. Warren and I would get up early, make our way through the heavy snow to the camp's kitchen and be fed by the Negro soldiers who would pepper us with questions about, *what's it like livin' in the woods in Awwstralia?*

Then the hammer dropped. Two hard-nosed officials from a German government department confronted us one day and demanded to see our green card, the one that gave us permission to work in Germany. Well we did not have that document and they told us we must leave the camp and Germany immediately, to avoid further investigation and possible ramifications. We couldn't argue the toss on that and we were given precious little time to say farewell to the many good people we had come across. Even so and I never knew who but I imagine someone didn't like us as much we might have liked them and for their own purpose they dobbed us in, Russian style again. I lost the rank of overseer.

We looked at the map and decided on a 550 km trip to Ostend in Belgium and from there to take the ferry to Harwich, England. It might be hard on the old Kombi. She hadn't let us down albeit this would be her biggest test and she would have to contend with snow covered roads in winter, as would we. In the morning we made the early start we needed and said farewell to beautiful Heidelberg. All things considered she had been good to us.

It truly was a long, long day and outside the weather slowed everyone up, not just us. The basic heater in the Kombi put in its best day by far because under our stewardship she had not been required to do too much up to now. As we drew close to the coast I think Warren and I were feeling pretty good about how the day had panned out. The short winter's day disappeared into the dark of the night and then we only had the final fifty km to see out.

Clunk. That one loud horrible sound told us in a split second that the engine had died. I'm no mechanic but I knew that was the end of the road. There was no other noise as the Kombi gently rolled to a stop but that last motion allowed us to at least get her off the road. It was amazing how quickly she passed away. Despite that accurate assessment we both tinkered with the engine as though by some miracle it would respond to our silent wishes.

That futile hope expired like a candle in the flurry of snow that constantly swirled around us. Our djellabas, especially the hoods, gave us a degree of warmth and protection from the freezing air. We packed up what we could carry and set out to walk to the next town whose lights we could faintly see through the gloom. We entered the nearest street where the lights were on inside only a few of the houses. Then we saw an outside light above a verandah. Its red glow looked soft and warm, inviting.

Warren and I trudged up the steps and knocked on the door. After a wait a lady opened it. She looked suspiciously at our attire and our worldly possessions before she asked what did we want? She spoke English which was a blessing and we explained our car had broken down while we were heading to Ostend and as we had nowhere to go we were seeking shelter for the rest of the night. She turned and called out to someone and when that woman came to the door I imagine she told her, in a language unknown to me, of our situation. She looked at us and then told us to come inside and shut the door, quickly.

We asked her if she could tell us where can we find a room for the night? She looked at us for a while and then said, *This house is brothel and you not find place for stay near here. Now weather is not good and we not busy and you no car. So I have room you sleep but no trouble and you go in morning. Follow me.* She led us down the long corridor to an open office and behind that she opened a door and showed us in to a storeroom, with packed shelves on three sides. Pointing at the floor she said we could sleep there and then she showed us an adjoining basic bathroom. At least we had our sleeping bags.

CHAPTER TEN

Jack the Ripper

A lady's imagination is very rapid, it jumps from admiration to love, from love to matrimony in a moment.

—Jane Austen.

In the morning a male member of the brothel staff drove us and our gear to the workshop of a mechanic he claimed would be able to help us. The mechanic, named Luc, said he would do what he could for us but we would have to wait at least one hour until he was available. It was nearer two hours before he came back to us waiting on a bench in the sun. The weather had turned around and the day looked promising.

We explained the situation to Luc and he was so good as to drive us back to the Kombi which he looked over. Yes the engine was kaput and in any event he could not do anything about it out there. He called one of his men who came out with a tow truck and took it to Luc's premises. The upshot was that we could write the Kombi off then and there or we could leave it with Luc and he would do what he could with it in due course. If he couldn't have it running again we would have to decide its future. If it could be fixed he would let us know and we would decide then.

Warren and I knew we wouldn't be back so we told Luc if he would take charge of the vehicle from now on we were prepared to let him have it along with all responsibilities signed for and if he could salvage it then good luck to him. We didn't want it hanging around our necks like an albatross. Luc agreed, we did the paperwork, shook hands and never heard from him again so hopefully both parties did alright.

His man took us to the bus station and we set off, again, for Ostend. There we boarded a ferry about two o'clock in the afternoon that would take us on the six-hour voyage across the English Channel to Harwich which is in Essex, East Anglia. We fell into conversation with a fellow passenger, a friendly, slightly chubby, fair-haired, middle-aged man by the name of Gerald. He had his car, a Volvo, on the ferry and when he asked where are we going, we replied to Battersea in London but we have lost our car.

Gerald was interested in that so we explained about the Kombi. He was going to London and it was no trouble for him to drop us off in Battersea, 144 km from Harwich. That's what happened. What a stroke of luck but that was just the first of three consecutive strokes.

It was about eight o'clock at night when we sailed into Harwich, which is a significant port and worthy of mention. Alfred The Great earlier defeated sixteen Danish ships in Harwich in 885, the harbour proper was created by a storm surge in the 12th century, Sir Francis Drake and other notable privateers sailed from there, in 1338 Edward 111 embarked from Harwich for France with 500 ships, in 1620 the Mayflower sailed from Harwich with the original 132 Pilgrims to America while its captain Christopher Jones was born and lived in

Harwich, Samual Pepys was the Member for Harwich and at the end of WW1 the German submarine fleet surrendered to the Royal Navy in Harwich harbour, in 1918.

Gerald placed our belongings and ourselves in his beloved Volvo and we set of to London. We came to Battersea at 11 o'clock at night and Saint Gerald dropped us at Nick's house.

You might remember Nick the Greek/English croupier of the gambling tables we had met on the island of Krk in the Adriatic Sea, not long after we had left Zagreb. He clearly said if we were in London feel free to call on him any time of the day or night. So we did, at 11 p.m.

Nick was as good his word. His wife was only slightly surprised, most likely because she had been asleep until we came a'knocking. Nick showed us to an empty bedroom, with two beds I might add and we slept the sleep of the deep until about eight the next morning. Battersea is close to the City of London, about five km from Charing Cross and Warren wanted to get to his bank near Australia House. Nick had been our second stroke of consecutive good fortune.

A bus took us most of the way and we were walking the last leg in the City when a bloke on the footpath handed each of us a flyer and at the same time asked if we are thinking of going on a tour of Europe? Without taking his question seriously I said to him, *Thanks mate but we've been on the road in Europe for the past ten months, so thanks but no thanks*. He said, *Are you serious? Have you really done that? Gospel*, I answered, to which he replied, *Are you interested in a job? My boss is looking for people like you.*

I looked at Warren and he said, *Not me mate, I just want to go back to Aus*. I thought about the offer for half a second and asked him what would I have to do? He took a card out of his shirt pocket, wrote a name on it and handing it to me suggested I go and see this man.

Warren went on to his bank while I didn't hesitate. I made my way to the address on the card, asked to see the manager, Henry Ballington, and five minutes later he was sounding me out. He was born in Rhodesia and still had the accent. I enjoyed talking with him, he was five years older than myself, just as tall but of darker complexion, well-mannered and spoken and I thought we were compatible on several fronts. His were all good questions and I was content with how I could answer them and perhaps more importantly with the suggestions and ideas I proffered to Henry. After no more than fifteen minutes he offered me the job, which centred on taking people on tours and talking to others about going on tours, tours that is with Adventure Travel.

Henry told me he wanted me to come back to the office at seven o'clock that evening. He had been advertising the position and had selected three men to interview that night in order to make his final selection. He said to me, *I feel I have to go through with the three interviews as those men have made it that far but I assure you that you have the job.* The due process was adhered to that night, even to the point that in front of the others Henry called me into his office to be interviewed. That caused me momentary concern but at the conclusion Henry announced to one and all that I had the job, true to his word. For a good while neither of us looked back. This success was the third consecutive stroke of good luck, with the brothel's accommodation, Gerald's delivery service to Nick's house and landing a good job within twelve hours of arriving back in London and for most of that time I had been asleep. The three events had occurred within a total of thirty-seven consecutive hours.

Nick had been adamant that we were welcome to stay longer at his house so we stopped there for another two nights and then Warren went back to Australia.

I moved into a flat with John, one of my new workmates and started to learn the ropes. I had to earn my spurs by being on the footpath at times, handing out the flyers and talking to potential customers about the options. We had our own bus and coach drivers and I was the guide, taking groups to see shows in London at night and venturing further afield on days and weekends. Comedy shows were a big hit and I took groups to see the Agatha Christe production, The Mouse Trap. The play opened on my birthday, 25th November, but in 1952 and is still going making it the world's longest-running play. We went to the Royal Albert Hall to see wonderful productions and there must be at least sixty theatres in the West End of London alone, such as The Palladium, Shakespeare's Globe Theatre, The London Colliseum, His Majesty's Theatre, the Theatre Royal Drury Lane and more.

Henry thought I was doing well and said he wanted me to go to a disco and chat up girls to go on even more of our trips and outings. The disco was in Kensington and not easy for me to get there on Monday nights and Henry wanted me to be there every Monday. With care I explained the logistics of its position did make it difficult for me. I shouldn't have worried. Henry gave me a car, a Mini-Minor, with an expense account. When I took people out for the day, the week-end or longer we invariably had to have meals along the way. I suppose it was the custom everywhere for I soon realised the café and restaurant proprietors would not charge me for my meals on account of the business I brought to them. That saved me quite a lot of money and I confess that I took that further. When I filled the car about three-quarters full with petrol and I paid cash the service station would give me an invoice for a full tank and I would be repaid in full. Another lurk was to arrange a phone call home to Australia for the homesick, new arrivals or anyone for that matter. If the regular phone call cost was £3 they could have it for have it for £2, cash. That came about because some of the workers at British Telecom would put the calls through so that no charge at all was incurred. I never took a penny of that but I knew other blokes did and the BT worker pocketed £1.

Now that I had the car I had to attend the disco every Monday night and I had a cash allowance to buy drinks for my prospects and myself. It was good for a while but in the end having to chat up girls and have drinks with them all became a bit tiresome but I battled on. At least my only expense was for rent so I was saving most of my fairly good salary.

Paul McCartney was playing at the Hammersmith, Cat Stephens was doing regular shows. Other performances were the Rocky Horror Show, Joseph and the Amazing Technicolour Dreamcoat, Gypsy, Two Gentleman of Verona, The King and I, and of course, Grease. I took coach loads of people on longer trips to Wales and to the beautiful Lakes district in the central north of England and elsewhere.

There was a fly in the ointment from time to time, there had to be otherwise it was all a dream. Henry was the perfect manager, for the business and I would say for me personally.

However the business was owned by Rupert. He drove a flash MGB and dressed like a dandy, too posh for my liking and that might have been alright if he had left me and some of the others out of his interfering, conniving ways. Let me give you two instances. Rupert liked to big note himself and at his company's expense he hired one of those well-decked out party boats that take people on a cruise along the Thames River at night, no expense spared as regards live music, alcohol, food and flamboyance. How could anyone complain about such a setting?

During the night Rupert was swanning around the main deck with an attractive woman on each arm while those of us he had previously called on to crowd around him at that particular hour were nearby. He had the air of being the man of the moment so it did not seem to surprise anyone when a journalist and a photographer appeared as if from nowhere to interview and film Rupert at the top of his game. But guess what happened? Rupert berated the two interlopers, ridiculing them for invading his privacy, lamenting the fact that he could not be left alone with his dear friends.

Professional as they were the two newspaper men were exposed for their thoughtless intrusion, an embarrassment to their profession. Words would be said. Chastened by Rupert's verbal attack they retreated to the nether parts of the boat.

It was all a put-up job. Rupert had invited the two men to come aboard, bide their time until he gave the signal and proceed to interview him. Then he turned on them. Why? Because Rupert wanted to impress those two young women, regardless of anyone else's feelings.

The second time I saw Rupert was on one of those extravagant

Chapter Ten *Jack the Ripper*

Monday nights at the disco. A man I had not met approached and asked if he could speak with me. He was different from most of the crowd, in his mid-thirties, well dressed and groomed, well-spoken without beating around the bush. He said he had heard I was a responsible, trust-worthy type such as he was looking for. I didn't ask where he heard that but let him, Nicholas, continue.

He told me that he had to have an A4 size envelope delivered by hand to a solicitor's office in Vienna, Austria, by the Friday afternoon of this week. There would not be anything to bring back to London, the job was simply the delivery, without fail. If I accepted the offer the return airfare would be paid by him and as the following day was the week-end I would have accommodation free of any cost, including meals, for the Friday and Saturday nights. This would allow me to stay in Vienna for the week-end and return to London on Sunday afternoon or evening as I desired. For the job itself I would be paid £100.

Now if £100 does not interest you let me say at that time Geoff was working as an accountant outside London and earning £40 per week. If he worked in London proper he would have been on a higher pay level. Nicholas was offering me the equivalent of two and a half week's good pay. Today a qualified accountant working as an employee in Australia would be on $150,000 to $200,000 a year. Being conservative I will say he or she has an annual salary of $160,000 or $3,076 per week. The 2.5 weeks pay would be $3,076 times 2.5 or $7,690 today. Lets round it up to a neat $7,700. That was a massive temptation and I don't deny I accepted Nicholas' offer. We shook hands on it and he said he would stay in touch with me. I would drop off a letter and have free flights London/Vienna return, all accommodation and meals paid and receive the equivalent of A $7,700. Sound too good to be true? Yes. Walk away? No.

I was comfortable with it because I did not imagine a letter of that shape would contain drugs. I went back to the girls but did not say a word about it to anyone.

One hour later Rupert walked up to me and said, *I hear you are going to Vienna on Friday*. I replied in the affirmative, by that I mean my one word of the conversation and he finished it by saying, *I can't stop you as you have an agreement with Nicholas but if you go you are fired*. Without further ado the ..... walked away. I would only see him once more.

Apart from him I was enjoying my London job so I backed out of the Vienna run. Ten years later I was in a business building in Pitt Street, Sydney, taking the lift upstairs when it stopped and three men entered. I recognized Rupert straight away and looked him dead in the eye but he was so busy impressing the other two he never noticed me. Hooroo Rupert.

Henry called a few of us into his office one evening, said Easter is coming up and he would like the firm to do something different for existing and new trips. He requested each of us to give the matter serious thought and come back with our ideas. All would be considered.

I gave it good thought and decided I would need to find something with a difference. I came up with four criteria to go by in my research i.e the past, present and future and the geographical presence of the place I would take the people to.

I settled on the Isle of Wight and I like to think you will understand my reasons why as the trip proceeds. I put the plan to

Henry and he liked it for the fact that the business had never sent anyone there and my proposed itinerary seemed appealing and practical. I had not included the costs but if the back-room people could make it work financially for both the business and the client it would be a goer. The trip was approved and a short advertising campaign implemented.

Eleven people applied and paid so the trip would be on. I was given a Ford Transit van and in those days there were many variants according to the wheelbase, windows, weight, seating, engine and the rest. In addition to the driver's seat there were eleven passenger seats with windows all around and ample luggage space. That was ideal for this trip and for the passengers who were eleven young women. Not one man applied to come with me. I re-read the advertising and could not understand why that would be so but off we went.

It was a good drive down to Southampton which has a strong connection to sea-faring. Henry V's army which won the famous battle of Agincourt sailed from there, the Titanic sailed from there on her fatal maiden voyage in 1912 and the Queen Mary left Southampton on her maiden voyage in 1936. In 2015 I sailed from northern Brazil in the previously mentioned 1911 built barquentine *Europa* and after forty-seven days we managed to make it around Cape Horn. I had earlier sailed four times around various parts of the world with the captain. This time owing to the nature of the voyage which would be that of sailing from east to west, against the wind and the current which is referred to as going *'round the Horn the wrong way,* necessitated that he call for volunteers and fifty sailors from the four corners of the earth came forth. My wife, Janice, and I applied and I was surprised he selected us to be amongst his crew of twenty-four. The resultant challenge, intermittent fear and exhilaration of success is the apogee of my every now and then stepping out of my comfort zone. Every year since then we have been invited to the annual dinner at Southampton to celebrate the rounding as we are official Cape Horners but we have not arrived. It is a long way for dinner.

Southampton is a great harbour and port, being situated near major shipping routes and having proximity to London and also providing rail and road links to Britain that bypass the congestion of the capital. It is at the warmer end of the country and is significantly blessed by having double tides. The tidal flow of the English Channel has Dover at one end and Land's End at the other, with Southampton situated nicely in between. The result is that Southampton experiences high water as the tidal swell moves west to east and another high water as the water reverses to flow from east to west each day.

This movement in time results in Southampton experiencing two high tides of four metres for seventeen hours in the day or seventy per cent of the time. Not as high as at Dover and Land's End but still of great natural advantage in that it is sufficient to handle the largest container ships and the many cruise liners. The port is also blessed by the presence of the Solent, that being the body of water between Southampton and the Isle of Wight. Whilst the latter adds to the favourable tide levels it is probably more important that its physical presence protects the inlet to Southampton from bad weather.

From Southampton I put the van on a ferry which took us on the twenty-five km, one hour crossing to East Cowes. I don't recall what that cost the punters but I know it wasn't noticeable whereas today you might choke on your smoothie as you pay anything from $148 to $437. From what the ferry company says that is one way and they list the return price as from $121-$397 plus a car is $289. Seems wicked to me, for one easy hour.

From there I drove to nearby Cowes which is internationally famous in sailing circles as it hosts the Fastnet Race, the Round the Island Race and Cowes Week. The former is the biennial offshore yacht race that starts in Cowes, goes around Fastnet Rock off the southwest coast of Ireland and finishes in Cherbourg, France. The latter is a world-famous regatta that takes place annually, in Cowes, with up to forty races daily and attended by royalty, the famous, the celebrities and plenty of public competitors and sailors.

Something else that makes the Isle of Wight so attractive is its temperate maritime climate of mild winters and warm summers with its 1,800 to 2,100 hours of annual sunshine. The island only covers 380 sq km and supports a population of some 140,000 residents.

We looked around East Cowes and came to Osborne House. The massive home was built by 1851 on 2,000 hectares for Queen Victoria and Prince Albert and the Queen lived there until her death in 1901. The land component today is some 137 hectares in a lovely environment.

A fraction of the eminent people who have lived on the isle includes the few I recognise as being the writer Charles Dickens, poet John Keats, inventor and radio pioneer Gugielmo Marconi, philosopher Karl Marx, poet Alfred, Lord Tennyson, inventor of the hovercraft Sir Christopher Cockerell, survival expert Bear Grylls, actors Jeremy Irons and David Niven.

When I was a teenager I often heard the Beatles singing *When I'm Sixty-Four*, written by Lennon-McCartney and sung by Paul McCartney. The words refer to renting a cottage on the island. I could never imagine being sixty-four and now I am eighty. Anything can transpire.

We moved on from East Cowes to the island's largest town, Ryde. I am told the Sydney suburb of the same name derives from the island's Ryde. Listening to Paul McCartney again we hear that the Beatles were there, in Ryde, and so inspired by that part of the island that they wrote the song, *Ticket to Ride*. The Rolling Stones came along to the Ryde Pavilion and played there. The island is renowned for its music festivals as you might imagine considering its climate, the space and the freedom enhanced atmosphere away from a big city. Jimi Hendrix turned up to play in West Wight and so did between 600,000 and 700,000 fans.

Tourism is the largest industry with multitudes taking to walking and cycling holidays on the island paradise. You can pretty much walk right around the 113 km coastline. The locals are still into the maritime and industrial traditions of boat-building, sail-making, manufacturing sailing boats, hovercraft and Britian's space rockets. Some of those activities may have come about due to the islanders having to take the brunt of the Spanish Armada as it tried to destroy Southampton and later contributing to the Battle of Britain and being attacked by Germany as it was close to occupied France.

Henry's office had arranged a lovely hotel for us, one so well placed that we could use it as our base for the entire visit. I had one problem. How was I going to entertain eleven attractive young women for five days and five nights?

Chapter Ten *Jack the Ripper*

One day we went back to Cowes and I took the girls to see some of the splendour of the Cowes Corinthian Yacht Club, the Royal Yacht Squadron where the club house is Cowes Castle and the Cowes Royal London Yacht Club, which was open to members only, so they missed us. I partially solved the problem of keeping the girls entertained at night by taking them to a club where a visiting team of amateur football, as in soccer, players were also on the loose. Their eleven players matched my eleven. I was only a few years older than the girls but I watched over them, discretely, and all went well. The next night at another club I let them have a good time with a visiting group of motor-cyclists, not motorbikes. The third night I came up with two teams of darts players and after that on the fourth and fifth nights I took them to a bar or a hotel and kept an eye on them from a distance. I believe by then they were more than happy to have me keeping an eye on them.

It was during the days that I thought we saw the best part of the island and I speak of the village of Godshill with its thatched roof houses and the most attractive private gardens and as a grouping I have never seen better. At times wherever one looked the household scenery was picture-postcard, unbelievably perfect and I do not exaggerate. I have heard people say the Isle of Wight is the most beautiful part of England.

We returned to London and the next night I was seconded to take a group of tourists to Whitechapel in the East End to go on a Jack the Ripper Walk. From April,1888, to February, 1891, eleven women engaged in prostitution in the most vile and dangerous part of London had been murdered and mutilated. The murderer or murderers were never caught let alone identified but at least five of those vicious crimes were committed by the man known as Jack the Ripper. In Whitechapel we met Trevor Seccombe, an acknowledged authority on those five events and he was to guide us to the site of each murder and graphically describe what took place. His tour was always conducted at night, for reality and effect. The darker the night the better for his description of each act of violence was so dramatic I heard one mortified lady say with horror writ clear across her face that by the glow from a lamp-post she could see the victim's blood welling up on the footpath as Trevor spoke.

After each murder we would retire to a nearby pub whereby we all imbibed in a strong drink to recover and prepare for the following gruesome happening. Otherwise I do believe some people could not have carried on without stepping into a well-lit bar where light and laughter were the norm. One of those pubs was The Blind Beggar Hotel at 337 Whitechapel Road. It does not serve food, only alcohol.

In July, 1865, William Booth heard a variety of preachers who were giving talks outside The Blind Beggar and in turn he was invited to speak. His stirring words were such a revelation and inspiration to all that they and his sense of destiny lead to the formation of the Christian Mission which soon became the Salvation Army. In 1904 Bulldog Wallace, a member of the Blind Beggar gang of pickpockets who frequented the pub, stabbed a man in the eye with his umbrella but the big play lay with the kings of the London underworld, the twins Reggie and Ronnie Kray.

In March, 1966, Cornell and Woods were having a quiet drink on bar stools in the pub when Ronnie Kray and Ian Barrie entered. To warn the barmaid and others Barrie fired two shots into the ceiling. Ronnie Kray walked up to Cornell and with his 9 mm Luger shot him once in the forehead, over his right eye, dead. That was where we had our drink.

The tour continued and at one point I noticed a blonde girl in our group wearing a rather fetching full-length cloak that streamed out around her as she briskly rounded a corner of the footpath. She was an English girl just days short of her twenty-third birthday and her Australian girlfriend had failed to turn up. Her name was Janice and fourteen days later I asked her to marry me. People have asked why was I so swift in proposing to her and in my direct way of looking at things I simply thought that I should do so lest I miss the boat. I was fortunate that she accepted as I have no doubt much of whatever I might have achieved in life I could not have done without the benefit of her constant loving and kind-hearted nature that supported and inspired me to not only accept life's regular challenges but to persist. In addition to raising a family she has committed herself to the Country Women's Association of voluntarily caring for others for the past half century. I was truly lucky.

We have now been shackled together for fifty-two years, thanks to Jack the Ripper.

I would have married her then and there but she told me of her work with St. Dunstan's which is an institution founded in 1914 where soldiers and sailors blinded during war are helped and trained to utilize their existing skills and how to use technology to make a life for themselves. By 1929 there were still 2,000 servicemen in their care and many of those were not gunshot or shell casualties but victims of German mustard gas. In addition she was undertaking the Cordon Bleu Cookery school of London and had three months to finish.

Marble Arch, London, where Janice's family lived

With all respect to St. Dunstan's I suggested we wait until she had finished her cooking class. It is not often one marries a girl who will hopefully keep one well fed for a lifetime.

Two weeks before the wedding Janice made certain that I had a decent haircut. After I had obeyed orders I walked into a pub to reminisce and ordered a beer. There were four men seated further along the bar and one of them said hello to me which began a conversation with all of them. They were off-duty plain-clothes detectives. After a while one of them said to the barman, *Have you shown him the cellar?* while nodding his head in my direction. The barman replied no and not wishing to be off-side with the police he said *but I will.*

The barman lifted up a section of the counter and told me to come though and follow him as he walked to the far end of the bar. There

Chapter Ten   *Jack the Ripper*

London fashions in late 1960s/early 1970s

he leaned down and lifted up a section of the floor to reveal a flight of steps leading down into the depths. We descended into a cellar that became a tunnel and we walked along until it was blocked off to stop further progress. This was where condemned prisoners underwent their death walk to Tyburn, now known as Marble Arch, to be hanged.

In days gone by the prisoners were taken from Newgate Prison and placed on a horse-drawn cart for the five km journey to Tyburn. Invariably the trip took three hours as an average crowd of 30,000 people would attend along the way. In 1724 the notorious and popular prison escapee and highway man Jack Sheppard is said to have drawn a crowd of 200,000. Due to the crush of people it was decided to transfer the prisoners underground for the last minutes of their life and a tunnel was built from underneath the pub I was in, the Masons' Arms, to the gallows at Marble Arch. We could not go the whole way as the tunnel, which still has some of the prisoners' manacles attached to the wall, has been sealed off. When a man was hanged some of the crowd would rush forward to either reach up to his legs and pull them down to ensure a quick death or to touch his hands for good luck, for themselves. As the procession stopped at the pub to transfer the condemned to the tunnel the prisoners were allowed a last drink, sometimes more than one. Hot spiced rum was a favourite. The expression *One for the Road* was first coined there as was the word *hangover*.

I walked to Marble Arch where there is a traffic island around which high volumes of vehicles speed past. In its centre, laid into the ground is a circular plaque which states *The site of the Tyburn Tree*, meaning the gallows on which those prisoners met their end. I marvelled at this footnote to history being no more than a blur to many of the drivers.

As with most Londoners Janice knew that and far more than I but she had not been to the Masons' Arms. She agreed to return with me and fortunately the barman was kind enough to take her down into the cellar to see for herself what had fascinated me.

One week before the wedding I took myself off for one last taste of freedom. I had found a package deal to Paris I could not pass up. It included return flights London/Paris, transfers to and from the accommodation which was a lovely one-bedroom apartment for two nights with a balcony overlooking a gorgeous garden in the heart of the city and transfers and entry ticket to Longchamp racecourse for the racehorse meeting of the year, the Prix de l' Arc de Triomphe, the biggest horse-race in France. All this for nineteen English pounds or thirty-one Australian dollars. I remember those numbers.

I also recall selecting the American-bred three-year old filly *Allez France* to win the Arc over 2,400 metres with twenty-seven starters, a big field in my eyes. She beat all but one as she could not run down the leader *Rheingold*, ridden by England's champion jockey, Lester Piggott. I had been reluctant to go against Piggott and I knew he was riding an English horse, *Sparkler*, in the upcoming Prix du Moulin de Longchamp, which I believe was the European championship over one mile or 1,600 metres. I doubled my bet on Lester and he duly won.

I remembered Claudette, the French girl who I ran into at the service station and who had invited me to call on her in Paris. I thought on the eve of my wedding that would not be appropriate, even if the building now had a lift to the seventh floor.

Janice and her mother intended to have the wedding at their church in Marylebone but at that time it was discovered that the Vicar was having an affair with one of his parishioners. It was announced the Bishop was instigating an investigation into the matter and placed nuptials and other services at that church on hold. Thus the wedding took place at the Marylebone Town Hall's Registry Office, a popular place for weddings. Others who signed on there include Ringo Starr, Antonio Banderas, Melanie Griffith, Cilla Black, Liam Gallagher, Ronnie Wood and Paul McCartney, twice. People always remark how stunning the building and beautiful the rooms.

Wedding of Janice and Bill, London

Mario and Wendy came from Italy for the wedding, a few mates from work were there and Janice and her family supplied the real numbers. The reception was at the nearby and rather swish, four-star Mandeville Hotel, Marylebone, a four-minute walk from Bond Street. Late in the night we drove to Haslemere, sixty km south-west of London and in south Surrey for a brief honeymoon. The town is set amongst rolling green fields and as the brochures said it is a charming market town with timbered and tile-hung houses and cottages. We stayed there for three days, returned to London and then with Wendy and Mario drove down to Brighton where Janice's cousin, Carol, lent us a two-bedroom flat for a week.

One evening we went out along the famous Brighton Pier to the Penny Arcade and played games and relaxed as it was out of season and not many people were out and about. It was a load of fun. Later that night a storm blew up and destroyed the theatre and much of the Pier which was eventually rebuilt. Today it is 525 metres long with 137 km of planking and so its annual repainting takes three months. At night it is lit up by 67,000 light bulbs.

I returned to work and Henry promptly wanted to see me. He looked well-pleased with himself as he asked me to be seated across from his desk. He said it was time for me to step up and to do that he wanted me, as a guide, to take a coachload of people to Russia. I knew from his perspective that was a significant opportunity and normally I would have accepted, free travel and all. He was still grinning when I resigned.

I know I disappointed Henry who had been good to me and I did feel bad about that but as I explained to him I had experienced problems in Russia and I had only confessed to what they charged me with. I had been let out but I was on the list and if they had caught certain people and my name came up they would hold me for longer if I went back. I could not risk that. As it was I had only recently been kicked out of Moldova, Ukraine and Germany.

I would go on to visit 120 countries and visas and the like were sometimes an issue. When I sailed from Argentina to Antarctica to South Africa I had no visa because the South Africans classed me as a sailor and said I could stay for seven days but no longer or they would be dealing with me. I entered North Korea without the use of visa or passport. The official North Korean line was that if something happened to me, or anyone else, they could say I was never there. I was in Syria heading for the Iraq border when insurgents were being chased by American helicopter gunships every time they attempted to cross the border, so Iraq was taken off the menu. In Boliva we were on the verge of crossing into Peru when our bus was stopped because rebel Bolivians were kidnapping foreigners at the border to force the government to share the national mineral wealth with the people. We could not enter there. In Sri Lanka I was invited to Saudi Arabia, by a Saudi family but their government would not allow me a visa because I was not a government official or a businessman.

I could have stayed on with Henry's team but I simply decided to go as much as I enjoyed it. In those days goods arriving by many ships came into London rather than the coastal ports. Janice's father sometimes had damaged goods, furniture, canned food, all manner of things to offload from the ships he salvaged. When necessary he used a London hustler by the name of Reg to distribute the goods to advantage as the Regs of the world know the highways and the byways that you and I don't even see. So I went to work as Reg's off-sider, loading and unloading his truck around parts of London that I would never otherwise have known about, doing deals delivering goods to people of certain character.

Reg was fair to me, I learned a lot about how others live and he paid me in cash, his world. One day I noticed an ad. in the newspaper regarding a hotel position at Gunton Hall in East Anglia. Something unknown about that interested me and I went up there for an interview.

Gunton Hall and all its lands belonged to the Gunton family in the 12th century, by the 16th century it was the Jermyn family who had control and the current house was built for Sir William Harbord, 1st Baronet in the 1740s. His son, The Right Honourable The Lord Suffield Sir Harbord Harbord, born 1734, succeeded him. When I arrived it was a charming 18th century manor hotel set amongst walled gardens and vast woodlands swathed in history.

I was shown to the superb wood-paneled office of the current operator, Andrew Brettingham, a gentleman to his immaculately polished boot-straps. After a polite investigative conversation Andrew proceeded to describe the available position, to which I rather tersely replied, without beating about the bush, *I didn't come here to be a waiter.*

Andrew kept a stiff upper lip and after a thoughtful silence he said, *I have a club not far from here. I open it for the summer season. Would the manager's position interest you?*

Andrew's offer was for me to manage the Magic Circle Club at nearby Hopton-on-Sea, a village of 3,000 people by the beach on the North Sea. The club itself was a huge building catering to many of the summer holiday-makers who flock there every year for the good times. In addition to a well-organized bar there would be live entertainment every night, without fail. Andrew's office would arrange that. It consisted of a variety of comedians, singers, ventriloquists, musicians, story-tellers, people of quality who could entertain with traditional British humour. They had to be good as no less than 5,000 Scots descend on the area for their annual summer holidays, let alone other visitors. He had a caravan park close by and for accommodation I could have my choice of caravan, rent-free, for the season plus a worthy salary. He asked if my wife would be interested in that line of work and I told him she would be a huge asset to the enterprise. However she was completing her Cordon Bleu school and we could not start for another ten days. Andrew assured me that was perfect timing and Janice would also be paid. I would find that I would need to employ at least two local people for the bar and also a no-nonsense security officer. Furthermore I would have a car, a Mini-Minor van for picking up supplies and orders, all expenses paid. We shook hands on the arrangement and I returned to London where I did another eight days for Reg, who made sure they were big days, God bless the rogue in him.

Before leaving Reg and London I took two hours off to go the Ritz Hotel and shout myself a prestige morning tea in the hotel's Palm Court. I duly entered the five-star hotel and I was rejected, politely but firmly turned away, on the basis that I was not appropriately attired. Fair enough but not the end of the road. I immediately rejoined Reg at work and requested I have the two hours on the morrow. He agreed.

Next morning I had a bath, washed that and my hair off with a shower, doused myself with deodorant, put on what was good enough to be married in, along with a dash of confidence and highly polished shoes. At the Ritz I was directed to a well-positioned table and served in style. Mission accomplished I changed into my working clobber suitable for the East End.

Janice completed her course and finished her horse-riding in London. For fifteen years, since the age of eight, she had been riding in nearby Hyde Park for horse-owners who had little time to ride their own horses. Owners who had placed them in surrounding stables came to know of her ability and reliability. In return for her

Chapter Ten *Jack the Ripper*

The Household Cavalry, London

riding their horses they did not charge her as they did with regular people. The fee at that time to ride a horse in Hyde Park was £1 for one hour. Today it is £115 for a one-hour lesson and up to £145 an hour for a private ride. Janice often rode horses from Ross Nye's Stables which unfortunately are now closed after 65 years. The stables were nearby on the other side of adjoining Bayswater Road. Coming from there she would usually enter Hyde Park at Victoria Gate and could then have a good ride to Marble Arch, which was where she lived. These days that end of the riding track has been reduced due to the placement of the roundabout and resumption of that corner section of Hyde Park, to Cumberland.

Amongst her many steeds were two white geldings Pall and Mall. Those two horses were used by Rothmans of Pall Mall to take their carriage around Knightsbridge, Mayfair and elsewhere to promote

The Rothmans coach horses, Pall and Mall, which Janice regularly rode to exercise them

Rothmans products. Good exercise as far as it went but they required more so Janice was hired to gallop the two horses around Hyde Park. That type of exercise was not permitted but she was told that the excuse was to be that the horse had bolted. She rode them many times and no one ever queried her early morning fast riding.

When Janice was riding in Hyde Park there came the time when she was approached by members of The Household Cavalry, the Queen's personal bodyguard then but King Charles' now, consisting of members of the Royal Horse Guards and the Ist Dragoons. Those units have seen action since 1660 including the Battle of Waterloo in 1815. It seems some of those men might have wanted to chat her up and so they would suggest they have a horse-race. Galloping was and is banned in Hyde Park but these races took place at The Mile on Rotten Row at dawn. Even so there were few if any people around at dawn and Rotten Row is lined with large and superb plane trees, so numerous that in the season their foliage would protect the riders from prying eyes. Roton Row is not what it sounds but a lovely 1,400 metre long, straight, track that connects West Carriage Drive to Hyde Park Corner. The track was constructed by bricks being laid as

Chapter Ten *Jack the Ripper*

Horse races at dawn between the plane trees

a base and then covered with sand, perfectly suitable for equestrian purposes. In the 18th and 19th centuries it was a favourite setting for the elite and others to ride, to parade their horses and carriages and for fashion.

At night it was another matter, a dangerous one for it was then frequented by highwaymen and robbers. King William 111 established Rotten Row in 1690 as he required a safe ride from Kensington Palace, where he lived, to St. James Palace, the seat of government. The track was lit by 300 oil lamps, thereby creating the first artificially lit highway in England. The name, Rotten Row appears to have been derived from the French expression, Rue de Roi, the King's Road.

The cavalry horsemen did not know that Leo, Janice's favoured horse, was an ex-racehorse. He had been trained by Harry Wragg who won three English Derbys as a jockey and a fourth Derby as a trainer. Mr. Wragg used Leo to educate his up and coming two and three year olds. I don't know what if any races Leo actually won but Janice tells me Leo never liked another horse going past him. Janice and Leo beat off every challenge by the cavalry. They never beat Leo and Janice and therefore the time came when they no longer challenged her.

After her usual riding in London's Hyde Park and when we later settled down in Dubbo Janice would ride regularly in Australia for thirty-seven years. When we had raised and educated our family and resumed travelling she would go on to ride in the desert sands of Egypt, at 10,000 feet in the Tien Shah mountains of Kyrgyzstan, in Canada, India, Bhutan, Peru and in land-locked Paraguay where

Rotton Row, Hyde Park, London when people and horses paraded

Chapter Ten *Jack the Ripper*

we stayed on a farm during a South American camping trip. I rode with her in the Pantanal wetlands of Brazil and she later rode with a friend we travelled with to the village known as Morro de Sao Paulo, on the northern tip of Tinhare Island, sixty km off the coast of Brazil. Most thrilling of all I joined her on a three-week horse-riding expedition across western Mongolia, with three Mongolian horsemen.

I was sorry for Janice's mother as I was taking her daughter away, temporarily but it would soon enough be permanent. The Australian girl, Clare, who did not turn up at the Jack the Ripper walk proved a good friend to Janice, and I, as she kindly drove us and our gear from London to Hopton-on -Sea. However the caravan was not ready so we were given a holiday cabin at Gunton Hall and we stayed there

Janice and her favourite horse, Leo

Janice and Leo

for several days with full board at no cost to us. That was a good start thanks to Andrew.

When we moved to the caravan and opened the club I hired a local couple, Roy and Iris. They had worked at the club in recent years, were a dream to be with as they were as honest as the day was long, knew the ropes and their good nature ensured everyone enjoyed their company, on both sides of the bar. They were that efficient I did not need to hire more bar staff, the four of us could cover everything. That left the security person. Hopton-on-Sea is eight km north of Lowestoft and six km south of Great Yarmouth, which has the bigger population. Today it has 100,000 residents. I went to the Great Yarmouth police station and hired a policeman to work the door at night for me when he was off-duty. This bloke, another Roy, had no neck. He was 1.67 meters tall, nearly as broad with meat-plate fists, a confident way about him and sired by a bull. To enter the Magic Circle Club the punters had to pass through a glass-walled cubicle which I could easily see into from the bar. Roy occupied the cubicle and everyone had to get past him.

One busy night but they were all busy, I looked up from the bar to serve the next customers and found myself confronted by three men with their faces painted exactly the same as the members of the rock band, KISS. My first reaction was, what's going on here? I looked across to Roy and he was ahead of me. He was already giving me the thumbs up sign, all OK. Another time I sensed something and looked across at Roy as he was confronted by an awkward customer who wanted in. I just had time to see Roy deliver one short blow to the man's solar plexus and he slid down the wall without a sound before being discretely helped outside. The fellow obviously wasn't well. If Roy couldn't be there he always sent me the next best man and that moment apart we never had any trouble that came to my attention.

The nightly entertainment ensured we had a packed house every night, thanks in no small measure to the visiting Scots who were great patrons. Unlike the stories I had heard about them being tight they were generous with their money. When they bought a round they would invariably say as they handed the money over the counter, *and have one for yourself.* So if they bought five drinks for five pounds I would pick up a bottle of beer so they could see it,

Janice, when Bill met her in London

acknowledge them and then place that bottle at the end of the bar where I already had a growing collection of unopened bottles of beer. Then I would charge them an extra pound to cover the extra drink and they knew that. After we cleaned up when everyone had gone home I would sell those bottles back to the bar. The four of us did that, Roy the barman and I buying beer by the bottle and Iris and Janice putting aside a bottle of Babycham each time they were tipped. It was all upfront, honest and allowed by Andrew. It meant that for the four months we were there we never touched our salary, it all went into the bank and stayed there.

We had been at the club for ten weeks when two men in suits arrived early one morning, unannounced. They said they were the auditors, I believed them and left them to their job.

Something else that made the club so good were the travelling show people. They came every year, set up their equipment next door and due to their high levels of competence never caused one iota of remiss. Two brothers, Ernie and George ran the dodgem cars which were always popular with kids and adults alike, others had a ferris wheel, zero gravity ride, balloon darts, weight guessing, ring tossing, the popular Punch and Judy show, clowns in whose mouth children place a ping-pong ball, air rifle shooting, fortune tellers etc. One of my favourite characters was Eddie who had a fish and chips takeaway. Every day he would come in for his favourite beer, a bottle or two of Worthington E. Eddie was so relaxed and fun to be around yet always with an appropriate remark when the talk might be serious. I did like Eddie and I never struck anyone else who asked for Worthington E but we stocked a few crates for him.

Sadly the day came when the season ended and once more there was a round of fond farewells. At the same time the auditors returned and silently did what they do best.

Janice and I drove to Gunton Hall to thank Andrew for the opportunity and the pleasure. The man did surprise me, saying that he had just received the auditors' final report. They had gone over the accounts with a fine tooth comb and he was pleased to know that we had not touched him for one penny. As it was mostly a cash business that was particularly good. So good that he said to me, *You may keep the car, it is yours and you have my thanks.*

We made our goodbyes with Andrew and I was able to take the car to the service station for the last time, having it serviced and replacing four tyres and the battery before returning to London. We had intended to leave for Australia but having the Mini-Van we opted to take it for a run around Scandinavia. I will not be writing about that trip for three reasons, being; 1 My last book ran to 162,000 words and that is probably too much when photos are added and I intend to make this book little more than 105,000 words. 2, Years later Janice and I would return to Scandinavia and I believe that trip which included sailing as crew aboard the barquentine, *Europa*, rather than driving was far more interesting than this one would be. 3 With all due respect to Scandinavia and Denmark in particular I do find that the wealthier and higher standard-of-living countries are sometimes not so adventurous.

Having said that I would like to mention one matter. We were driving through the mountains of northern Norway when in an isolated area with no apparent settlements for many km we rounded a bend in the road and came upon the flags of New Zealand and Australia proudly flying at full stretch in the breeze and some twenty metres apart, large flags. We partially learned their story. It appears that New Zealand and Australian airmen died there in World War Two while fighting the forces of Germany.

We returned to London and I continued to use the car for a couple of weeks for getting around. Geoff was now in London so Janice and I went to Swiss Cottage in north London a few times with Geoff and his girlfriend for dinner and real ale. It is such a great all-round

Chapter Ten *Jack the Ripper*

pub with ambience galore and much appreciated by many as it is no more than a two minute walk to the nearest train station, making it easy for those patrons to make their way home. I then had no trouble selling the Mini-Van to an eager South African traveller. Having studied the possibilities of returning to Australia by an interesting route we signed up to travel with a group by the name of Sundowners who had acquired a retired London single-decker bus and intended to drive it from London to Kathmandu.

CHAPTER ELEVEN

Mary of the Mongols

I am the punishment of God. If you had not committed great sins, God would not have sent a punishment like me upon you.
— Attributed to Genghis Khan.

Janice and I left her mother's Marylebone home early in the morning and made our way to Earl's Court where we met our fellow travellers and departed from there at 7.30 a.m. Almost immediately we fell in with two other newly-wed couples, being Charlie and Natalie Szabo from Canada and Glen and Anne Mitchell from Sydney.

The journey would take forty-four days but there was no guarantee as Sundowners had never done the run. If we made it there then we would fly home via Singapore to Sydney. We didn't mind if it was a camping trip although that wasn't to be but we could expect the accommodation at times would be only a notch above that. Should be interesting.

It had been decided that as most of us had been around Europe beforehand that the bus would proceed quickly though those countries and allow us more time in the Middle East and beyond. We began by

Chapter Eleven   *Mary of the Mongols*

taking the ferry from Dover to Zeebrugge, in Belgium. That went well for us and I say that because a few years later the ferry capsized near Zeebrugge with 650 passengers on board and tragically 193 of them died. From there we drove on through the night across Belgium, a corner of Holland and into Germany via another favourite of mine, Cologne, and then Frankfurt and arrived at Munich twenty-four hours after we set off. We continued on and were in lovely Innsbruck for which I also have a soft spot, for an early lunch, having already covered about 1,300 km. We stayed there for the rest of the day as it was Austria's national day. In the town square we watched 150 performers dressed in black-buckled shoes, white stockings to the knees, black breeches with light green jackets and soft felt hats rolled up at the sides and with two white feathers at the back.

The following morning we departed Innsbruck and its surrounding snow-capped mountains, drove over and down the Brenner Pass and into Italy, passing by Trento to Verona, over to Trieste and into what was then Yugoslavia to Zagreb, where we had an awful lunch but stayed in a top hostel. The next day saw us driving on to Skopje, the capital of Macedonia, through part of Greece and into Turkey. The country was celebrating its national day and having a public holiday with flags everywhere and also the Turkish Army being prominent.

This was my second time to Turkey and whilst it came to be my favourite country all too often I was appalled by the local driving. On this day three coaches overtook our old bus, all tightly packed nose to tail while going into a blind corner, uphill. The road going up was single lane while going downhill it was somehow one and a half lanes. Death was waiting.

Innsbruck, Austria

We made it to Istanbul and settled into a rough hotel near the Sultan Ahmet Mosque. We had dinner on the Galata Bridge which is a great place to dine being over the water with harbour views. It is in the Golden Horn. Charlie and Natalie, Glen and Anne joined us.

In the morning the muezzin chanted the six o'clock call to prayers for the faithful from the balcony of a minaret of the Blue Mosque, which allowed him to move around and call in all directions. The words are not in Turkish but Arabic and unchanged since Islam began.

The Blue Mosque is one of Istanbul's main attractions. From the outside it takes the eye with its central dome surrounded by four semi-domes over the prayer hall and edged by not four but six minarets. The many thousands of tiles inside the mosque are what gives it the blue title. The tiles were manufactured by potters in the town of Iznik, which by road is 200 km south-east of Istanbul. From the last quarter of the 15th century until the 17th century the town's potters

Chapter Eleven   *Mary of the Mongols*

Hagia Sophia, the Church of Wisdom, Istanbul

produced these extraordinary tiles painted with cobalt blue under a transparent lead glaze, which I presume ensured their longevity. Later other colours were included. The tile designs combined traditional Ottoman arabesque patterns with flowing Chinese elements. They are beautiful but sadly during the 17th century the quality of such tiles fell away and they were no more. In fact when the Blue Mosque was completed in 1617 is believed to be the last significant building to be decorated with Iznik tiles. They can also be seen in sections of the Hagia Sophia, the Rustem Pasha mosque and the Topkapi Palace such as in the Circumcision room and the Baghdad kiosk.

We returned to the Topkapi Palace for our second visit, with the others and then went to explore one of the many features of Istanbul that you will not find in other cities, leastways of comparable size. I refer to the cisterns of the city. Similar to other cities Constantinople received much of its water supply via aqueducts and storage facilities outside the city. The first underground cistern within the city walls was built by the Emperor Theodosius between 428 and 443. More followed that success and in 532 the Emperor Justinian, helped by 7,000 slaves, constructed the large Basilica Cistern. This underground chamber of some 9,800 square metres could hold 80,000 cubic meters of water.

To support the underground ceiling no less than 336 marble columns, each nine metres high were arranged in twelve rows of twenty-eight columns each spaced five metres apart. Some of the columns were of various marble types as well as granite. The weight of the cistern is carried on those columns by way of utilizing cross-shaped vaults and round arches. We entered the Basilica Cistern and went down into the depths where boats have been used to carry

The underground Basilica Cistern, Istanbul

people across the water. It is fascinating and to the citizens and the defending soldiers the cisterns must have been life-saving during the centuries when Constantinople was besieged by no less than twenty-three armies.

Istanbul's Grand Bazaar is one of the world's largest and oldest markets, with sixty-one covered streets and close to 4,000 shops over an area of 30,700 square metres. Daily visitors number are said to be anywhere from 250,000 to 400,000. Many people claim the city that has the most visitors a year is Las Vegas with 39.6 million visitors. The Grand Bazaar is closed on Sundays but even with its daily average of 292,500 it welcomes a reputed 91,250,000 people each year, more than twice Las Vegas.

Within reason and budget the Bazaar can be a shoppers' paradise and especially so when there are streets where all the shops are offering similar products, such as streets that sell jewellery or perfumes, leather goods or lamps, gold or shoes, carpets or ancient coins. We stepped up and made a few purchases such as a small hand-made rug from central Turkey. We still use it inside the front door of our house for people to wipe their footwear, so it has been durable for over half a century and wonderful value. Our major purchase, for Janice and I individually, was a three-quarter length Afghan coat, lined with sheep's wool. Janice's coat is a rare colour of light burgundy with blue embroidery and it is still in close to pristine condition. Only recently our daughter and grand-daughter were admiring it. I can only describe my coat colour as a cross between lime and mustard yellow with cream embroidery which really set it off. Lord knows how the lime mustard yellow colour was produced but it was superb, too good for me and unfortunately I eventually wore it out.

It is easy to spend a lot of time looking at the goods on well-organised display when the thousands of shops are under one contiguous roof. In Indian markets men come and hustle you to their master's shop but in Turkey they usually call out the advantages of their goods. I found that of interest because there are so many tongues to be heard let alone understood with millions of visitors from wherever. One caller in particular caught my attention as he was a dark-skinned man with a good number of light-skinned, blonde headed customers speaking in a language I did not know. When his customers had gone I jumped in and asked him about that. A local Turk he told me that not so long ago he had heard a language new to him but more often as the weeks went by. He inquired and realised such people were coming in from Denmark on cruise ships, in ever increasing numbers. So after hours he studied the Danish language, learned it well enough and when he heard Danes talking as the crowds of people passed by he was able to hail them, invite them to see his goods and definitely increase his already numerous language skills and his sales. Industrious man.

In the early 1970s most, if not the majority of the buildings in Istanbul, were constructed of timber and on our way back we passed a three-story building which was burning fiercely. The fire brigade arrived and salvaged what they could. Fires had long been a problem when timber buildings were so close together and accidently or not quite a few churches had suffered that fate but many of them literally rose again from the ashes.

Armenia was the first country to convert to Christianity, in 301. followed by Georgia and Ethiopia, and there are thirty-five Armenian churches in Muslim Istanbul. Janice and I walked to one of the largest Armenian churches but I cannot be certain now if it was the 14th century St. Gregory the Illuminator Church or the St George Armenian Church. Based on its city location and my liking for good old St George who pops up in many parts of the world I do think it was the latter. No matter.

We tentatively entered the church. As a service was not in progress it was surprising to see many people gathered inside. They were all smartly dressed irrespective of their age, standing in small groups and talking quietly. A few people approached us and realizing we did not speak their language conversed with us in excellent and politely spoken English. The more of their friends they introduced us to the more welcomed and at home we felt.

Of course Constantinople was a Greek city long before Istanbul became a Turkish city and whilst the Muslims destroyed all too many Greek churches some still exist. On Sunday we saw a number of buses coming into Istanbul from Greece. We were told they are Greeks coming a long way to worship where once their ancestors and churches dominated, most important of all and in big numbers, at the time of the Greek Orthodox Easter.

Having resumed our walking we came to a tea house where a young couple were sitting by the open window looking out on to the street. I was so taken by their appearance and relaxed manner with each other I presumed they must be in love. Furthermore I had the distinct impression theirs would be a marriage that would joyfully carry them into old age. I asked if I could take their photograph, from the street and through the open window. I still have that photo as I do my faith in them to justify my perception.

Janice and I then entered the tea house and partook of tea in the

Bill and Janice joined this young couple at a Turkish tea house in Istanbul.

Turkish manner, without milk as they do but in my case without sugar whereas Turks love sugar in tea. They should know what is good as on a per person basis Turkey is by far the highest consumer of tea, averaging nearly twice as much as third placed Britain. The tea is normally consumed in a glass which in winter warms the hand and in summer the indentations in the glass permit it to be easily and comfortably held by two fingers. The tea houses are constructed of loving timber that is smooth and easy to maintain and keep clean. Thus they are extremely popular family gathering places to meet and greet and where men often play backgammon.

I was told the early morning is the best time to have a Turkish massage as they are not busy then. I am not talking about a Turkish bath or some other pampered therapy treatment. I was after the real McCoy where an old hand with all the techniques of centuries

Chapter Eleven   *Mary of the Mongols*

The fabulous Cemberlitis Turkish baths of Istanbul

past would pummel my body to the nth degree but ensure that all the kinks, aches and pains and other unwanted contortions I have accumulated over the years would be long-time removed.

I found the Cemberlitas Hammam or bathhouse, which was built in 1584 and has been in continuous use ever since. I met my torturer and after stripping me down to a loin cloth and sandals he placed me in a hot-house to loosen me up and perhaps soften me up. He then took me to another room with a large circular marble slab which is also heated to make you work up a sweat before the treatment begins. I did observe that the slab slightly rose towards the centre so that it had a mild but definite hump to it. I don't know why that was so and once the brute started work on me I didn't care. Two other men were being similarly massaged, Andy an Englishman and Hiram a Canadian.

He began by using a coarse mitt to scrub my entire body. The idea was to remove dead skin cells and I was glad I had the three major levels plus about seven minor layers of skin for it felt as though he had scrubbed the epidermis or external skin clean off me. When he rolled me over, which was far quicker than I could at the time, I found myself looking up at the domed ceiling. It was perforated by hexagonal holes that let glowing beams of sunlight into the room. I had never experienced anything like that and somehow even it felt healthy.

That moment of brief relief was the signal to test the other side of my body and then for the real work to begin. Putting his mitt aside, the one that had previously been used in place of a wire brush to scrape corrosion off abandoned tractors for spare parts, he took hold of my limbs, one by precious one.

A full body massage includes your arms, legs, hands, feet, neck and back, stomach and buttocks. If you have had a regular massage I assure you that you were let off rather easily. These willing warriors go at you for the best part of an hour as if they respect you, in other words they assume you will not concede one whimper as they pound, pummel, pull and pulp every facet of your body. I might have let a soft groan escape but I was adamant I was not going to orally concede one sound to the master. You might say I am boasting but to the best of my mind I held my ground silently. It became a challenge to take the punishment and even to look forward to the next onslaught just so I could stay the course. I believe I did that. Otherwise I suppose I would not mention it.

The master finished his work, spoke to me in Turkic with a sly grin and slapped me on the back as he directed me to the showers. I was incredibly sore but already feeling the benefit. The sensation of being resurrected increased over the next few days. I felt fabulous then.

Hiram took his medicine well but Andy was always groaning as his masseur worked him over. He told me he was on his honeymoon but he wouldn't be able to perform for a while.

Janice was also given a solid massage, by a man, but she survived it and was happy she had experienced the process of a genuine Turkish massage. Good on her. The English rose was proving herself tough. She would need to be before too long.

Prior to leaving London and after enjoying my first visit to Istanbul I had carried out research into the city and having learned something of interest, as soon as we had arrived in Istanbul on this occasion I contacted the headquarters of the Turkish First Army at their Selimine Army Barracks across the Bosphorus. I had discovered that during the Crimean War when England and Turkey combined in war against Russia that Florence Nightingale served as a manager and trainer of nurses in that cruel conflict.

She brought thirty-eight nurses, new ideas and a determination to do good for wounded British Army soldiers and others in Turkey in the 1850s. She became known for her devotion to nursing and health reforms and epitomised the Victorian feminine ideal of good works, cleanliness, compassion and godliness. Due to her regular checking on every ill or wounded soldier in her care during the night, when she did her rounds while carrying a lantern, she became known as The Lady with the Lamp. The principal hospital in Constantinople in which she and her nurses were stationed was at Scutari, these days known as Uskudar, Istanbul.

Florence Nightingale was credited by Henri Dunant of Geneva, Switzerland, as his inspiration for founding the International Red Cross in the 1860s and for his co-working that resulted in the creation of the Geneva Convention. Whilst Florence Nightingale was stationed at Scutari the Turkish Army maintained private rooms for her at the prestigious Selimine Army Barracks and whilst it was unlikely, we were keen to see them, if that might be possible.

Turkey has four armies spread across the country and the Selimine barracks are the biggest and as it would defend Istanbul, the most important. To gain entry permission we needed to submit

Turkish First Army headquarters at Istanbul where Florence Nightingale was granted quarters on the third and fourth floors of the north-west tower

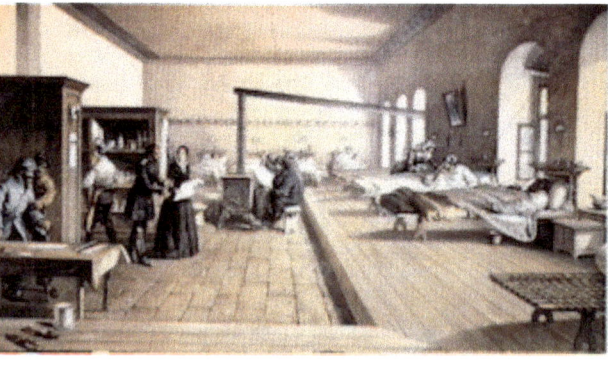

Florence Nightingale's Treatment Room in the tower

to interrogation, repeated identification proving, security scans and inspections by armed guards. This took two days overall and then we took a ferry across the Bosphorus, were admitted into the base, handed from one soldier to another before being issued with red security approved tags and taken through the base. It is huge and at one time was said to be the biggest army base in the world, bigger than the Pentagon. Eventually Janice and I were escorted into the office of a Lieutenant-Colonel.

After we underwent yet another grilling of no less than fifteen minutes he smiled and accepted us. Not only that but he and an escort marched us down a corridor that must be the length of the enormous building with framed photographs of former Army commanders looking down on us from both sides. At the end of the corridor we came to one of the four corners of the building, the one that converts into the north-west tower and the First Army Museum. From there the Lieutenant-Colonel led us up a winding staircase and on the third floor we came to Florence Nightingale's treatment room where she also tended wounded soldiers, the officers. Here we saw the antique chest tube that was for the drainage of certain wounds and used by Nightingale herself. The officers took us up to the fourth floor with its glorious views overlooking the busy waters of the Bosphorus and we entered the spotless rooms formerly occupied by Florence Nightingale. Her bed, desk, twenty personal letters, etc are exactly as she used them. Wow, how good was that. At least that was how the situation struck Janice and I, far better than we ever imagined it might be.

Overcrowding, poor sanitation and rampant diseases caused a high death toll among the soldiers. Florence Nightingale implemented strict hygienic practices, improved patient care and a systematic approach to nursing thereby reducing mortality rates dramatically. She is regarded as having laid the foundation of modern nursing.

Selimine Army Barracks is a military installation officially closed to the public although a few people do gain admittance. For some reason the gods ordained Janice and I could also.

As I wrote in my book, *Skirmish Hill*, Prince Alfred, second son of Queen Victoria was on a walkabout at Clontarf in Sydney in 1868 when a gunman shot him in the back from close range, the bullet lodging a fraction to the right of his spine. His life was saved in good part by the presence of six nurses who had arrived in Sydney one month earlier after being trained by Florence Nightingale.

Further research into the history of Constantinople uncovered the life of Maria Palaiologina. She was the daughter of the Constantinople Emperor Michael V111 who sent her to be married to Hulegu Khan, as a means of keeping the Mongols from attacking Constantinople. Hulegu Khan was a grandson of Genghis Khan and his armies ruled the western Asian lands of the Transcaucasus, of Persia, Iraq and Syria. He totally destroyed the great city of the time, Baghdad. Maria was in select company for Hulegu Khan's brother Kublai Khan ruled over all of China while another grandson of Genghis Khan and brother to Hulegu and Kublai was Batu Khan whose empire for 250 years was what would be Russia.

As fate would have it Hulegu died as Maria arrived so she was then married to his son, Abaqa Khan. She had a position of power and influence but when Aqaba Khan died fifteen years later, in 1282, she took advantage of the temporary uncertainty amongst the vacant leadership to make her escape. She was able to return to Constantinople and refused to allow her father to trade her off again. Instead she rebuilt a nunnery and church, which is still in the same shape as it was after her rebuilding, in 1285. She retired to that complex until she died. The church is on the top of a hill that on 29th May, 1453, saw the last defenders of Constantinople valiantly trying to hold off the attacking Turkish Ottoman army in that very street. The Turks call that church *Kanh Kllise* or Church of the Blood and the street leading to it from the Golden Horn is still known *as Sancaktar Yokusu* or the Ascent of the Standard Bearer in honour of a Turkish standard bearer who went down fighting there.

The Turkish commander was Mehmed II aka Mehmet the Conqueror and because the Mongols had been highly regarded for centuries he spared Maria's church. It is the only surviving Byzantine Christian or Eastern Orthodox church in Istanbul and I wanted to find it.

It wasn't difficult to obtain the address of the church known to the Greeks as *Panaghia Muchliotissa* or Mary of the Mongols but finding someone willing to take us there was. It is in the district of Fener which is an acceptable area at ground level but it rises up to the top of the Fatih Hill and as we were told the higher you go up the hill the more you find how fundamentalist the Muslims who live there are. They do not like outsiders of another religion and for a while we could not find a taxi driver who would take us there. Eventually we did but the Turkish man made it clear he was not happy in doing so.

It was not only a winding road but the higher it went the steeper the road became. At length we arrived at the top of the hill from where one can look down on the Golden Horn. The church is surrounded by a high wall and part of that was a big timber door. I knocked several times but nothing happened. The taxi driver reluctantly left his car

The firman or document in the Church of Mary of the Mongols signed by Mehmet the Conqueror of Constantinople in 1453 that states the church can never be converted to a mosque or other

and walked to the wall beside the door. He then reached up and pressed a buzzer which I had obviously missed. He was back in his car before a young man named Michael opened the door.

I told him who we are and from where and asked could we please enter to see inside. Michael, a rare Christian in Turkey, let us in and said he was the only person here. He showed us around and we inspected several icons, many paintings, several mosaics, a statue of St Barnabas and a dozen or more portraits of religious figures that seemed to be edged with a shimmering silver effect, quite unusual. A 500-year old mosaic of Jesus and Mary retained most of its original colour. The item that I sought and found was the firman

Chapter Eleven *Mary of the Mongols*

or document signed by Mehmet the Conqueror that granted everlasting protection to the Church of Mary of the Mongols. It states clearly and strongly that no one is allowed to convert this church to another religion as has happened to others.

Michael took us down into the crypt and from there we were able to move into and along a tunnel for some distance. It is said to be five km long and lead to the Hagia Sophia but like tunnels elsewhere it was blocked off at a later stage.

Janice and I thanked Michael sincerely for we were well pleased with our historical visit and we made a donation in memory of Mary of the Mongols. We were also pleased to find our now anxious taxi driver still there and he was glad to drive on.

In the afternoon we visited the Spice Bazaar with its outstanding variety and presentation of spices, herbs, teas, dried fruit and its most expensive product, Turkish saffron spice. The best Turkish product grown is in specific areas and is hand-picked from the purple or dark red saffron crocus. It is highly regarded for its vibrant colour, rich flavour and apparent health benefits. I recently saw, in Australia, five grams selling for $40 and fifty grams for $320. Janice says she prefers the Spice BaZaar to the larger Grand Bazaar. Perhaps she is swayed by the tempting Turkish Delight which is served as dessert in Turkey.

While eating out the air was very cold and snowflakes fell on us. We ended up at the Pudding Shop where Europeans tend to hang out but after the first fist fight we left. Went home and packed up to be ready for an early departure the next morning.

We made a good start and were soon in mountains at 1,500 metres. Turnip harvesting was underway but unlike Yugoslavia where it is done by mower-type machines here it was done by hand and there were literally truckloads and cartloads of turnips. All day we were in snow, usually thirty cm of it. We arrived in Ankara the national capital to be welcomed into a pretty ordinary hotel but it supplied a great meal. We had roast beef off the spit, kebabs, tomatoes and beer for $1. That was for the two of us, fifty cents each, as good as Morocco.

Ankara seemed disappointing to us as little of it was modern and advanced as expected. Most of the people appeared unkempt. Sorry but true. Continued driving the next day, courtesy of Garry and Les who handle the bus in turn and appear to be more than capable. We stopped in a small town for lunch and were the centre of attention to the locals. I had the best soup ever, chicken flavoured but with lamb, carrots and potatoes. The local taxis were two-horse drawn surreys and carriages, no cars. We drove down to Samsun on the Black Sea coast. Samsun was impressive and we enjoyed a dinner of fresh fish and Turkish ice-cream. We continued on to coastal Trabzon and as we slowed down at our hotel a man pulled out his gun and shot another Turk, dead, sitting in his car. Welcome to Trabzon.

This time the hotel was good and at $3 a double even better. We were about 150 km from the Russian border and again were the centre of attention but not to the point that someone shot at us. We were surprised to see so many women who were only 1.47 metres tall, on average, poorly dressed and with their faces all but covered except for their eyes. However they usually surrounded us and were friendly, especially the younger ones.

The next morning was cold and snowing and after fifteen km we put chains on the bus and headed back into the mountains towards Erzerum. Soon the snow was a metre deep and by the time we were

Chapter Eleven *Mary of the Mongols*

at 2,000 metres we could not see through the falling snow for more than a few metres. Decided to push on but often had to stop and back up or move over precariously as a hay-laden truck, petrol tanker, council truck or bus came the other way towards us. This happened fifteen times. At one stage we passed a loo, like an old out-house. It was perched off the side of the road and over a 200 foot or sixty metre drop.

As darkness fell we came to the town of Gumushane and because the road ahead was so dangerous we stayed there, having covered 110 km in a full day. Our room was directly over a smoke-filled bar inhabited by the usual noisy Turkish drinkers. The room had two antique metal beds and one small table plus a wood-burner fire which had enough fuel for fifteen minutes. The window curtains, or their remnants, hung in tatters and during the night things scurried across the floor, whilst we again heard the prayers being sounded from the local mosque. Snow ploughs were out and about on the roads.

As early as we could the next morning we continued on over the Canik Mountains through rugged country aided by the chains again. Along the way we passed no less than three Army camps, with hundreds of tanks, trucks and jeeps. They all looked to be in excellent condition so the Russians shouldn't catch them out one day. I say that because I know the camps form a line of defence, in conjunction with the mountains which were now at a genuine 4,000 metres high. Now and again we came upon people using horse-drawn sleighs and sled transport and cattle-drawn carts with wooden wheels. Rugged people living a tough life.

After 220 km we reached the University and industrial town of Erzerum which has 35,000 hardy souls. It was immensely cold with snow and ice everywhere. It was difficult to walk without slipping and sliding. Our hotel was reasonable even though few lights worked, the bathroom was filthy and all the rooms could be opened by one key. Across the street and opposite our fourth floor level were 1.5 metre long icicles hanging off the ledges.

Erzerum was a fascinating town with troikas and not just because they are the traditional Russian sleigh or carriage but because they use three horses harnessed abreast. This method of using three horses abreast increases their stability and reduces individual strain. It was developed so as to enable quicker crossings of Russia's lengthy and hazardous roads. There is more to this mode of travel. The middle horse of a troika is harnessed in a horse collar and shaft bow while the two outside horses wear breast-collar harness. There is more again. The middle horse trots and the two side horses canter. Extraordinary and it must be the only harness combination anywhere with different gaits of the horses. When Janice and I later went on a three-week horse-riding expedition across western Mongolia we learned Mongolian horses do not have four speeds like our horses, they have eight speeds.

The horse-drawn troikas with their carriages went clattering through the streets, their bells jingling and whips flashing as they conveyed their passengers through the snow. Riveting stuff. The Turks in Erzerum seemed more like the real thing, being much bigger and broader. Men have thick, black moustaches and a strong independent look about themselves with solid facial features and clear resolute eyes which seem to take everything in. Most were friendly to us and physically more appealing than Turks from elsewhere.

The next morning we were up at five o'clock and there was ice on the thin panes of window glass in our room. We left at six and

Chapter Eleven *Mary of the Mongols*

there was still a heavy covering of snow everywhere. For the first three hours the windows of the bus were frozen. Morocco was a long way behind us now. After forty km the countryside opened up into rolling hillsides with magnificent scenic views, when we could see. As we came up the side of one of those valleys a dozen hard-riding horsemen appeared beside the bus, yelling loudly and waving furiously. One of the men galloped past us, whipping his horse to the crest of the road where he turned and sat his horse, waving us on enthusiastically.

When passing through several villages we saw what appeared to be haystacks but were in fact heaps of cow dung collected during the summer months to be used as fuel during the winter as everything is then under metres of snow and the only available wood is higher up the mountain. The houses were all built of stone with some local hand-made bricks. The leaves, bushes and branches are so covered in snow that they look like snow-white coral. It was a winter wonderland, in Turkey. We were getting our money's worth. Fabulous.

As we drove the bus over the Agri Pass at 2,600 metres we were stopped by air in the fuel line when a London taxi appeared and resolutely drove by. As they do. We cleared the line and drove on, passing another three army camps, the last one being at Dogabayazit. This camp may be the largest in Turkey away from Istanbul and it completes the line of defence as it is only thirty km from the border with Iran. It is also all but at the foot of Mt Ararat, which is part of the Russia/ Turkey border. After America, Turkey has the second largest army in NATO, which it joined after Stalin claimed Turkish lands and now Putin claims Ukraine lands. If required Turkey can blockade Russia at the Bosphorus.

Mt Ararat, eastern Turkey, near the borders of Armenia, Azerbaijan and Iran. Russian border is 30 kilometres from Mt Ararat.

We had an excellent view of Mt Ararat with its 5,800 metre height and seven km distance from us so we stopped for photographs. More than a few people believe Noah and his Ark came to rest on Mt Ararat. It is featured in the Koran so the Turks go along with the idea.

We had a two-hour delay crossing the border into Iran and on top of that a time change of one and a half hours put us well behind the clock for the day. Tabriz is only 270 km over the border and we had intended to stop there to see the world's largest bazaar, larger than Istanbul. As a result of the lost three and a half hours we decided not to delay in Tabriz. It was always an important stop on the ancient Silk Road as confirmed by Marco Polo being there in 1271 and my Moroccan mate, Ibn Battuta in 1330.

We decided to push on into the night to reach Hamadan. The better roads in Iran enabled the bus to go significantly faster than when she was struggling over the Turkish mountains. In addition to having the lower section of the radiator still frozen when we left Erzerum the desert wind was colder, there still being snow around.

The faster we went the colder the radiator and we came to a freezing halt. Thank goodness for our Afghan coats.

We had no option but to patiently wait for the ice to dissipate, to thaw out. While we were outside the bus we could hear wolves howling in distant hills which made the girls uncomfortable when they needed to go to the toilet. Some of the boys gave them a hard time about that, verbally but the girls silently put up with that as well as the call of the wild. Due to the desert air we stayed in the bus for a long time until five of us decided to brave the cold and stretch our legs, perhaps a walk would warm us up. Before we left the bus Garry turned the parking lights on so that we could see a short way and hopefully not stumble. We stood around talking, our breath hanging like mini clouds in the still desert air. After some time we saw what appeared to be small lights on the road ahead. They seemed to be coming closer.

They were coming closer so Les went back to the bus and turned the headlights on to reveal that the lights were eyes. A pack of wolves was now no more than fifteen metres from us. Fortunately no one spoke or panicked but walked steadily backwards to the safety of the bus while keeping an eye on the seven or eight wolves. What else could we do, it was impossible to take your eyes off them. Les had the door open for us and we silently and gratefully closed it behind us without being attacked.

After the engine defrosted and the wolves seemed to have moved on we refilled the thawed-out radiator which had four litres of antifreeze in the previous twenty-four hours and we push-started the bus. We continued on and after sunrise we were past the snowline but in mid-morning we ran out of fuel. We then discovered the fuel tank was dirty. Diesel was costing us two and a half cents a litre but there was a higher price to pay because it was of poor quality in Iran, then. Petrol cost a touch more. We arrived in Hamadan at five o'clock in the afternoon and we tucked into a hot meal of soup with chicken in it plus two raw eggs followed by Iranian peaches and cups of tea. We had time to look around and noted that the streets had open drains beside the footpaths and a number of beggars nearby. The city looked better than it must have when Genghis Khan totally destroyed it in 1220.

The following morning was gloriously sunny and relatively warm. The road to Isfahan was uneventful so we had our lunch by the road without a wolf in sight. Arriving in Isfahan we found our hotel was directly opposite the truly magnificent Chahar Bagh Theological school. It is a major tourist attraction being the largest theological school of its time and renowned for its architecture and mosaic work along with Persian gardens in the quadrilateral style, so they are divided into quarters and surrounded by pools and arcades. The school's entrance is decorated with gold and silver, the dome and the walls are made of bright yellow bricks and the tilework is seen as a masterpiece.

As this was the first Sundowners trip to this part of the world they knew no more than us so we went on a guided tour of Isfahan at the incredibly low price of one Aussie dollar each for an entire day's outing. First up was the elegant Royal Mosque with its iconic blue-tiled mosaics and perfect proportions. It has fabulous photographs of Mecca where non-Muslims are not allowed to go. Next was a display of carpet-weaving so fine that the best weavers can make 164 silk or wool knots per square centimetre or 900 per square inch. A 2.4 metre by 1.8 metre or 8 by 6 foot carpet takes three women two years to make.

The people of Iran can pray at home instead of in a mosque except on Friday when they must attend. At noon they go to the Friday

Chapter Eleven *Mary of the Mongols*

mosque as did we. As one enters the suspended chains over the entrance force everyone to bow their head. After that we were taken to a large building that housed a camel oil press, where a camel walks around a circular slab turning a large stone to which it is harnessed. The stone we saw weighed three tonnes and was crushing linseed. While the timbers of the building and other apparatus may have been refurbished this press had been in operation for four hundred years.

Another age-related item was pointed out to us. The guide explained that the minarets were originally placed on and at the corners of a mosque so that a fire or beacon could be lit on top of them to guide the caravans in at night. He then took us to two old-style Persian houses, one with the harem room full of beds. The other belonged to a wealthy merchant who donated his house to the government. When he died and as an exalted favour his body was allowed to be buried in the house.

It takes a special bridge to be as beautiful as the Khaju bridge constructed about 1650. I have never seen the likes of it since. For the record it is 133 metres long and twelve metres wide with twenty-three arches. Poets would go there to paise and describe it but that is beyond my ability without taking too long. Shahs attended there on picnics, to sit and enjoy.

Speaking of food we enjoyed a late lunch at the top drawer Shaharzad restaurant, said to be one of the best in Iran. The eye-catching coloured glass windows, extraordinary mirror work on the walls and ceiling plus the culinary delights do reflect Persian culture and cuisine. The afternoon was spent at the bazaar for shopping opportunities too good to pass up. Then a representative of Sundowners arrived from London. He was surprised at our itinerary and outings and though we were getting outstanding value but perhaps the company wasn't. That night we hit the Sahara Club for a fantastic night out after some of the testing times in eastern Turkey. The dining, the accompanying wine and even our dancing made for a fun-filled night to remember.

In the morning it was back to the bazaar where Glen and Janice had minor repairs to their coats before purchasing more goods such as necklaces at rather low prices and then taking to the streets on our own. At night we were escorted to the magnificent Shah Abas Hotel, now known as the Abassi. It was constructed in 1716 and has been ongoing ever since but obviously with updates. We were told the renovation before we arrived cost seven million Australian dollars, a huge amount of money more than fifty years ago and it could have been earlier, seventy years or more, perhaps. Anyway you can imagine the hotel is on the grand scale. We reclined on carpets and cushions in an illuminated red room to the scintillating sounds of Persian music and were well and truly spoilt.

It couldn't last and the next morning we reluctantly left Isfahan and headed north. After passing yet another army camp, a large one as they all seem to be, we had lunch at an ancient caravanserai, part of which was still occupied. We found a tea house of old and entered. It was a plain room with basic furniture but there was nothing ordinary about the three middle-aged men in their tribal robes who were seated within. Each man sat bolt upright, their craggy faces lined with character and a hunting falcon either on their shoulder or on the top of the long staff beside them. If ever I missed the photograph of the year, that was it.

Next was the city of Qom, which in Shi'a Islam has the second most holy mosque to Shia men and the most holy to women as the Imam Ali ibn Musa Rida's sister, Fatimah bint Musa is buried there. Non-Muslims are not allowed to enter but there were long lines of pilgrims as twenty million come every year.

The old bus now came to the Dasht-e-Kavir or Great Salt Desert which occupies an area of 800 km by 320 km in the middle of the Iran Plateau. We did not have to go across all of it but enough of it and we did before arriving in Tehran, capital of Iran. Driving into the city we encountered two incidents, the first being a traffic jam and the second courtesy of the jam. A woman in a Mercedes Benz started blowing frantic kisses to us, until the man she was with started hitting her. He fair dinkum walloped her. Then six bicycle riders followed us, acting the goat until one ran into the back of the bus.

We saw men carrying the most enormous loads on their backs to the bazaar, of course. After we had checked in to the hotel we went straight to the Central Bank of Iran, where we were able to see close up and freely, the Iranian Crown Jewels. They are staggering in their beauty, shape, style and value. I could not list or describe them all and even if I did try my hardest I could not do them justice but they do take one's breath away. I might give you an idea of their worth. The Crown Jewels of Britain's estimated value is US $4 to $6 billion. The Iran Crown Jewels are said to be worth US $30 billion. They are so prized the Iranian government is able to use them as security for international loans. The Peacocke Throne, of solid gold inlaid with jewels, is regarded as one of the world's most valued assets. It is said that the Peacock Throne, stolen from India by Persian conquerors, is worth twice as much as the Taj Mahal and I know it was recently claimed it would cost one billion dollars to build the Taj Mahal today. The Peacock Throne was commissioned by Shah Jahan of India who also built the Taj Mahal.

Next on the agenda was a visit to the Zurkhaneh, the ancient Iranian house of strength that dates back for two thousand years. This is a traditional venue for physical fitness and spiritual cultivation. It incorporates elements of martial arts, gymnastics, calisthenics, spirituality, ethics, art, literature, devotion and music to train the mind, body and soul. We were allowed in and shown the central pit which is below ground level where much of the physical action takes place and a lot of that has to do with wrestling. The laws and techniques are numerous and require much learning and understanding as it is also an exercise in morality. Heavy clubs are used for strength conditioning, exercising and preparation for wrestling. It would seem that it would take decades to master the intricacies of the noble art. We were impressed.

Many of the ways of Iran that I have mentioned are worthy of note and reflective of how some, the better-off live, but the reality overall was that excluding the up-market suburbs the rest of Tehran was dirty, untidy and in some areas not safe. In fact it was the dirtiest city that we had yet seen in Asia. Of course that can change with time and good government.

We left Tehran the next morning and after forty km came to a village. While the good old bus slowed down as you do in a built-up area young men began to throw rocks at us. Somehow the glass windows held up but it was an unpleasant sensation. We came to a better village and I say that because it had been crafted out of the side of a hill as we saw in rural Spain. The difference being in Spain it was several houses dug into Mother Earth while here it was a village. Having to do that exemplifies how difficult life is for some people.

Chapter Eleven *Mary of the Mongols*

It was a long drive from Tehran to Mashad in north- eastern Iran. As we came down from the Iran Plateau we saw the Caspian Sea but did not go to it. What we did see were thousands of sheep with their shepherds and they with their tents, all the way. The countryside flattened out, dried out and produced barely any water for irrigation to help out. That may have been why we started to see so many camels.

We were approaching the city of Neyshabur. About five km from Neyshabur was a small encampment of black tents and roughly erected timber poles and skins which served as shops. We stopped there for a break and to again stretch the legs. Whilst walking around we came to a heap of human skulls. They looked old and Garry who did some of the driving but was also a part-time guide said they would most likely have been from the time Genghis Khan was there. They must have been under cover to survive that long although the teeth are always hardy. I later researched that suggestion and Genghis Khan was there in 1221. After his son-in-law, Tuquchar, was killed by an arrow at Neyshabur Genghis Khan was so outraged he asked his distraught daughter what did she want him to do. In her grief and rage she ordered the city be utterly destroyed and every living thing within its walls killed. The Mongols decapitated every person, placing the heads of the men in one heap and those of women and children in another. They killed every cat and dog and laid waste in such a manner that afterwards the site could be ploughed. Such was the destruction that Neyshabur was later rebuilt five km away.

We came to Mashad the holiest city in Iran as the eighth Imam, Imam Reza, lived and died there. We drove out to see the mosque where he is buried, being the only Imam, an Islamic leader, buried in Iran. As we pulled up at the complex a crowd of men rushed the bus, throwing rocks at us. Janice and I were in the back seat with Janice nearest the side window. I can still see the young man, about twenty years of age and at the head of the mob, with the anger in his eyes flashing like lightning as he drew his right arm back. He then cast the rock in his hand at the bus and I was mortified as in an instant I followed its trajectory and realised it was heading straight for Janice. It hit the window in line with her jaw and only after we escaped and stopped when well away did I read the fine print on the exterior of that window which said this section is armour-plated. I don't know why that should have been so but oh what a relief. The bus had been peppered but Garry had responded instantly to the attack and as he still had the bus in gear could not have done better to get us away.

We learned, afterwards, that seven million Muslims a year then made the pilgrimage to Mashad, coming from Iraq, Iran, Afghanistan and Pakistan. Consequently it was mostly dirty, untidy and in parts, unsafe. It was a great place to buy the world's best turquoise so it was not surprising to see the dome of the mosque built of turquoise. The Imam's mausoleum is of gold but the surrounding land is not suitable for cultivation. Oil is the area's chief export followed by carpets. Mineral deposits are substantial but not developed.

The mosque at Mashad, Iran, where we were stoned

CHAPTER TWELVE

Afghanistan

An eye for an eye will only make the whole world blind.
— Mahatma Gandhi

The next day we reached the border with Afghanistan at 11 a.m. but were not able to pass through until 4.30 in the afternoon. Not that we did anything wrong, unless word had been passed along that we had transgressed at the mosque. It was in that part of the world where time means nothing. We weren't even searched by customs but border officials and medical personnel took their own sweet time. Some of our group did have to cut their hair.

Mashad is almost due west of Kabul but the terrain in between is so rugged one is compelled to go south-east to Herat, then south-east to Kandahar before north to Kabul.

There were no towns along the way but scores of black tents which were of goat-skin. As a few were close to the road we stopped several times and received an inquiring welcome. One man challenged us, by hand signals, to take him on in one of their main pastimes, which was heavy rock-throwing. Well apart from blood feuds and fighting

Black goat hair tents of Afghanistan

perhaps there isn't much to do for entertainment. Back then they were serious about the rock-throwing. One of our blokes stepped up for the challenge and carefully selected his rock. He might have been a bit out of condition because the Afghan cleaned him up.

In the first 1,000 km of driving on the roads in Afghanistan we saw six cars. Five of them were well-worn, somewhat battered Mercedes, of the type favoured by local dictators.

Eventually we came to Herat after seeing a wolf crossing the road ahead of us. 1,000 years ago Herat was the centre of Central

Chapter Twelve *Afghanistan*

Afghan mode of travel

Asian intellect. Herat is typical of the countless wars that have been waged in Afghanistan. It has seen both substantial victories and losses, two of them in particular. In 1221 it was destroyed by Genghis Khan, who was busy that year. By the time it recovered it was all but wiped off the planet by an even more savage opponent, Tamerlane, aka Timur, in 1383. I have looked at Tamerlane over the years and it is calculated he killed or had killed on his orders, seventeen million people. He was said to be constantly thinking of new ways to eliminate others. By the time those two predators had finished with Herat it was in bad way and it didn't look much better when we arrived.

We stayed in what was called a hotel but it wasn't. There was a hotel in Herat which was said to be better, which wouldn't be difficult.

However it was a Russian-built hotel and while it looked alright we were told hardly anything actually worked, so we stayed put.

Glen and Anne and Janice and I hired two horse-drawn carts with local drivers so we could go off on our own and have a look around this rather wild town. We set off and the horses did seem to respond well so Glen and I were able to convince the Afghans to let us take the reins, and the whips, which we did. After while I noticed Glen pulling ahead of us so I gave my horse a bit of a touch-up. He responded with interest, Glen looked across at me as I went past him and it was on. In no time both horses were going flat out and the Afghans seemed to be calling us to do something but we couldn't understand their language. One thing we did respond to was the police car which chased after us and signalled us to stop.

It was no good the police talking to Glen and I as we know nothing so they took one of our shotgun co-drivers away in the police car and we walked back to the accommodation, with our annoyed wives.

Some of the bedrooms had canvas ceilings but ours had a few supporting timber beams. The shower was something else. Without electricity it was an ancient wood-burner or chip heater with a pile of wood beside it so that you could feed the wood into it and keep the water hot. It was curiously placed beside the wall as was a bucket of water. It only took a few minutes to realise that as you showered you fed the wood through the opening by the wall. Before long the heat started to burn the wall and so every two to three minutes you had to throw the bucket of water over the wall to put the fire out. True. Went to sleep listening to the bells on the horses as they raced their passengers home. It was a cold night.

The first thing we saw in the morning was a group of three

camels and six donkeys carrying as much as they could along the street. Breakfast was inedible and the bus would not start. It took ninety minutes to clear the fuel line of air so while Les and Garry handled that we went walkabout. A knife-sharpener was busy on the footpath, brick-layers were building a mud wall, shabbily dressed soldiers ambled by which reminded us that yesterday's border officials, the ones who took four and a half hours to let us pass, were minus all their buttons and shoe laces, were dusty and dirty themselves and had rips or tears in their uniforms. Fruit sellers were out in force as were those with birds in cages to sell and those who simply drifted around. Overall an awful assortment which included many casually carrying their rifles. Some of the rifles were old but beautifully engraved on the long barrels. The bright spot was that a high percentage of the trucks were superbly covered with designs of glorious colour. A lot of work must go into that presentation, something to be proud of.

The fuel line clean again we hit the road to Kandahar and would have seen at least 1,500 camels during the day including about 200 at one time, grazing like a herd of cattle. There were large mobs of sheep and goats and the people lived in mud huts or the attractive black tents which dotted the dry, barren and flat landscape. We had lunch by the road and then walked to a nearby tribe or community who had stacks of firewood for sale. It was impossible to see timber anywhere so they must go into the distant hills which were a fair way off to cut and collect the wood. These people were scruffy and poor but quite friendly except for the man who unfortunately insisted on throwing stones at Allan. Janice was able to go up to some of the donkeys and feed them carrots, without being stoned.

Afghans collecting and selling rare firewood

Back on the road the Afghans got at us in another way. Someone must have sent smoke signals ahead to say we were coming as from then on we were repeatedly stopped at hastily erected toll gates. We also stopped for those of us who were now suffering diarrhoea. As this morning's breakfast looked appalling, which curiously is only an e away from appealing, I had not touched food and that might have saved me, for the time being. It was dark when we rolled into Kandahar and another modest room. It consisted of a concrete floor, plastic walls, two single beds, a small table and two hooks on a fragile wall.

Chapter Twelve *Afghanistan*

Kandahar is in the south of Afghanistan and connects Iran to Pakistan and India. The one constant about the place would be the many wars it has seen. It is amazing people still live there. It has been fought over, defeated or fought off everyone bar the Salvation Army. i.e. The Persians of Darius 1, Alexander the Great, the Bactrians, Parthians, Sasanians, Arabs, Turks and Mongols. As with Herat, Genghis Khan thought he had destroyed it but more than a century and some recovery later along came Tamerlane again who reduced it to rubble. The Mughal empire was followed by the British empire, the Russian empire and then the Americans in having a crack at the place before it ended up as the centre of Taliban power.

It was still a rough-house when the Sundowners arrived. Shortly before we descended on the city four Frenchmen were invited to a local home by some Muhammadans who murdered them. The murderers had only just been hanged and we received warnings to be particularly careful in Kandahar and Kabul.

The Russian-built road from the Persian border ended at Kandahar and we moved on to the American-built road which was better as it did not have the concrete joints of the Soviets. That took us nor-nor-east to Kabul, following the lovely Hindu Kush mountain range off to our right. I don't recall how much bribe money we had to pay but once again there were numerous toll gates to hinder us as well as more cases of diarrhoea. The two seemed to go together by now.

For all that discomfort it was a fascinating drive with extraordinary scenery and local life. The Hindu Kush mountains begin in the north where China, Pakistan and Afghanistan meet, then run south-west through Pakistan and into neighbouring Afghanistan for some 800 km. The mountain peaks, which average

Typically decorated Afghan truck

4,500 metres but top out at 7,708 metres in height give off a feeling of strength and dominate the skyline with the dark blue colouring they exude. They were wonderful company to travel with and it is not surprising that there are an estimated 35,000 plant species and 200 or more animal species amongst them.

In case you don't know the Hindu Kush are commonly referred to as Killer of Hindus or Hindu Killer. My man from Morocco, again, Ibn Battuta, travelled that way and wrote that slaves from the Indian subcontinent died in the harsh climatic conditions of the Hindu

Chapter Twelve *Afghanistan*

Kush while being taken from India to Turkestan by Muslim traders. On our passing at lower altitudes we came to many, many camel caravans that were all loaded up and accompanied by men, women and children of several tribes. Exciting time.

We also came to several graveyards out there in the open and usually there would be one or two large stones on top of each funeral mound. Somewhat desperate we stopped at Ghazni town for lunch. Today it has 190,000 people and I hope a reasonable standard of living but we found it to be filthy and smelly, so awful that we could not bear to eat anything there.

Our good bus continued on until we stopped to meet some local tribesmen. Dave was right into mixing with them so he was challenged to another bout of rock throwing. The silly bugger lost. We would often see a man in the middle of nowhere down on his mat praying to Allah and once a group of thirty men, out in the open-air praying. Rather impressive.

 As dusk gathered we arrived in Kabul, capital city of ancient Afghanistan. We checked into the reasonable looking Metropole Hotel, where an Afghan engagement party was in progress. Across the road we were able to have food that we could stomach, literally and the first for two days. Chicken broth was followed by turkey meat with quality vegetables and a surprise, chocolate ice cream.

The following day started well with wonderful warm sunshine after all the wintry weather we had recently experienced. Glen and Anne joined us on a Kabul walkabout and probably wished they hadn't. It had to be the dirtiest, the filthiest and the most unhygienic collection of human and public garbage we had ever seen. Unless someone cleaned it up I find it hard to believe the Russians and then the Americans would go there and stay as long as they did. I wonder how worse it was in decades and centuries long gone. The open sewers which separate the footpath from the road were forty-five cm wide and sixty cm deep. On average half of that was human excrement. A nearby side street was used as a public toilet with the saturated and excessive excrement climbing up the wall, like volcanic lave flowing in reverse. The smell in the air was so vile and disturbing that one felt an infection in the throat within a few hours. The buildings were of plaster and rotting timber. In the worse areas the beggars, the blind and the crippled were numerous. The clothing of thousands of residents was ragged and filthy. Even the army and the police were scruffy.

The wares of the usual fruit and vegetable sellers were covered by clouds of flies but outdone by the butchers' shops. Those consisted of a rough wooden bench in a timber or tin shed in front of which hung either whole animal carcasses or parts thereof. In the already vile atmosphere the flies would have had a hard decision of what to feast on, spoiled as they were for choice. The kebab vendors were not much better off while the numerous barbers were to be found sitting on the footpath, beside the open sewers, using rusty cut-throat blades to shave their clients' heads completely bald, while endlessly talking and seeming to be inflicting new cuts to the head.

Some of the fruit vendors had huge baskets of produce loaded on the backs of donkeys which stand amongst the human flotsam all day if need be. The carpet sellers displayed their goods along the wall beside the Kabul river and then enticed you across the road to their warehouses. Women are rarely seen unless selling beads, trinkets and bangles. The men make up ninety-eight per cent of the crowds and it seems as though all of them spit. They continuously spray a brown or green mixture on to the ground while young boys occasionally sneak up behind you and yell like mad, amusing themselves while trying to frighten you. People continually wander all over the streets or footpaths while sometimes making way for a rare car or a usual hand-drawn cart. Every now and then one or more of our girls was touched, patted or felt. Every Afghan must have a good supply of knives as all the many knife-sellers had hundreds of the sharpest knives imaginable.

On the far side of the river we came to small shops that sold antique coins, knives and swords as well as gold and lapis lazuli, the world's best of the latter being extracted from the Hindu Kush. Lapis lazuli, a dark blue stone similar in colour to blue opal, is used to make daggers, game boards, bowls, hair combs and amulets. There is a catch to lapis lazuli in that the powerful vibrations emanating from the dark blue stone when near one's head, can cause an increase in pressure of the head. Live chickens are bought in the street and bread is baked in charcoal ovens before being slapped onto the counter and then hung on a nail protruding from a post. In Morocco one is openly accosted by people trying to sell you hashish while in Afghanistan someone is always asking you to change money as in dollars, pounds, marks but unlike Russia not at competitive prices. Indian rupees can be bought but if one is found taking them into India one can expect to be thrown straight into prison.

We came across craftsmen making furniture of timber and treated rope, all by hand. Well done but perhaps ridiculously cheap even though we are used to low prices. We could not take them home but without bargaining the chairs were A $2.50 and settees or lounges for three people were priced at $7.50.

Many of the men have a distinct Mongol or Chinese look to their face while older women still wear shroud-type cloth over their heads with a lattice-work piece over their eyes so that they can see out but can't be seen themselves. That manner of clothing continues down to their ankles.

Herbs, dyes, soaps, shirts, teas, hand-woven covers, dress belts, leather Afghan coats, silks and Chinese toilet paper are all for sale. The wailing music of Islam was to be heard continually in the crowded streets of Kabul.

Next morning Glen, Allan and I went to Chicken Street, a popular tourist venue for those on the so-called Hippie trail from Europe to Kathmandu in the 60s and 70s. It was a narrow street where foreigners could look for and expect to find antiques, carpets, handiwork and hashish. I don't believe any of our group were after hashish as they were more concerned with staying healthy and alert so as to learn and appreciate where we were going. I may be wrong but I could never smell the stuff or even hear it discussed. Chicken Street did offer leather goods, coins, rifles, swords, pistols and the like but if you wanted to buy a chicken you went to adjacent Flower Street.

On the way back we passed the Czechoslovakia Airlines building which was blocked off by a full-blown riot. There were several riots in Kabul while we were there and with so many poor and agitated people I was not surprised. After that Janice and I joined Glen and Anne on a two-hour taxi tour of Kabul's outskirts, just to see more of the city and its environs, for a cost of ninety cents each. The driver took us to see the enormous Russian Embassy and then to the Kabul Museum, where there was a fist fight in progress at the entrance to that building. Apart from old coins and rifles there was little else to see except for coloured clay paintings from the Bamiyan valley and intricate ivory carvings which had for some reason unbeknown to us, been sealed away in the second century AD in the mountains to the north of Kabul but we were permitted to see on the day. There were statues of Buddha, that religion having been strong from the second to seventh centuries when Islam arrived and then the Taliban later disgracefully destroyed the meticulously carved 55 and 38 metre tall statues of Buddha that had existed since 600 AD in the Bamiyan valley, which is about 130 km to the north-west of Kabul.

The driver took us to the other side of Kabul for another camel market. They were there in their countless hundreds and perhaps he thought we hadn't seen camels up close before. Anyway we left the car and strolled among them which was after all something of a revelation. Some of the lumbering beasts of burden were not in good condition and had cuts and sores about the head. Unlike the camels of Morocco they made for a rather messy and sordid scene. Others were in better shape and Janice walked amongst them, patting and talking to several. Then she saw a black camel, an unusual sight. As she walked towards it an English-speaking Afghan stopped her, saying, *No touch camel. This bad, bite, kick you.* He told us that is why he was selling it at the market. Thank goodness he saw Janice in time.

Our man then drove up a perilous dirt track to a hill that overlooks the city to see the Noon Gun being fired. The gun was fired every day at noon by the occupying British forces in the 19th century to tell the people of Kabul what the time was. The Afghans carried on with

Overseer

An eight year old Afghan girl at work in a brick factory in Kabul.

Another eight year old Afghan girl after her school was bombed.

that tradition as we saw and heard but I wonder if it is still carried out. I believe the ancient and rickety-looking piece is a British Navy twelve pounder gun. It is mounted on a field carriage. At 12 noon we stood by as a huge flash of flame exploded from the ancient barrel, a large cloud of white smoke, a loud crash and a shock wave nearly knocked us off our feet.

Back in Kabul for the afternoon Glen and I went to the carpet area but after quite some time had not seen anything of interest. Until we came to a large warehouse and entered through its double doors. The centre of the building stood empty but on all sides were endless rolls of carpets. When selected they could immediately be rolled out and displayed. The burly forty-year old owner, whose name was Gulru, called to three men who rolled out carpet after carpet but none appealed to either of us. He then told two of his men to go upstairs and bring down small carpets and rugs. One rug instantly caught my attention and after assessing it I offered to buy it, without a word of English from Gulru and less Afghani from myself. Not being sure of how to proceed I produced one of those beautiful blue English five-pound notes, current at the time in England but not Afghanistan. The man inspected it and after some time he accepted it. He then handed me the rug and we left.

Back in the hotel I unrolled it and was happy with myself. I just knew I had something special but not what that was except that it was genuine and aged. Charlie, our good Canadian friend walked by, saw it and asked would I be able to take him to that warehouse?

Charlie and I walked in and Gulru in company with one of his men quickly came to meet us. Something wasn't right and Gulru spoke angrily as he produced the five-pound note and shook it in front of me. By drawing with his finger on the dusty warehouse floor he traced out the numbers 5 and 50. Then he put a line through the five. I gathered he wanted and expected to be paid fifty pounds. I knew he did not speak English but I told him, *No. It is a done deal.* He understood that and I understood what he meant when he and his off-sider reached into their robes and each pulled out a rather large knife and held them at our stomachs, just below the rib cage actually.

It is amazing how quickly things can happen. In less than a second overall I turned my head ever so slightly to the left, where Charlie was standing beside me, caught Charlie's eye and in what remained of that second we both turned and ran. The first thing we had to do was to get through those double doors and to confirm that, Gulru called on his other two men to cut us off. We had a good ten years on them and both Charlie and I were still in reasonable shape from our Rugby Union days. I was concerned they might have thrown their knives at our backs but possibly they were more for stabbing and cutting than throwing. We made it through the doors and I looked back. The pursuit was on and the knives were still evident.

Outside we hurdled the open sewer. How bad would that have been, to stumble and end up in there and at the mercy of Gulru and his men. It was pointless trying to run on the footpath as it was already occupied by the barbers and their waiting customers. We opted for the street with its oxen and camel-drawn carts and wagons, figuring we might have an edge by dodging and weaving faster than our pursuers and with a bit of luck they might not see in which direction we had gone when hidden by the traffic. We did not stop or look back for five minutes at least before taking a chance

Chapter Twelve *Afghanistan*

and turning into an alley. We stopped to regain breath, waited some more and then peeked back around the corner. No pursuers were in sight but they might also be waiting so we continued on but in a roundabout way so as not to lead anyone directly to our hotel.

We gradually closed in on the hotel via several lane-ways and streets before walking slowly and openly over the road to our hotel. To be on the safe side we did not go out that night and it was probably fortuitous that Sundowners left in the morning.

After leaving Kabul we plunged in to the Kabul Gorge, a magnificent series of hair-raising and breath-taking views and turns along the American- built road, which is for the most part directly carved out of the sides of the cliffs. The country then levelled out as, still following the Kabul River, we came across occasional sheets of water in the shallow but often wide river. At the border we were confronted by hordes of Pakistani money-changers who had huge wads of money at better than government rates.

We entered the historically famous Khyber Pass, which is thirty-four km long. While the pass is winding and guarded by high and solid cliff walls it is up to a kilometre and a half wide in some places and narrows to seventy metres elsewhere which can cause bottlenecks. We stovpped at a heavenly viewing point where we could see down into Pakistan and while we could not define it as such, the imagination says probably into India beyond. The only other long distance view I have seen to equal that is from the top of the Simien Mountains in the north of Ethiopia, known as the Roof of Africa.

The Khyber Pass had forts about every kilometre in advantageous positions, the most famous being the Shagai Fort where the Khyber

Overhead photo of the Khyber Pass area

The Khyber Pass as it exits onto the Plains of Peshawar, Pakistan

Rifles were stationed. The British Army formed the Khyber Rifles in 1887 and it came under the control of Pakistan in 1947. Today its role is to defend the border with Afghanistan and to guard the Warsak Dam located on the Kabul River which supplies water to Peshawar.

Chapter Twelve *Afghanistan*

*The Bukhara, Uzbekistan, prayer rug of 1803
fortuitously obtained in Kabul*

While it also has other duties the Pakistan government from time to time grants it the power to arrest and detain criminals.

They say the Pakistan town of Darra Adam Akhel is the gun manufacturing and gun-runners town of Pakistan. It is not for me to say otherwise and we did not go there but we went to Peshawar which is the next town north and it seemed to us that every second shop was a gun-shop and that absolutely every man in the street was carrying a gun, a rifle or both. None of us had ever seen anything like it. Every man and his dog was prepared for war.

We stayed in Peshawar so when I found a decent-looking carpet shop I took my rug there. By the grace of the Almighty the owner spoke excellent English but when I unrolled my rug he was at first speechless. *Where did you get this?* he finally gasped, his eyes still bulging outwards. I told him I bought it from a warehouse in Kabul but I did not mention the circumstances. *Can you please tell me what it is?* I asked. He replied, *It is a prayer rug from Bukhara, in Uzbekistan. It was woven in a village over time. You can see that, if you look carefully, as the colours and the weave changes here and there, when they worked on it. The building that it shows is of a mosque. When a mosque is done they usually show the outside of the mosque on the top half of the rug and the inside of the mosque on the lower half. But here they have put the same outside of the mosque twice, top and bottom, very unusual. It is 170 years old and in good condition. I will pay you US $1,000 for it.*

I had to tell him that I did not buy it to sell. *I do not know the finer points of paintings, ceramics, jewellery, books and artefacts. I only know what I like and I liked this rug as soon as I saw it. I would like to help you as you have helped me and I shall remember that.*

On the exchange rate I had paid a touch over A $7.60 and he was offering me A $1,500. In twenty four hours I could sell the prayer rug for 200 times what I paid. Now I realised why Gulru was mad at me. Even at fifty pounds he would have short-changed himself.

In Peshawar there were then often riots and foreigners would not be allowed on the streets. Trouble did come our way when once again our bus was inundated with rocks and stones.

That night we risked a fish meal and the next day we left the lawless and mostly dirty town and followed one of the great rivers of Asia, the Indus River. We crossed the strategic Attock Bridge which led us to Attock Fort that was built to protect the river. As the fort is still a military base it is not open to visitors. It sits nearly 300 metres above the water, extends for one kilometre in length and is 135 metres wide. It is impressive to say the least and was the main British fort for a long distance in any direction. Cultivation came into view with water buffaloes and oxen pulling large carts.

I must mention the Indus for I find it to be one of the world's great rivers, not as many are measured by the length or volume of its water but for its place in the world for all so many. The word or name, India, is derived from the Indus River, which begins its 3,200 km journey in Tibet before flowing north-west through Kashmir and then changes course quite significantly to head sou-by sou- west to Pakistan and its extraordinary Punjab region after which it passes close by to Karachi and then tumbles into the Arabian Sea.

The Indus is an antecedent river as it existed before the Himalayas and it feeds off endless amounts of material eroded from the mountains. This allows over fifty per cent of agricultural produce in Pakistan's rich Punjab region to be irrigated by one of the largest contiguous irrigation systems anywhere in the world. That Indus River irrigation system services 8.8 million hectares of cropping land. In total Pakistan has 18 million hectares of irrigated land and fifty-two per cent of its agricultural land is irrigated. By comparison Australia irrigates 1.9 million hectares of its agricultural land or 0.535 per cent of its total agricultural land. What must it be like to have water volumes of that preponderance?

People were crowding the roads like ants and driving became

even more of a hazard. Head-on collisions seemed so often to be inevitable as the crowded trucks and buses, their drivers preferring to blow the horn rather than adhere to the rules of the road, although to do that you would first have to know the rules, careered down as much of the road as they felt like. To add to that distraction the fish from Peshawar's dinner last night came back to tickle us.

We came to Rawalpindi in time to line the street with hundreds of thousands of Pakistanis to see President Bhutto's carriage hasten by. It was accompanied by his body guard of cavalry, pennants flying atop their deadly lances glittering in the sunshine. Rawalpindi was awash, ironic word, with professional beggars which was quite disturbing. English is widely spoken but in the south it is hot, dusty and overcrowded with multitudes of the poor. As it was then, what might it be like now amongst a larger population?

The bus took us into Lahore at dusk and then us through a tree-lined entrance to the sprawling and former British Empire hotel, Feletti's. The order of the day was large, no, huge comfortable bedrooms that can each sleep six people in king-size beds with marble baths and the grand dining room with red suited and white turbaned waiters. This luxury was created in 1880 and was something unexpected by us on account of Sundowners group.

As we unloaded in front of the hotel, off to our right a wedding procession approached across the manicured lawns and impeccably arrayed gardens. Normally the bride is the centre of attention but here the groom held sway, at least for his mode of transport to the wedding venue. Immaculately clothed in traditional eastern attire he was riding a white horse across the green lawn with his colourful followers, dancing as they were in his wake. A lively band brought up the rear and off to the side and still on the endless lawn, not far from us stood a snake charmer and an elephant. The procession turned on to the enormous horseshoe driveway by which we had arrived and the groom went on to his expectations.

I do not wish to be seen harping on about prices too often but when that occurs it is usually due to the great value of the market and Feletti's was definitely up-market. So for a three-course dinner that night, with the band playing, and in the morning a full English breakfast, both at Feletti's we each paid A $1 in total. Goodness knows what the accommodation tariff was but as you know, by now Sundowners thought we were getting the trip too cheaply.

We weren't done with yet. Feeling much refreshed and in good health we set off the next morning in a fleet of chauffeured Chevrolet limousines on a tour of Lahore and yet again, the price per person was the now regular A $1. We sat back and enjoyed the ride to the Shalimar Gardens, built 1641-1642. The design is that of a Persian paradise garden and as it relies on vast amounts of water a 160 km long canal was built to carry water from the foothills of Kashmir. I learned there are 820 fountains and eighteen varieties of fruit trees.

In the Pakistan language *La* means bring and *hore* means more money so Lahore together means bring more money. We moved on to the historic Red Fort. A minor fort was there in the 11th century and a substantial fort by the 14th century, allowing for rebuilding here and there, courtesy of the antics of some of the following. We begin with the conquering Mongols and the follow-up prince of death, Tamerlane, the Mughals, Emperor Aurangzeb, the Sikhs and the British with apologies for the missing. Rudyard Kipling named his Vermont home Naulakha in honour of one of the fort's pavilions.

At one time Lahore was home to the 105.6 carat diamond the Koh-i-Noor which is now kept amongst Britain's Crown Jewels, specifically in former Queen Elizabeth's crown.

We then attended the Badshahi Mosque, the largest in Pakistan, built in the reign of Emperor Aurangzeb and estimated to hold 100,000 people. There was a remarkable gathering in 1974 when the rulers of thirty-nine Muslim countries attended on one day. They included King Faisal of Saudi Arabia, President Bhutto of Pakistan, Muammar Gaddafi of Libya, Yasser Arafat of Palestine and Sabah Al-Salim Al- Sabah of Kuwait.

Rudyard Kipling's stories were generally about the life and times of the British Army in India, which then included the land of Pakistan. His most successful book was Kim and tells of the gun named Zam-Zammah. It was made of green bronze and known as a fire-breathing dragon. We saw the gun where it sits on a brick platform opposite the Lahore Museum.

Third bomb blast in Peshawar, Pakistan, in one week.

CHAPTER THIRTEEN

Varanasi

I'm the one that's got to die when it's time for me to die, so let me live my life the way I want

— Jimi Hendrix

We left Lahore the next morning and travelled twenty-four km along the Grand Trunk Road to Wagah which forms part of the border crossing into India. It is then thirty-two km to Amritsar in India. It might sound a regular procedure but there has long been friction between the two countries and to lighten the atmosphere that border crossing has become one with a difference. Every day at two hours before sunset both countries have a stylish and colourful flag lowering ceremony with exaggerated marching and rituals, to outdo the other in a pomp and ceremony exhibition. India erected a 110 metre high flagpole so Pakistan made theirs 120 metres. I think India won the grandstanding with their stand that can seat 25,000 spectators. It was at the border that a few of us met Pakistan's tallest man, a veritable giant of 2.23 metres in height and with thick red hair.

We had left Lahore at 8 a.m. and waited until almost 3 p.m. to

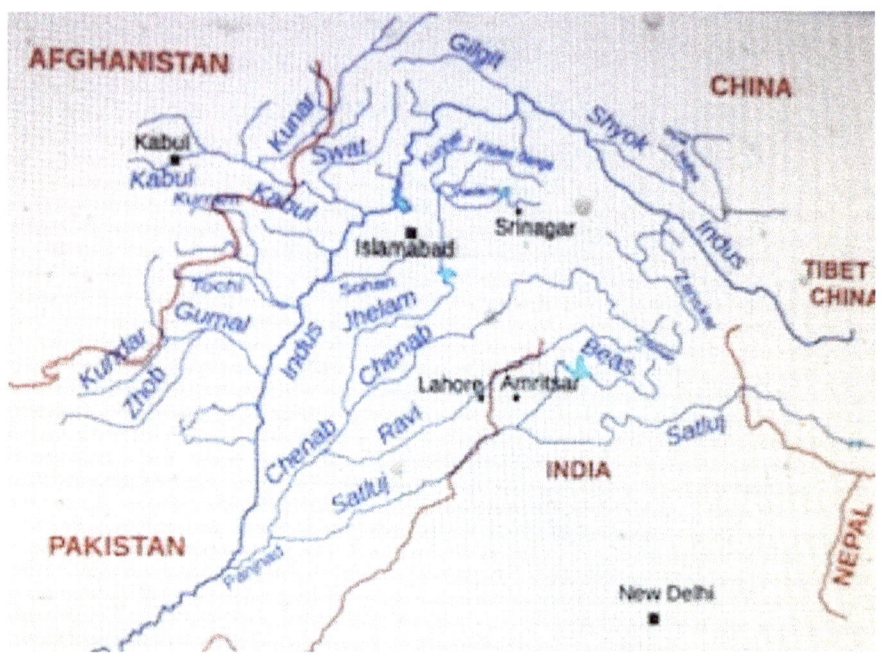

Part of our journey, showing Kabul of Afghanistan, Srinigar in Kashmir, Lahore in Pakistan, Amritsar and New Delhi in India and on to Kathmandu, Nepal

cross the border. This was brought about by having to take all our luggage out of the bus, have the riot act read to us and then be searched. Nothing untoward was found and we lost another half day due to local differences. You can plan for these border delays but you cannot do much about them.

We crossed into the Indian section of the massive food producing Punjab and went immediately to Amritsar's Golden Temple of the Sikhs. The temple is spiritually the most significant shrine of the Sikh world. Whilst we have come to cities that have been destroyed it is amazing to know how often the Golden Temple has suffered destruction and yet been rebuilt in no time at all although it is not so large. I am told that the Sikhs are an off-shoot religion of the Muslims

Chapter Thirteen   *Varanasi*

A pilgrim at the Sikh's Golden Temple, Amritsar, India

and the Hindus, combining the best of both religions. Perhaps.

The Golden Temple was essentially built of marble and copper and overlaid with gold leaf. Surrounded by water except for the footing leading out to it, the setting is memorable. The Holy Book of the Sikh religion is read non-stop, from cover to cover which takes forty-eight hours. At the temple live music is played and sung to amplifiers but more important is the community kitchen. Staffed by volunteers the kitchen provides free meals to between 50,000 and 100,000 people, every day. We would see many such kitchens across India.

That night we stayed in a former private home, an Indian bungalow with all conveniences. That was pleasant, especially as we were given a typical curry dinner in the open court-yard.

Refreshed once more we set sail from Amritsar for Jammu, which is 200 km to the north and sits at an elevation of 234 metres, just

Above, below and facing page: Travelling the Jammu-Kashmir road

inside Kashmir. Having arrived at Jammu we decided to press on for another 266 km to Srinigar at 1,585 metres. If we could do that by nightfall we would have an extra day in fabled Kashmir.

We didn't know what to expect but soon realised it was a challenge for Garry and Les who like us had not been there before. It was a winding, narrow mountain track of extremes. It wound so much that you had scarcely a brief reaction time to a vehicle coming

Chapter Thirteen *Varanasi*

from the opposite direction and it was so narrow that for most of the time it was impossible for two vehicles to pass by alongside each other. Thank goodness in those days vehicles were rare.

There were heart-stopping moments when several times our rear off-side wheel was so close to the edge that the bodywork of the bus was literally over the edge of the road with nothing but cold air below it for hundreds of metres. When that sunk home it was scary and miraculously another vehicle never forced us to back up in reverse and in despair. We had reports of landslides across the road that had blocked traffic and left vehicles stranded up there for three days. Most travellers take all day to traverse the Jammu-Srinigar road and so it was 8.30 p.m. for our grateful arrival. Garry and Les did a great job of handling that road. As I think back I would rate that the most terrifying road I have encountered.

We were transferred by canoe-like boats to houseboats on

Srinigar's Lake Dal where our two houseboys showed us to our rooms, one each for Anne and Glen, Natalie and Charlie and Janice and myself. We appreciated them serving dinner to us in the houseboat's dining room. After a welcoming hot dinner we retired to the living room where a glorious fire was keeping the freezing night-time cold air outside at bay. It had been an absorbing day.

In the morning Janice gave me a birthday card, which she had carried with her from London.

Kashmir is the northernmost geographical region of India and it is a disputed land, claimed by Pakistan which has one third and India which controls two thirds of the land. I would say most residents overall are Pakistan's Sunni Muslims but India's Hindus have the strength. Since then China, as usual, has stuck its oar in and having illegally annexed Tibet now claims land to the north-east so the dispute over land today is between Pakistan, India and China.

Houseboat, Lake Dal, Kashmir

Chapter Thirteen *Varanasi*

Boating on Lake Dal, Kashmir

The houseboats, made mostly of cedar are 24 to 38 metres in length and 3 to 6 metres wide, an ample size. They have an exclusive shikara, a boat for ferrying guests ashore. The house boys, not really boys but men in their 20s to 60s live and cook in their attached kitchen boats.

After an English breakfast of ample porridge and eggs courtesy of the houseboys we set off on a four-hour tour of Srinigar's Lake

Dal. Srinigar comes from the ancient Indian Sanskrit language and has two meanings. One being City of Sun and the other translation Shri, the Hindu goddess of prosperity. Lake Dal comes across as Lake of Flowers possibly on account of its many floating gardens of lotus flowers as well as fishing and water plant harvesting.

After lunch we took a boat to the old city which still exists in good condition with its Mughal gardens and home-made papier mache, carpet weaving, dried fruits, jewel making, wood-carving and Kashmir shawls. The latter are made of the soft underbelly of Himalayan goats and cashmere wool. While we were walking around the old city Janice and Charlie were unfortunately stoned by Muslim children, incurring mental damage as much as physical.

When we returned to our boats bands of hawkers descended on us but we were able to repel boarders. After an on-board dinner we went next door to Garry's houseboat for a party as it was his birthday following mine of yesterday. Due to a little exuberance at the celebrations we missed the early morning start to the planned pony-trekking in the surrounding Himalayan hills. We decided to make up for it at the golf club.

To have a little exercise after the bus trip to Srinigar and I suppose last night's excitement we walked to the Kashmir golf club and hired the golf clubs and a caddy plus bought golf balls, tees and paid the green fees for the nine-hole course, which set each of us back all of $1.40. My young caddy was very knowledgeable but only one other person was playing the course.

After the rather drawn-out but fun-filled match we had a packed lunch prepared by the houseboys, using tables and chairs by the clubhouse. Later we took a water taxi back to our houseboat where

Chapter Thirteen *Varanasi*

the houseboys were so good as to make afternoon tea for us.

The locals often wear what looks like striped pyjamas under their robes. On the cold days and at night they wear their robes while carrying a small lamp between the pyjamas and the robes. As street lighting was almost non-existent that seemed practical, certainly at night but I gained the impression it was also a rare form of heating for them. Not that you might think that when you noticed their feet for on the coldest of days it was obvious that they did not wear shoes or any footwear. I suspect they could not afford to. Many locals lived on rough-looking houseboats along the creeks and waterways amongst the mud and the slush which abounded there. Houseboats first came into being for those without land.

The following morning we began the return trip to Jammu and were stopped in a 2,700 metre long, dark, mountain tunnel for twenty minutes that mentally totalled an hour, especially as more than a few of us were unwell after the ravages of lake water. It was a long day drive to reach New Delhi and once there we went to the famous Red Fort. The fort is significant to India and its people, it has a long and worthy history and if I were to tell you now what its attractions are it is another of those stories that would have me engaged with you to the point I might not know where to stop. I suggest you try to see it for yourself but be warned, I have heard more than once that it is closed. Check it out, it is well worth it.

I wasn't well in Delhi but I guess I had a charmed run up until then. You could say I had Delhi belly, as millions do. I wasn't to know then but what I missed on that visit to Delhi I would recoup in later years when I returned, thankfully with a stronger stomach or better luck.

After two full days we left Delhi and drove straight through to Agra bar a slight mishap. Once we cleared Delhi it was a drive through mainly agricultural areas. On such a road our bus was minding its own business when a truck came at us, head-on in our lane. Les flashed his lights and blew the horn but the truck driver never altered course. It was as though he was on a suicide mission. By now we were all aware of the oncoming situation. At the last possible moment Les had no choice but to allow himself to be run off the road and that is what took place. That truck held its line and stayed in our lane as though nothing happened.

Without hesitating Les drove the bus back on to the road, then swung it around and set off after the truck. The truck may normally have been more powerful but its load slowed it down while Les was a man on a mission and not conditioned to failure. He wound the good old London bus up to the maximum and kept the engine revs there as the bus gradually caught up to the truck. When he judged it safe to do so, with oncoming traffic at times, he pulled out, caught up to the other driver and then swung the wheel hard to port, cutting across the front of the truck and at close range. The driver had to wear the collision or pull over. He did the latter and he was then run off the road, exactly as he had done to Les.

Quicker than a brown snake Les jumped out of the bus, leaving it in neutral for Garry to take care of. He ran hard to the truck, jumped up on the running board, put his arm through the open window and wrenched the keys out of the ignition before the now startled Indian driver knew was happening. Continuing his non-stop and silent response Les ran seventy metres to a lake, brought his arm back like an Aborigine with a woomera and threw those keys as far as he could into the lake, where they sank without trace. Relaxed, Les drove on.

We were at our hotel in Agra for lunch and spent the afternoon doing the only thing possible, exploring and marvelling at the Taj Mahal. Janice and I lived in an old fibro-weatherboard farmhouse for thirty-seven years before she said to me, *it's time*. We moved into Dubbo and I built her a pretty good house to perhaps make up for past years but no one could build a better monument to his wife than Shah Jahan did for his Mumtaz Mahal.

Statistics abound for unique structures such as the Taj Mahal and millions of people know more than I do about it so I shall be brief. Construction took 20,000 men more than twenty-two years, completion was in 1648, built of white Makrana marble inlaid with semi-precious stones including jade and brown and black marble. Four minarets flanking the mausoleum lean slightly outwards so if they fall it will be away from the main structure.

In late 1978, during the Pakistan-India war, the Taj Mahal was closed to the public for the first time in more than 300 years. It was camouflaged with straw matting, leaves, vines and grass as Pakistan bombers were using the reflection of the Taj under moonlight to guide them to important Agra targets. A red sandstone mosque to the left or west is matched by an identical building, with a guest house to the right, for the sake of architectural harmony. Around the nine-metre high portico are quotations from the Koran in Arabic script. Inside the Taj Mahal is an intricately carved marble screen that shields the tombs of Mumtaz Mahal and her husband, Shah Jahan. The original screen was removed as it was of solid gold and tempting to thieves. The tombs are fakes, being over the real ones,

Sundowners at the Taj Mahal, India, with Bill sitting on the extreme right while behind the girl next to him is Janice

the sarcophagi, which are in the chamber below. The marble walls are exquisitely decorated with Pietr Dura inlay, the method of inserting precious stones into marble. Some of the decorative lotus flowers are composed of as many as sixty-four separate jewels.

Behind the mausoleum an open terrace looks across the river to a crumbling red stone wall which is believed to have been the site for a planned replica of the Taj Mahal but in black marble, the two to be linked by a black and white marble bridge. Before this could be built Shah Jahan was deposed by his son Aurangazeb. When Jahan died in 1666 he was buried beside his beloved wife, Mumtaz Mahal, which translates as Crown of the Palace. She died in childbirth after she had borne him fourteen children.

Chapter Thirteen *Varanasi*

Our satisfactory accommodation in Agra was an apartment in a city block with a flat roof. I twice went up there for the view and to look over the city. Each time I did so I was met by a group of low-flying vultures circling overhead. Death is never far away in India but I found this surprising. In the afternoon we went to Fatephur Sikri, about thirty km away. It was the first capital of the Mughal Empire under Emperor Akbar and renowned for its architecture. Even with that auspicious beginning it was to become known as the ghost city and later abandoned, possibly because it did not have a reliable water supply.

The next day was a pre-dawn to post-dusk drive of 600 km from Agra to Varanasi, one of my top ten places on the world map. Varanasi is the holy city of the Hindus. Although Indians will tell you they have thirty-three million gods but can never explain how that works, at least to me, in Varanasi they concentrate on three. One of these is Shiva, known as the destroyer and Varanasi is dedicated to Shiva. The holy Ganges River flows through Varanasi and it is the desire of most Hindus to visit it at least once in their lifetime and if possible to die there. They believe in reincarnation but if they die in Varanasi they will be free after death. The people flock to the river every morning from 3 a.m. in the summer and from 5 a.m. in winter to bathe, wash their clothes, fill ornate brass jugs that they take home as holy water, exercise their bodies with intense physical work-outs or simply sit cross-legged gazing at the rising sun with their hands clasped and their minds free.

Back then the permanent city population was 800,000 and at least 2,000 pilgrims arrived every day. Now on holy days people are at the river in their millions. We went to the river early the following morning. It has to be one of the great walks. Dull streetlights shed a little insight on the most humble of dwellings that edged on to the side of the road along with homemade hovels as well as cardboard sheets that were home for some. I imagine they were better off than the men who were sleeping on the cold morning road. So many exist by a fragile thread of life's greatcoat. Firelight flickered through the hessian doorways of the dwellings while outside strong flames subsided into hot ashes as hundreds of men used scarce and valuable firewood for their stoves, preparing the first meal of the day for themselves and for the thousands who were already on the move, hustling to sell everything from food to flowers to the unimaginable to make it through another day.

After walking the last 300 metres past a continual line of beggars holding out their metal trays, for food if not money, we arrived at the riverbank at 8 a.m. Forty-five years later Janice and I returned to Varanasi and set off for the river at 5 a.m. Traffic was so intense that we had to leave our car and walk the last two km, still in the dark. In those forty-five years India's population had increased from 695 million to close on 1.4 billion people, an extra 700 million mouths to feed and bodies to shelter. Six men passed me riding their donkeys with short whips and long words while I was constantly besieged by others sticking to me like flies and trying to exchange something for my rupees, still in the pre-dawn darkness. At times the congestion was such there was no more room for me to walk than might be found on a tightrope.

Craft akin to large rowing boats took us out on to the Ganges and along the waterfront where there were pilgrim houses in which visitors can stay for four days free of charge. If they can then find another pilgrim house with space they can also stay there for four days. Countless pilgrims who come to visit end up staying until they die and receive their wish.

With the other Sundowners Janice and I walked down the large broad steps to one of the river's eighty-five ghats on which the bodies of the dead are cremated. You can step forward and see the workings close at hand. The shroud is removed from the body which is then lowered into the river on a green bamboo stretcher to be washed. Only one member of the deceased's family can be in close attendance at the actual cremation. That must be a male family member and he must have his head shaved and be wearing white clothing. Women are traditionally not permitted to be present for fear they will become emotional and cry and thus ruin the respectful atmosphere. When brought out of the water the body is left out in the open air to dry, then wrapped again before being placed on the prepared logs, usually of sandalwood which by its popularity and scarcity is becoming expensive.

The feet of the body must point south in the direction of the realm of Yama, the god of the dead while the head faces north to the realm of Kubera, the god of wealth. The workmen, the Doms, a sub-caste of the Untouchables, use heavy bamboo sticks to make sure the body is broken and to stir up the flames. It is dirty work and death in India is believed to be contagious. As no one else wishes to work in that occupation the Doms have formed a union and having a monopoly funeral business they have become wealthy. The poorest of the people will, if necessary, borrow money to ensure their relatives have the best send-off possible. There are no defaults in payment where death is concerned. The Doms also take a cut from the sale of the firewood.

Above and facing page: Cremation at Varanasi, India

Chapter Thirteen *Varanasi*

A regular wood cremation requires 400 kilograms of firewood but modern ghats have metal frames on which to lay the timber. This keeps the wood off the ground and the flames have more oxygen and burn better so that only 260 kilograms may be required. With nine million deaths per year in India the cremations are said to burn fifty to sixty million trees a year, although this latter figure seems too high, to me. Due to the rising cost of sandalwood it is being replaced by cheaper wood from mango trees. The heaviest wood is placed on top of the corpse as heat causes the muscles to contract and this can cause the body to sit up.

Men are wrapped in white shrouds, women in red. While the corpse is drying on the riverbank it runs the risk of being urinated on by wandering cows, which we saw happen and, being holy, they are untouchable and knowing this after centuries, they go where they please. That includes on the ghats amongst the bodies and into the neighbouring houses. I once looked up and saw a cow on the fourth-floor patio or terrace of a house calmly looking out over the river. The cattle will also eat the deceased's flowers.

To the rather romantic creaking of wooden oars a young man

slowly but powerfully rowed our open boat out into the river from where we watched professional laundrymen slap and wash the cotton garments on to the rocks at a cost of one and a half cents each. We passed Beatle George Harrison's riverbank house where he lived for many months so as to immerse himself in Indian culture and playing the sitar. George Harrison died of cancer and left instructions that after his cremation his ashes were to be cast upon the Ganges at Varanasi. We came to the elegant foreshore home of *the caretaker in charge of burning.* His house is enriched by the painted presence of two huge tigers across the facade, a symbol saying that one is never far from death. All the while the absorbing sounds of the river accompanied the widows singing farewell hymns with the tinkling of bells and the clashing of cymbals.

Despite the city's obvious, even outrageous, rank pollution the river water seems to be of a different ilk. Our boat took us to many sites and sights while we watched the bodies burning and others laid out awaiting their turn. On the water it was different.

Coffins do not exist in the Hindu world and children up to the age of four, holy men, lepers and those who die of smallpox cannot be cremated and we did see a man who had died of smallpox disposed of. After his body had been washed, straw was placed on his face, which was burned, extinguished with water, and the face such as it was, re-covered. The body was laid across the prow of a skiff and a rock tied to it. The boat was then rowed towards the middle of the river and the body dumped over the side, while the relatives were wailing on the bank.

There were times when we were in the city streets that we would see a body wrapped in a shroud and tied to the roof of a car as it raced its passenger to his final resting place. Just as on many occasions we witnessed a group of young men running fast through the streets while carrying their shrouded responsibility to his finality. In winter a body has to be disposed of in twenty-four hours but in summer in four to five hours so time is important.

The ropes binding the bodies that are dropped in the river are loosened and then they float down the river. The comparatively clean or perhaps pollution-free water is said to be due to the high sulphur content of the river water. I don't know if that is so but it is widely told and believed. The locals trust it as they will not drink any other water and we know they take it home for that purpose.

Going ashore and stepping past the ashes of the deceased which are heaped up before being cast into the Ganges we made our way to the holiest temple of the Hindus. Hereabouts the streets and alleyways are so narrow it is necessary to walk in single file. The Vishwanath or Golden Temple as it is called is forbidden to non-Hindus but we had a good look at it from the roof of an adjoining house. Monkeys roamed the outside and cows were to be seen through the open doorways on the inside. After that we went to the University of India, one of the largest in the world with 566 hectares of land but not many students, probably because many of them are residing in Australia.

Next on our list was the beautiful white marble Temple of Shiva. That building was somehow organized by one man. They say a beggar gave a loaf of bread which was auctioned for US $1,600, the money being donated to the temple and so it went. After that we moved on to the Durga Temple, which is widely called the monkey temple as quite a few simians congregate there. I found it remarkable as its large exterior has been stained red with ochre, stunning colour. Continuing on foot we were confronted by an elephant, as you do. Robin and Ellen climbed up on it while Janice fed it an orange and a banana.

Back to our current accommodation the Hotel de Paris, which is described as a throwback to the British Empire with its perfect lawns, superb gardens, mango trees and first-rate rooms running off the wide verandahs, where we enjoyed another four-course feast. I recall at one Indian hotel seeing a team of eight women in a line and on their hands and knees, weeding the hotel grounds not with garden tools but with their hands.

After lunch we played touch football on the exquisite lawns and then watched an exhibition by a yoga expert. At one point Jim and Garry held his arms palm down on the ground while the man turned himself through and through his shoulders, that was rather unreal. Next we were introduced to three snake-charmers who played music as their cobra snakes rose up out of their baskets. Janice joined in by allowing a two-metre long python to wrap itself around her neck and a green snake was passed around to the willing. A dangerous snake escaped its handler and nearly reached Virginia before being caught by the tail, the snake that is. The deadly opponent of snakes, the mongoose, two of them actually, made an appearance that could have helped Virginia if need be. After all that exertion it was time for afternoon tea, on the lawn of course. A band provided the background music, featuring tracks such as Daisy and The Isle of Capri. All this cost us a contribution of twenty cents each and while I thought we were being somewhat spoiled there was more to come.

Yet another wedding party appeared with the groom impeccably dressed and wearing a turban bedecked with garlands of beads and feathers while seated atop another white horse as the groom's friends

Chapter Thirteen *Varanasi*

danced before him. Not to be outdone the steed sported a red plume and a magnificent saddlecloth on which he bore his charge off to his destiny.

We departed Varanasi for the drive to Patna. It was a shocking road, as narrow as a ribbon, all the way. We arrived in Patna at dusk and were not impressed. Our hotel was as simple as could be. The bedrooms for three couples had two beds, the lights were more often off than on and while they partially worked, nothing else did. Service was not an issue for it did not exist but perhaps the Hotel de Paris had spoiled us.

In the morning we ventured out and about and were astonished at the numbers of people. Nowhere in the world have I seen so many brethren clog the footpaths, the streets and the great variety of transport vehicles and it was endless. I don't recall the population then and now it is in the millions for they must breed like rabbits and simply stay put. Extraordinary.

I don't wish to be offensive but Patna was claustrophobic to us and we hurried on to the India border which we found as easy to leave as it had been difficult to enter. By that I mean the next border, that being with Nepal. We stopped in the Nepalese town of Birgunj and stayed at the Birgunj Hilton. Unfortunately it was then the only hotel in town. The usual six of us shared the one room and the whole place was crowded. Shades of Patna. We had to eat our meals in shifts, again perhaps because of there being so many people.

The next day we clambered aboard two local buses after the bags-on-heads porters had loaded the luggage for our final destination, Kathmandu. It would be a long climb into the Himalayas and seven people opted to fly there in twenty minutes at a cost, I think, of $20.

The road was winding and slow as we climbed to 2,440 metres

from where we had a splendid view of the Himalaya mountains, of magnificent Dhaulagiri, Annapurna and Everest. Then we dropped down to a large valley, going down one side and up the other before levelling off slightly below the valley rim. The road took us into the Kathmandu valley and at dusk we came to unreal Kathmandu. Two different authorities say the road was 180 km and 135 km. I don't know which is correct but I assure you it took ten hours on the road to complete the journey, as against the 20 minutes for those who flew up the hill.

Our accommodation was the three-star Blue Star hotel with a double room this time. Most of our group had a rather large steak dinner followed by a party in the hotel for Sundowners at which we helped Reg empty his bottle of brandy. As the trip was officially over the next day Janice and I moved into a large room with Anne and Glen and relaxed for the day.

That relaxation is no good for you as Janice was then ill and I had to ask for a doctor to visit. The doctor came and treated her with medication and an injection and while he was there he cared for quite a few others, mainly with stomach problems. I paid the doctor and he gave me a Nepalese receipt but with the services and invoice written in English. I didn't look at it properly until we were back in Australia. It transpired he was the personal doctor to the King of Nepal and he had been so good as to make a house call to Janice.

Next morning as I couldn't do any more for her I hired a bicycle and went off riding around Kathmandu. I have to say that cost me twenty cents for a full day and that night I dined out at the Mandarin restaurant. As the bike-riding was such a change from bus travel and the sight-seeing so enjoyable I resumed riding early the next morning, Janice being close to good but not 100 per cent. I rode out to the neighbouring city of Patan in glorious weather and surrounded by Himalayan mountain peaks. It was a magical experience and the air always so fresh. After some of the places we had been to I suppose that was fair enough.

I cycled on and came to a Tibetan refuge camp where I stopped and was made welcome. It was not exactly a camp but an area where the Tibetans had settled and were allowed to make their handicraft rugs, carpets etc under government supervision at set prices. I found them to be the nicest people I had met in my travels although in later years I would come to rank the everyday people of Syria, without their government, on a par with the Tibetans.

I spent quite some time there and gained the impression the Tibetans are honest, straightforward, open people who have had their country overrun by Chinese soldiers who murdered their monks by the thousands as well as the citizens who objected to the unprovoked assault on their peaceful way of life and their ownership of Himalayan rivers. Naturally they wished to return to their homeland in peace but as with the Dalai Lama that was not possible. I noted they are brown-skinned, of stocky build and slanted eyes.

I continued my cycling on a day to remember and returned to Kathmandu late in the afternoon with memories that hopefully will survive for years to come. Janice was now up and about so we joined many of the others for dinner that night at *Aunt Jane's* restaurant on Freak Street where we had buffalo steaks, pumpkin pie and vegetables. Jane was an American and she would tell you that her staff have been so well trained in food selection, preparation and cooking that you would not be sick from eating at her place and if you were you could afterwards eat free for ----a bloody long time. I forget how long. It was good Jane.

The next morning I hired a rickshaw and took Janice on a tour of Kathmandu. It was and hopefully still is so full of variety, colour and interest the only way I can do it justice is through your eyes, put it on your list. I can say in general we went to temples, fruit markets, Buddhist shrines, stupas, the gigantic bell that summoned the people to hear announcements or warnings and a gigantic statue of Kali who is the Hindu goddess of time, death and destruction, on one of her many hands, while on the other she deals in creation and fertility with her four, eight or ten arms and somewhat wild or fierce appearance. A post-card seller from Bangladesh took us around for two hours pointing out items we would have otherwise missed and he refused to accept any payment.

The one thing I will dwell on is the Living Goddess for if you travel to Kathmandu and seek her out you will have to be extremely lucky. Kumari or The Living Goddess is the worshipping of a chosen virgin as manifestations of the divine female energy in religious traditions. A prepubescent girl is selected from the Shakya clan of the Nepali Newari Buddhist community. The worship of the goddess in a young girl represents the worship of divine consciousness spread over all creation. A young girl is selected over a mature woman due to her inherent chastity and purity.

Young girls are selected to be considered for the position of Living Goddess when they are four years of age. That selection is courtesy of the combined assessment of five senior Buddhist priests including the Chief Royal Priest and the Royal Astrologer. Eligible girls are of the Newar Shakya caste of silver and goldsmiths.

Chapter Thirteen *Varanasi*

*The Kumari or Living
Goddess of Kathmandu*

The selected girl must be in excellent health, have never shed blood or been subject to diseases. She is also assessed on thirty-two perfections, some of which are as follows: A neck like a conch shell, a body like a banyan tree, chest like a lion, a voice as soft and clear as that of a duck, thighs like a deer and the eyelashes of a cow.

Her hair should be exceedingly black and she should have dainty hands and feet, small and recessed sexual organs and a set of twenty teeth. Then 108 buffaloes and goats will be sacrificed to Kali after which masked men will dance around with the severed heads. Next she must spend a night alone in a room with the heads. If she exhibits fear she is dismissed. Finally she must pick out the personal belongings of the previous Kumari from others.

Her family can only visit her rarely and she will always be dressed in red and gold with the fire eye painted on her forehead as a symbol of her powers of perception. Crowds of people wait below her residence hoping she will pass by the latticed window on the third floor and glance down on them. These rare appearances last a few seconds at most and only once or twice a year so the atmosphere in the street below is charged with the devotion and awe of the people that she might appear. She remains as the Living Goddess until puberty.

After she leaves her palace/temple home she may marry but not anyone locally. We were told it can be bad luck for someone who marries the Living Goddess but it is good luck for anyone who manages to make eye contact with her. She receives a grant from the government and with her dowry will be financially secure for life. I don't know how to tell you this without arousing doubt in the minds of some but I give you my word that when I passed by I looked up at her timber-framed window which had just been slid open by someone who was already sliding it shut and in those two seconds I not only saw the Living Goddess but I made eye contact with her as she looked down on me.

The following morning we flew to Calcutta in a DC8 and then to Bangkok for a few days followed by a similar stay in Singapore. Next and last was Australia and home for me but a new life for Janice. She would be my ultimate overseer.

www.ingramcontent.com/pod-product-compliance
Lightning Source LLC
Chambersburg PA
CBHW061724070526
44583CB00024B/3002